SELF-CARE

YETTA M. BERNHARD

SELF-CARE

Introduction by Virginia Satir

CELESTIAL ARTS
MILLBRAE, CALIFORNIA

Cover design: Abigail Johnston

Copyright©1975 by Yetta Bernhard

Published by CELESTIAL ARTS, 231 Adrian Road,
Millbrae, California 94030

First printing: October, 1975
Manufactured in the United States of America

Library of Congress Cataloging in Publication Data

Bernhard, Yetta, 1909-
    Self care.

        1. Interpersonal relations. 2. Intimacy
(Psychology) 3. Self-actualization (Psychology)
I. Title. [DNLM: 1. Behavior — Popular works.
2. Self concept — Popular works. 3. Psychology —
Popular works. BF145 B522s]
HM132.B466   158'.2   75-9448
ISBN 0-89087-110-8
ISBN 0-89087-111-6 pbk.
    2 3 4 5 6 7 8 9 10 — 80 79 78 77

Foreword

I feel very privileged that Yetta Bernhard asked me to write a foreword.

All of us in some part of ourselves know that caring for ourselves is an essential part of our lives. It is a cliché to say that even though we know about it, we somehow do not do much about it. I believe that there may be two reasons why this is so: one is that even if we know it is important, we do not believe it; the second may be even more significant and that is that many of us who believe it may not know how to do it. The subject of self-care obviously has many aspects. But like everything else, there are some aspects with a greater priority than others.

I think that Yetta Bernhard addresses herself to the central issue which is how to define, to limit, and to make specific your every-day interpersonal negotiations with the people with whom you live. I think that in the way she presents her material, it is possible to get a deeper appreciation for the relationship between belief, knowledge, and human practice.

Another outstanding contribution of her book is the specific and practical methods she offers which, if followed, cannot help but produce practical results. Implied in her book is the assumption that human beings in daily work with one another will meet conflict and differences as a part of the ''givens'' of being human. Coping with this difference in the way that Yetta demonstrates is a central point in the development of maintenance and self-care. Perhaps this book will heighten the awareness that the presence of differentness is a natural expression between two human beings—not a comment on who loves whom. It is not a comment on human perverseness. If we are to honor the fact that we are all unique expressions of humanness, then we have to expect the naturalness of difference. Understanding this and accepting it as a basic human fact will then help us to develop ways of coping that make this part of our humanness work for us instead of against us.

I have long been interested in the phenomenon of human differentness and the part it has played in the erosion of human relationships. To find a way to be able to not only survive this difficulty but to make it a growth point is a continuing challenge. I think Yetta takes giant steps in practical application.

She brings a new dimension to the meaning and practice of self-care.

Virginia Satir

Contents

To Pat, Ed, and Eric
And to all who have the courage to face their own
creative ways of making themselves and others
miserable, the intelligence to consider alternative
modes of behavior, and the will to invest in the
pain of change.

Acknowledgments

Acknowledgment, appreciation and thanks:

To Virginia Satir who skillfully guided me to new realizations and new worlds.

To George Bach, who (during the years I was his co-director of the Institute of Group Psychotherapy and co-developer of the Fair Fight Training System) taught me the realities of confronting aggression.

To Jane Levenberg Gerber, Dick Cook, Rose Brandzel, and Ray Robertson who aggressively persisted, encouraged and made my commitment to write this book an HONOR.

To Cathy Bond, my student and colleague, who took time out from a busy schedule to read the manuscript and whose suggestions for deletions and expansions were most helpful.

To Jean Twiest, who typed the manuscript, suffered through and participated in many of the thought processes of construction and reconstruction.

To the many participants of my workshops and therapy sessions who gave me permission to tape and publish our work—a mutually enriching experience. I taught and was taught!*

To my daughter, who, upon being admitted to Psychiatric Residency asked, "Will you help train me, Ma?"—beginning another growth process for me.

*All names have been changed to preserve anonymity.

Preamble

Studies of conflict in intimacy and families in discord give repeated evidence that messages are frequently distorted in transit from the mouth of the sender to the ears of the receiver, that assumptions are questionable and need to be checked out; that styles of living differ and negotiation may be possible; that needs for closeness, at times, conflict with another's need for distance; that tests of trust need to be explicitly stated; that assurances of mutual importance in a relationship need to be verbalized as positive reinforcement of the relationship; that areas of separateness of power need to be established to avoid the feeling of being used, abused and exploited; that unquestioned and unchallenged "knowing" of the intimate other is a fantasy that has to be exposed in order to deal with the reality of each other's BEING.

The system of Self-Care (utlizing the concepts of Fair Fighting*), focuses on person and pair-responsibility in a significant relationship.

Self-Care deals with the what and how of BEHAVIOR of people in conflict in order to attain a more effective relationship of binding or breaking it. Self-Care combats the unreality of "romantic love" as a concept and guide for intimate living.

The assumption "If you loved me, you would (or would not) do . . . ." incorporates a basic sabotage in intimate relationships—that of failure to hand the script of the "woulds" or "would nots" to the significant other. In this fantasy concept a role is assigned to another, but no details explicitly stated as to specific actions the assigned role implies. The assumption "You ought to know," must be supplanted by "I ought to tell you what you ought to know."

---

*Fair Fight Training System was originally formalized by George R. Bach and developed into a Therapeutic Educational system by George R. Bach and Yetta M. Bernhard. See: *Aggression Lab—The Fair Fight Training Manual* by Bach and Bernhard, Kendall/Hunt Publishers, Dubuque, Iowa.

The assumptions "If you loved me you would not *feel* sexual interest in another" or "so close to your parents" or "such dedication to your work" are based on an assumption that the love or interest given to others is at the expense of the mate, that one person can be everything to another, fulfill *all* needs.

In spite of the uniqueness (difference) of each person, pair, family, and group, some general human qualities and needs are shared in common. Among these, I believe, are a desire for power, a feeling of significance to another, and a search for meaning in living.

To feel power one must have a sense of worth (I am somebody); to be significant to another one must have impact (you are aware of me); to find meaning in life one must transcend self, expand into a larger world (a created ability to go beyond the limits of private concerns).

Basically I find people searching for connectedness—to another and to the world in which they live. This involves pair, familial, and societal relationships to counteract the often-felt despair of "aloneness." Where a relationship is in trouble and bringing more conflict and pain than joy and freedom, connectedness is threatened. This poses specific problems for consideration:

Is the relationship worth keeping?

Am I able to critically challenge my own behavior patterns?

Will I work at creating the ability to act beyond and over relationship-sabotaging feelings?

When there is a commitment to a relationship, in spite of the pain, turmoil, and conflict immediately apparent, the message is: THIS RELATIONSHIP IS WORTH KEEPING, and so becomes the first building block to connectedness.

Challenging current unproductive behavior patterns implies a choice of alternative ways of behaving—opening new concepts:

I can learn to do things differently.

I am willing to invest the work and pain it takes to change habits and ideas and expectations, especially those that operate to alienate me from intimate others.

I will work at creating the ability to act beyond and over relationship-sabotaging feelings:

Jealousy and possessiveness,

Rage at past actions currently remembered,

Distrust, constant suspicion of words and motives of another.

The how and what of attaining worth, impact, transcendency and connectedness is the art of Self-Care.

Basic considerations are the specifics of Conflict, Confrontation, and Communication.* The system of Self-Care teaches processes of dealing with emotional dynamite more safely and with greater purpose:

1. The process of ventilation and catharsis.

2. The process of information-giving.

3. The process of correctly placing rage, anger, and aggression—picking the correct target.

4. The process of control and containment.

The task, as I see it, is to turn the very real acid produced by alienating encounters into the honey of a bonding relationship. At least we can neutralize the acid. This is an alchemist's job based on some very practical considerations.

The alchemy I am proposing is in the work of:

The action of change—ideological and behavior change.

Challenging of attitudes—admitting another perception or point of view is possible.

Recognizing and confronting your own prejudices.

Checking out assumptions.

Verbalizing expectations.

Releasing rage by *consent* and *safety* (within stated bounds).

Finding person-specific rage de-escalating exercises.

Building trust.

Maintaining authenticity.

Establishing autonomy.

Negotiating differences.

To me, Perls' Credo:

I do my thing, and you do your thing.
I am not in this world to live up to your expectations
And you are not in this world to live up to mine.
You are you and I am I,

* Virginia Satir's three "Cs"

And if by chance we find each other, it's beautiful.
If not, it can't be helped.

is a paean of individual autonomy which misses the major striving of human beings—*an interrelationship* with significant others—which involves individual responsibility to self and to the relationship in order to achieve a greater richness and expansion of being—an independence and an interdependence. These I do not leave to "chance." I teach ways and means, the "how" and "what" of *making* a relationship and starting and maintaining a growth process. The system of Self-Care emphasizes individual and conjoint responsibility to MAKE A RELATIONSHIP PAY OFF in intimacy, creativity, and growth potential.

Yetta Bernhard

Chapter 1

About Bernhard

As a therapist and participant in growth-change, I take the risk of personal openness and vulnerability to the extent that it "fits" in the current encounters. My dedication to the techniques I teach grew in large part out of my personal stresses and what I learned in the management of them. This, to some extent was the content of a paper presented to the Western Psychological Association, San Diego, California, on March 30, 1968. It was an exposé of a marathon experience (part of a Virginia Satir workshop, a 24-hour non-stop session) which went, in part, as follows:

IMPACT OF MARATHON GROUPS ON THERAPIST'S GROWTH

YETTA M. BERNHARD

My role as marathon group facilitator is conceived as a commitment to interact with group participants as a person—as well as a technician in keeping the group on the course of significant work—utilizing group pressure to productively change self-sabotaging attitudes and behavior. I see this as a technical and personal challenge of my own authenticity very much different from the 50-minute interview which can be easily controlled. In this open commitment of myself to the group I make myself vulnerable to attack, to expressions of hate, acceptance, and love. Inevitably, I, too, was molded by the various groups—in various stages—to greater openness, greater fearlessness, greater self-understanding, and greater change.

1

A revolutionary change of life style occurred in this process. My personal growth increased my professional value. Overcoming my own shock of aggressive encounter allowed group members to be more confrontive with one another. Overcoming the stress of my "FOUR D" life style (DISCIPLINE, DUTY, DIGNITY, AND DISENGAGEMENT) allowed me to relate more intimately with my groups, thus facilitating release of their defense mechanisms, self-exposure, and realistic attempts at problem-solving. I learned that discipline per se is not necessarily a value in itself, but is more productive as a frustration tolerance for that which cannot be changed.

Turning *duty* into reality-assessed-and-accepted commitments made me happier. Turning objective dignity into self-respecting actions—not always dignified—made me freer. Disengaging from, rather than escalating, another's rage, anger, hostility—*temporarily*—to allow a cooling off period—made subsequent engagement more meaningful.

Through my own experience as marathon participant I have learned that tearing down a defensive structure opens the door to emotional growth. The marathon experience is potent in that it allows time for change to emerge and be validated through open contact with others.

I personally have experienced being attacked, fighting against giving up a comfortable fantasy, feeling the despair and agony of the loss of a defensive armor, and finally emerging into a new freedom of BEING.

Preceding my experience on the "hot seat,"* I had presented myself to the group as being content with my current living, as glorying in my favorite role of "mother," of enjoying the dividends of my mature years: freedom of movement, disengagement from competitive struggles (socially and economically. I was a widow and had come to terms comfortably with living in a social world that was primarily female.

I found myself attacked by a man I had deeply antagonized. "Yetta," he charged, "you are a phony!" In one way or another many colleagues joined in a stream of negative feedback including the comment: "You talk as if your husband was alive. I didn't know he had died." In one way or another they were telling me I was giving off ambiguous messages—projecting an image of self-containment and contentment that didn't quite come off.

This part of the attack left me unshaken. I was secretly proud that I "could take it;" that I didn't need everyone's love was being validated

---

* Group's focus on one member

by my composure. They weren't getting to me, until a non-verbal discrepancy was exposed (an incongruence between eye message and word message). The original attacker crossed the room to my side and said: "There's a sadness in your eyes. There are unshed tears. Are they for your husband?" The impact of these words had the effect of a battering ram shattering a defense structure. I dissolved into sobs that seemed to well up from my toes.

The target hit was the emotional unfinished business of my husband's death. I had not fully accepted the reality and finality of this fact. Immediately following his death I was busy functioning, being heroic, taking over his job of running a convalescent hospital, returning to private practice a year later, and priding myself for the modeling of such superb discipline, especially to my daughter. Little by little I found myself functioning with more ease and less pain. I found myself thinking, "Bernie would be proud of me." "Would be proud" became "is proud" in a gradual, imperceptible manner until by the time of my marathon experience I had built up a very private, deeply satisfying inner emotional life "as if" my husband were alive. This shut off any real intimacy with others. The sexual aspect of living was turned off. On the surface, I continued in greater depth, a style of living long in building, an observer rather than a participator. This life style had its very real pay-offs: I was invulnerable to emotional hurt and uninvolved. I was existing comfortably.

Now I was in agony, stripped naked, and shattered. At this point I had tunnel vision. I was convinced that the wrong target was hit, that a therapeutic error had been made. I protested there was no purpose in destroying this particular fantasy, my private Shangri La. It brought me happiness and harmed no one. It didn't affect my productive functioning as therapist or mother or person. I had given myself a job: to make my husband and daughter proud of me. I felt applauded as I went about functioning so very admirably.

At the marathon for the first time in my life I could not control the tears. I felt as if the agony would never end. Loss of control was itself image-shattering. One door was closed; somehow I knew I could never rebuild my fantasy. I had to, once *and* for all, face the fact that my husband was dead and the agony was the burial of the "AS IF ALIVE" fantasy. In the beginning I could only see what the fantasy did *for* me. I did not know what it did *against* me. The fantasy made living a comfortable duty without emotional risks and with the deep satisfaction of being approved. The "AS IF" structure was a warm, insulating cocoon. It was also a distance-making structure, an almost symbolic suicide, a cut-off of an "I and thou" relationship.

Gradually I became aware of the concern, guilt, and fright of the group. I began to feel expressions of warmth and caring. There seemed to be something to go to, another door to pass through, other alternatives, choices, options, and FEELINGS.

The very able group leader's NO COMMENT listening to my protest, "The wrong target was hit," led to my own suspicions and reappraisal of this conclusion. The group had picked up the discrepancy between the brave words and the non-verbal message which was the "phoniness"—the fantasy "AS IF LIVING" had created.

The destruction of the fantasy let me out of the box into which I had put myself. The fantasy permitted only one secret structure. The reality permits the building of many structures—many avenues to explore, many choices and alternatives. I began to see people as persons to relate to and not as objects to observe and study.

In great joy I wrote to my daughter who was then vacationing in Europe. I present this letter to you, uncensored, as example of my first feeling of exuberant freedom:

> My darling,
> I'm bubbling over with things to tell you. It's now four days since I returned from the workshop and marathon with Virginia Satir. I was the first to be put on the "hot seat"—and I got blasted, excavated and renovated and I feel alive and energetic and bouncy. Also—for the first time that I remember I'm *enjoying* writing a paper which I'm going to submit for publication. The major focus of my private living was built around the created fantasy (an internal secret) that your father was alive to me. This affected nothing but my very private lack of involvement on an emotional-affect basis— with my age-level peers. It was also very comfortable and safe for me—I was totally disengaged.
> Obviously I was 'ready' for the next step in living for me. The transition was agonizing—four days of the deepest emotional pain I have ever known—but already *I know* that it was worth it. I feel alive and creative and I do have loving, realistic *memories* of your father—but he's no longer part of my everyday living. An awareness of the world about me is emerging. I'm noticing signs on the road! One client remarked to me, "Your eyes look washed clear!" A created fantasy is smashed and a new energy is released in me—like

a vital part of me has come alive. Now—for the first time—
I am understanding what you meant when you said to me,
"I talk to you, but you don't talk to me." Honey darling,
when you get home I'm going to talk and talk and talk. Have
fun darling—all goes well with me.

Your ma.

My daughter has often kidded me that I go about half blind; that I am
not observant. I now am more aware of the world about me.

As a person I've relinquished the stress of my FOUR D style of living. In the process I have opened a many-splendored door to human
contact. The fantasy destruction loosened the bonds of the cocoon in
which I was so tightly wrapped. The difference is mainly internal. I
FEEL MORE ALIVE; more enjoying of life and more participating. I
feel less a mother and more a woman. I feel initiated into a state of
BEING in a relationship. I have thoughts to stimulate me, projects to
excite me, and memories that please me.

PROFESSIONAL GROWTH

In addition to personal growth, my marathon experiences have been in-
strumental aids in my professional growth. From a tendency to be too
accepting and protective (and thereby sometimes colluding with and
reenforcing the client's defenses). I now attack, expose, and build.
From a BE-ing of disciplined disengagement, I now encounter and
take the risks of punch and counter-punch.

After listening to the complaints of a jealous lover: how he "proves"
his sweetheart is betraying him by every glance at another male,
whether passing by in an automobile, or conducting a business engagement, or at a social affair, I openly reflect the self-image I am sensing:
"You must think you are a turd—to be so threatened by every passing
male!" In my first marathon session I would have more or less gently
reflected a destructive self-image—à la Rogers. The shock of direct confrontation facilitates the work at hand.

I have noted a distinct change in life style as I currently participate in
encounters. In an attempt to elicit a feeling reaction (instead of an intellectual analysis) from a seemingly cold, emotionally uninvolved, ar-
ticulate, frustrated, and frustrating husband. I *feel* the equally desperate
frustration of his wife—I FEEL what she is up against and loudly pro-
claim in exasperation, "Fuck you—I feel like climbing the walls!" the
exact expression his wife had used earlier. My feeling reaction had the
impact of an explosive new awareness. For the first time this husband

was listening and trying to understand. And for the first time I was totally involved. Never before had I used such words!

I have become more aware of the significance of timing interpretation—becoming more keen in picking up clues of "readiness." I find myself sharing more of my own person and becoming more adept at assessing when it would be less productive to do so. When the group is actively engaged in the process of pressure to change, self-revelations are untimely—actually intrusive. They should be used to spark action, that is, "I've travelled this road and this is what worked for me"; to show common humanness—"me too!" variety; to demonstrate risk taking—making oneself vulnerable.

I feel a greater depth of skill as a therapist and group facilitator. I have personally experienced the meaning of a therapeutic dictum that tearing down a defensive structure must include tangible evidence of compensations—growth development. Time must be available for this—as it is in the marathon sessions and on-going group sessions—for demonstration of emergent change, actualizing and internalizing the new way of being.

A radically different behavioral change has taken place in relation to physical contact. For the first time I experienced going over to a sobbing woman and putting my arms around her and rocking and cradling her. And we were both enriched. The importance of the reassurance of body contact is an element of therapeutic worth I had discounted.

I find myself zeroing in to the healthy core of my clients and am considerably less up-tight at hysterical demonstrations and temper tantrums. I am more tuned into the pain behind the sometimes emotional hurricanes than I am to their noise. But I sometimes miss. I make errors.

Very recently a group participant communicated the fact that his marriage was at an end—he was moving out the next day at his wife's request. He had come home very late and very drunk the night before and his wife said "I have had it—this is it!" He was feeling depressed and also somewhat relieved. Working at the marriage again (after a six month separation) was, he said, "Like being on a yo-yo—sometimes making it and sometimes not—a constant up and down—and I'm glad I'm off it." I let the group take over without intervening. He was getting support for the conclusion he presented—along with a few very mild suggestions that he could try again later. In effect, I had permitted it to become a leaderless group.

At the end of this session I was greatly dissatisfied with myself. On hindsight, I think I failed to detect an unspoken message: "Don't let me get out of this so easily—keep me in the fighting ring with my wife —don't let me give up so soon.'' In the past I would be stewing in self-condemnation—severely pulling myself apart for not being more keenly perceptive. Now I can more freely admit goofs and go about the next productive step with less agitation and more self-acceptance.

At another time I prided myself on deliberate non-intervention when one group participant said to another, ''You are really sick—you need special intensive psychiatric help—the problem is in you, not in your husband—we cannot help you.'' The shock value of this open confrontation was immediately apparent. This particular ''victim'' was literally pulled into more productive attitudes and behavior through the trauma of seeing herself as others saw her. Coming on as emotionally sick was an image she wanted no part of—and consciously began work changing that image.

As group facilitator I have options and decisions to make in determining when to sanction group pressure, intervene against it, adopt a *laissez-faire* attitude, or give a new direction. I see the real value of being direct and involved as mutually stimulating to growth.

In still another area of living I had not related my own sexual anesthesia to insurance against future hurt. This phenomenon was merely an intellectual curiosity, so I missed the significance of a sentence from Sidney Jourard's *The Transparent Self:* ''The person who effectively guards himself against pain from the outside just as effectively ensures virtual sexual anesthesia.'' Making a connection between outside isolation and internal feeling affect has further increased my professional value in dealing more holistically with sexual problems and problems of alienation from others.

Through my own feeling experience that growth and pain are usually go-togethers, I am less fearful of hurting—if I can survive, so can you! The price of emotional growth may very well be pain—and it's worth the price!

Any fantasy concept of living is a box—a fenced-in enclosure which shuts off—it is a miniature death. Reality is living—it has no fences— there is freedom, choice, contact, and limitation. Basic to living is risk-taking.

I have attained a freer way of being—I hang loose more—I like being alive. The glow and excitement of new awareness is gone. An inner feeling of freedom remains. I have a greater acceptance of all of me. My less than perfect performances do not shatter me. I don't like it when I'm not performing at a level of excellence in my professional work, but neither do I condemn myself for it. I am more productively critical of myself and more tuned in to others. It is good to know that I usually have another chance.

Because I have been there, I feel able to empathize without colluding, attack with less fear, and facilitate growth with more confidence.

Meaning and Action

The tools and ammunition developed for the productive management of conflict evolved in my therapeutic application as a system of responsible Self-Care; an individual growth process and a relationship growth process. I maintain the practice of Self-Care is the process by and through which self-respect, self-worth, and self-liking are developed. This process involves an investment of work in:

> deepening awareness of self
> assessing cost of goals set
> risking hurt and rejection.

Such an investment in work gives an impactful message: I AM WORTH BOTHERING ABOUT!

In order to practice Self-Care one must be aware of one's own tensions, stresses, conflicts, pains, and deprivations and one must take the responsibility of dealing with them. It means risking the impact of authenticity. It is a process by which we enhance a relationship. The focus is MY RESPONSIBILITY TO MYSELF AND TO MY RELATIONSHIP WITH SIGNIFICANT OTHERS.

Self-Care means: Detective work on self —GETTING TO KNOW
> ME
> Daring to BE
> Risking another's displeasure
> Maintaining areas of privacy
> Accepting limitations
> Realistically assessing "oughts" and "shoulds"
> Creating areas of power

Self-Care includes acceptance of oneself as a human being. As a human being you will love and hate, be constructive and sometimes destructive, be at times serene and at times tempestuous, at times rational and at times irrational—and at all times BEING YOU in the many dimensions and facets of YOU. How can you best enjoy your lovable parts and manage more productively your unlovable parts—your errors, your goofs, your rages, your conflicts? The what and how of this communication can be the bridge from you to your significant other or the barrier that separates you.

When I talk about my emotional aches and my gripes and my complaints, I'm talking about your impact on me—this is information-giving. When I talk about hurts in the past that are no longer a problem today, I'm giving yôu information of *change* in me. When I say "This gripes me and it's a big problem. . . " I'm telling you there is something about you that I'd like to change.

When I say what hurts I am surfacing a problem—exposing it (an act of awareness). Dealing with it as a problem to solve opens the way to alternative courses of action. Making a choice implies a risk. Taking a risk implies "I AM WORTH IT." A feeling of worth is basic to self liking. So we have a sequence of: awareness of a problem, consideration of the problem, a choice of action, a possible resolution—THE PROCESS OF SELF-CARE and Self-Validation.

Chapter 2

Ways of Beginning and Tools with which to Work

The starting point in an attempt to rebuild a stressed and conflicted relationship is the client's decision to do something about hurtful behavior. I present an educational/therapeutic process of re-conditioning behavior with set tasks that are reality-tested and goal-directed. Pinpointing the hurt in relationship uncovers behavior, attitudes, or "sets" that are causing the pain. The client knows where it hurts; the therapist "fishes" for information in order to uncover the behavior pattern involved.

From this information about a pattern of pain-producing behavior, I focus on one realistically attainable goal as a target for change. The Inventory of Corrosives or Museum* (a list of aches, pains, and gripes in the relationship) provides the *what* of the process, the content with which one needs to deal. I ask "What do you want to change first?" or "Where do you want to start?" As therapist, I make no value judgment as to appropriate starting points; I work with whatever material the client selects.

As I see it, therapy is an educational procedure. In the relationship between client and therapist, the responsibility of the therapist is to listen, to empathize, to respect the individual, to probe for meanings and purpose, to focus on alternatives, and to make interpretations. I see the responsibility of the client as one of accepting, rejecting, or modifying these—or of presenting a different interpretation. I balance on a tightrope between direction and non-direction in this relationship, for I do not attempt to insist on my interpretation, but I cannot deny the value of my background, education, and experience in making such interpretations. When I am consciously directive I feel I am using the long years of clinical training and life experience that have shaped me.

*"Inventory of Corrosives" and "Museum" are used interchangeably

10

I do not refuse to use the resources that all this has given me, nor do I negate all the lessons my clients have taught me. My clients have taught me to listen to them carefully—to trust that they know themselves better than I do; that my "insightful wisdom" has value only to the extent that it has significant meaning to the person concerned.

Of course, any decision that involves offering an interpretation of another's behavior is always a risk. I risk being "wrong" many times a day. Yet in an attempt to define a system of behavioral therapy that is growth-producing for an individual, I maintain there is really no one "right way." There is only a pragmatic way, one that will work for the client in his relationships. And this pragmatic way is always tested and tried in action. What works in creating a feeling of self-worth, self-liking, and bettering a relationship with another is productive; what works to devaluate self and a relationship is destructive.

Since I often work in groups, I also have the advantage of group "feedback" as an added mirror of a client's impact. I teach my clients to listen in order to learn how they come across to different individuals. There is no effort at corroboration. Rather, I try to show the importance of all aspects of communication in conveying a message—not just the words. The group often responds to the extra-verbal messages, and what they perceive may not be how the individual intended to convey his message at all. It may not even be *what* the client intended to convey. The person's own perception of what he is doing is limited by what he thinks he is doing or hears himself saying—without benefit of a mirror that discloses body tensions, and facial expressions that may be dissonant from his verbal message. In reality, the message-giver is often unaware of the total message given.

The receiver—intimate other or a group member—is equally limited, but in a very different way. He, too, is hampered by selective perception due to his emotional state; this can be sometimes revealing of certain "listening limitations" or "sets." But the outside vantage point is helpful in order to get a fuller picture of the communications —a picture that can help focus problem areas or blocks in the communication system of the individual or pair under scrutiny.

The therapist's role in these situations is paradoxical. I can neither abdicate my own learning experience nor assume responsibility for another's. Therefore, I consider it of primary importance to emphasize that I know I'm fallible and I expect my client's out-front acknowledgement of my humanness! The responsibility, then, for taking or refusing to take direction is squarely upon the shoulders of the client. I want my clients to "try on for fit" (both emotional and cognitive) any interpretation, direction, or suggestion I make—and to feel free to modify or reject it if it doesn't "fit." To this end, I always ask "How does this seem to you?" (in one form or another) after offering an interpretation. I try to preface my remarks with some version of "This is what it seems to me."

I am most interested in teaching people how to ingest a process of communicating with others as well as a process for modifying behavior. The latter relates to doing what you are committed to do regardless of how you feel. A process of working over and beyond feelings to attain a self-set aim: caring for baby at four A.M.; giving a free gift of love; listening and making oneself available to significant others because of their needs (always limited to avoid exploitation or martyrdom). One essential element in learning to communicate effectively is learning to listen carefully. So accurate hearing involves both clear feedback of messages and the checking out of assumptions about the other. What happens when you do this is the process. It results in an increased personal and interpersonal awareness.

When you ask and receive permission to express your hostility in some specified form you have begun a process: 1) of considering the other when seeking permission to verbally vent your emotions at that particular moment; 2) of acknowledging, to yourself and your partner, when you are in need of such an emotional outburst; and 3) of actually releasing the pent-up feelings in a predetermined and prescribed form (time limited).

Again and again I return to the question: are you willing to pay the price for the relationship or goal you want? In any style of living there's a price to pay. Two examples that are often contrasted may serve as an illustration: living alone versus living with an intimate other. If you choose to live alone, you have the freedom to do as you please at your own option, offset by occasional loneliness and unconnectedness. If you choose to live with another, you have intimacy (connectedness and belonging) on an ongoing basis, but your freedom is curtailed; another has to be considered and dealt with. Within a relationship the same question arises: "What are you willing to give up for what?" If you want to get along with your intimate, you need to learn how not to harbor past grievances that smolder in hidden resentment. What I teach in this case is that you *can* learn to forgive—by a shift of focus, replacing the old with the new. You can minimize the past by a commitment to productively act in the present. And you can feel better about burying the past if you are actively engaged in improving the present. This also involves learning new alternatives of confronting each other, less lethal methods than the ones you used to practice.

All this involves concentrated effort—not to repress feelings, but to switch behavioral gears, to direct and control what you do for a reason. The message is: "Get off that track. It's non-productive." I have learned that as soon as a person realizes that his behavior is not producing the results he wants, he is usually willing to try something else. But to try something else you often need an ally, since the old way has the power of habit (unconscious reaction to stimuli). To break unproductive behavior patterns you need to bring them to conscious attention. In my system, partners learn how to become working allies in each other's efforts to change. The base for change is the courage and intelligence of the person in conflict: courage to face oneself and acknowledge that what he is doing is not bringing the results he wants (an act of self-criticism), and intelligence to contemplate change through enlarging the horizons of alternatives and choices (risking change).

My focus is on conflict, confrontation, and communication. The communication techniques are structured methods through which the corrosives that separate people are diluted or eliminated—a process of decreasing the individual's sabotage of his own potentials and his relationships with others. It is also at the same time a self-care system in order to better tolerate and deal with differences of significant others.

No matter how well or how little you know *why* you do *what* you do, you still have the conditioned unproductive behavior with which to deal. Behavior can be changed at your option. The how and what of behavior change is the focus of my work. The base of this work is the courage to face oneself critically and the intelligence to open alternatives and make choices for more effective living.

BASIC PREMISES

1. Hostility, rage, aggression, frustration, and anger are givens—natural manifestations of BEING. Anger is not something to be deplored but something with which to deal.

2. Hostility can be used destructively or it can be constructively managed and released non-lethally.

3. Behavior modification and change are learned processes and are possible at any age.

4. The what and how of behavior change are implemented by learned communication skills.

5. Good will between intimate others and a commitment to a relationship are sound foundations upon which to build desired behavior change.

6. Absence of good will and commitment to a relationship make behavior change between intimates difficult but not impossible. There are always alternatives and choices to be made in meeting issues— less destructive ways of living and *being*.

7. Concepts to consider:
   a. "As If" trust (taking the risk of believing, acting "as if" you trust in order to engage in the process of new behaviors mutually agreed-upon; a testing of the reality "fit" of a commitment).
   b. Self-expansion (working over and beyond "feelings") the created ability to do what you do not feel like doing in order to attain a self-set goal as well as to attain intimacy.
   c. Specifics of Self-Care (the how and what of building self-worth, self-liking and self-respect).
   d. No matter how much or how little you know *why you do* what you do or think, you still have the behavior to deal with, and behavior can be changed by your option: accepting responsibility for what you do, assessing the cost of change (is it worth it to me?), and investing in the work of change.

8. Hostility rituals, impact procedures and techniques of the Fair Fight System are ammunition for productive living and tools with which to work.

AMMUNITION FOR PRODUCTIVE LIVING—TOOLS WITH WHICH TO WORK

HOSTILITY RITUALS (EMOTIONAL RELEASES)

In practice they de-escalate feelings of rage through cathartic release and give information of the specifics of the anger, frustrations, and hurts. Through this process, avenues are opened to increase the bonding capacity of the relationship by such procedures as specifically naming a future time to deal with specific issues of discord.

Every ritual follows agreed-upon procedures with time and content limitations—and can be engaged in only by mutual consent, thus assuring a listening ear. The petitioner for the rage-release, when granted permission, has the freedom to express and release his hostility within the time boundaries set by the receiver. Freedom to rage is wedded to the discipline of containment within clearly stated boundaries of one, two, or three minute's time duration—according to the emotional tolerance of the receiver and is *verbal only*. Every procedure and ritual is bound by specific rules of freedom and safety—liberty within contained boundaries!

The Haircut (Terminology from Synanon Games)

This is a time-limited verbal rage-release confined to one *specific current happening*. It is a "dressing down," a scolding, by permission, for some specific "sin" committed by the partner. This ritual starts with a request, "May I give you a Haircut?" The receiver of the request has the right of time-limitation as well as the right to refuse acceptance. If the Haircut is accepted then the receiver is obliged to listen without defense for the time contracted. When commitment of the "sin" is acknowledged (owned up to, such as, "Yes, I did humiliate you") and the person seeks reprieve from the alienation it caused (being in the "doghouse"), the possibility of compensation for hurt presents itself through the mechanism of the "doghouse" release. When good will exists between partners the possibility of turning acid (hurt) into honey (some "goodie") always is present. For instance: "You may get out of the 'doghouse' (isolation by my displeasure) by doing the dishes tonight—or bringing me breakfast in bed." This is a making-up procedure. The "doghouse" release must never be excessive, must not stress the relationship, and must be relationship-suitable and acceptable.

When the Haircut is rejected: "I did not do or mean what you are accusing me of," a careful listening to the other view may clear the air, or a time is set (within 24 hours) to discuss the issue further if necessary.

When permission for a Haircut is denied, the problem of what to do with frustrated rage arises. A specific assignment early in the work of Conflict Management and Self-Care is to find alternative idiosyncratic rage-releases.

Idiosyncratic Rage-Release

This is a person-specific and solitary way of letting off steam when permission to do so by another is denied or a listening ear is unavailable. This involves an exploration into the self to determine what effective method fits in deëscalating rage. An exercise in self-knowing, through trial and error to find meaning is involved here. For many this release becomes a double-barreled asset: a catharsis *and* an accomplishment of a necessary job (weeding the garden, scrubbing the floor, cleaning windows, jogging, punching a punching bag). These engagements use up energy and help deëscalate rage with the possible added bonus of a cleaner house, a more beautiful lawn, or firmer muscles.

The Vesuvius

This is a verbal and time-limited rage about many things—inside and outside the home. This is an information-giving release, by permission, about frustrations, angers, and humiliations suffered during the day. It offers the comfort of a listening and respectful ear with no thought of retaliation, advice, or blame. The mate gets information about the partner's hurts, and limits the hearing according to his or her own time-tolerance. Any information that needs discussing is dealt with by making an appointment for such consideration at a later time (usually within 24 hours and not later than 48 hours). The purpose of this time separation is to avoid contamination of a rational process by irrational emotion. It is a way of letting off steam—clearing the way to rationally dealing with specific problems.

The Pickbone

This concept, as I use it, is the mutually agreed-upon right to grumble and complain about a specific behavior pattern of the significant other, without the obligation or request of the other to change. This ritual is a practical means of living around what a partner refuses to change, with the right to "bitch" about it given to the other. Designating a particular behavior as a "pickbone" gives each person the freedom to *be* in a specific area—one to do as he must and the other to verbalize displeasure. This becomes an acceptance of idiosyncracies and may even admit humor into the situation.

IMPACT PROCEDURES—RATIONAL CONFRONTATIONS

These are confrontation exercises that emphasize the what and how of *being* in a relationship. They are based on pair-specific tasks to create intimate involvement as well as independence. Behavior modification is used here, aimed at decreasing defensiveness, increasing openness, increasing explicit communication, and increasing assertiveness. The base of change is authentic communication, open encounter, confrontation, and negotiation. When partners differ and are in a state of conflict, there can be no productive resolution without aggressive confrontation of differences and finding pair-specific solutions. Impact procedures are techniques by which we help to make ourselves known to each other and effect change for our mutual benefit. Each has specific ground rules—mutually accepted.

The Museum—An Inventory of Corrosives*

This is a list of all grievances accumulated to date from the start of the pairing relationship. It is an historical, chronologically ordered record of the acid hoarded in intimate living. Confrontation of the partners with their separate Museum lists may be an initial assignment for a couple in conflict—to give information of hurts—past and present. The Museum then becomes the working base upon which to make the present more productive. Each assignment is pair-specific—based on the emotional readiness and "state of the union" of the couple. The Inventory of Corrosives is used as a base of information for change and growth tasks.

The first step is to determine which items on the list are no longer negotiable—which cannot be replayed, modified, or changed. On these items a burial ceremony is conducted, incorporating a commitment to forgive and eliminating their use as partner-punishing weapons. In all courts of law there is a suitable punishment for each crime. And when the punishment is carried out, it ends at the expiration of the sentence. In marital unions, too frequently the punishment for sins (crimes) is endless. This suggested procedure offers an escape from excessive punitiveness and opens the way to a change in the state of the union.

The next step in utilizing the I.C. information is to list the negotiable items of grievances in hierarchical order. This procedure may elicit the establishment of *belt-lines* (hurts too painful to absorb) and *beefs for change* (specific current gripes), starting with that which is immediately most practical to negotiate.

Dealing with the contents of a couple's Museums starts the process of unloading the emotional garbage that is suffocating the relationship and making barriers against intimacy.

---

*"Museum" and "Inventory of Corrosives" (I.C.) are used interchangeably.

Beefs for Change (Negotiation for Change)*

This is a communication technique aimed at establishing a process to deal with any specific issue—an item of discord. It is a zeroing in on a single gripe about a specific alienating behavior with a demand for change by partner ''x'' of ''y.'' It begins (as do *all* conflict management procedures) with a request for engagement: ''Will you engage me in a beef for change?'' A ''yes'' answer begins the work and learning of a process of communication. The therapist acts as coach in the encounter.

The first step in this process is meditation on the exact thought and wording of the request for change. This often involves an oral monologue by ''x'' giving background and feeling about the beef or gripe to ''y,'' as an introduction to the presentation of the beef. The beef is presented: ''I feel trapped and overloaded and would like four hours of free time from the children each weekend. Will you baby-sit at the cost of some of your weekend leisure so I can have some time for myself?''

Accurate *feedback* follows the message for change: ''I hear you say you feel trapped and overloaded and you would like four hours of free time each weekend at my expense.'' The response from ''x'' is ''That was not my exact message.'' The correction and addition again is clearly stated, followed once more by verbatim feedback. This process is repeated until the message given and the message received are identical.

Following the *assurance* of accurate hearing, ''You heard me correctly,'' the response is requested. This may be denial, total acquiescence, conditional acceptance, or alternative suggestion: ''I will give you four hours of free time and baby-sit if I can choose whether it will be a Saturday or Sunday of any week.'' This message is now fed back by ''y'' to ''x'' and again checked out for accuracy by ''y.''

The process of negotiation now is under way. Should ''x'' become enraged at a seeming hesitancy of ''y'' to accede to the request made, time out for a ''Haircut'' or a ''Vesuvius'' may be in order, provided this is granted by the partner and time-limited by the partner. The use of rage rituals during a Fight for Change often results in a clearer ''hearing'' of one by the other.

Before replying to the conditional acceptance of the requested change a ''Huddle''** with the therapist acting as coach may be necessary. A ''Huddle'' is a dialogue between the participant and the coach,

*''Beefs for Change'' and ''Negotiations for Change'' are used synonomously.

**''Huddle'' and ''dialogue'' are used interchangeably

the purpose of which is to give information of feeling content and problem background in order to clarify a situation—the other member of the confronting pair listens without defense or engagement—*and in silence!* The "Huddle" exposes the difficulties of the conditioned acceptance: "If I allow my free time choice to be on a Sunday, this limits my activity considerably. I would rather choose alternate Saturdays and one free evening instead." The "Huddle" may result in a counter proposal which is then presented and checked for accurate reception. If accepted, the negotiation is sealed by whatever nonverbal expression the couple can manage, usually a kiss, sometimes a handshake, depending upon the emotional state of the union at that particular time.

The "Huddle" may occur at various stages of the encounter with either partner or with each partner in turn. It enables each partner to immediately deal with and verbalize feeling content that might otherwise escalate into anger or rage that cuts off and derails from the immediate issue. The "Huddle" is an antidote to emotional escalation and provides a time-appropriate airing of internal steam and content. It prevents the contents of the "kitchen sink" from being thrown into the specific item of negotiation.

A negotiation may be premature or may be unworkable due to unconsidered circumstances—or it may need to be periodically reinforced to ensure a continued behavior pattern change. Therefore, each negotiation is checked weekly to determine the time readiness and "fit." There is no closure. Each negotiation is subject to re-negotiation for better "fit" in the reality space of the couple concerned at a later time.

The key element in this process is the feedback technique. It is direct practice in eliminating the process of interpretation or "set" in the mind of the message receiver. A message may have to be restated many times before an alienated mate hears it correctly—uncontaminated by his own lacerated feelings of negative expectations and hoarded hurts.

When a Beef for Change has been successfully negotiated, the transaction has now become a *commitment to act.*

Every commitment to change becomes part of the homework of the week. The following week's report on assignments determines the reality of the commitment and the extent to which it was carried out. Sometimes a commitment is premature in a stressed relationship, although given in good faith. It then becomes necessary to back-step to the point of what is actually possible. A re-negotiation takes place. In this way commitments are pragmatically tested and realistically changed if necessary—week by week.

The Beef for Change is an exercise in communication uncontaminated by the invasion of extraneous emotional injuries unrelated to the immediate issue. It's aim is to prevent the escalation of rage (when the "kitchen sink" contents are thrown in) by a studied, precise attention to the immediate issue—the current interaction. The emphasis is on exact feedback of each message with corrections clearly stated when the message given is altered in passage to the ears of the receiver. The procedure is contrived to start a PROCESS of keeping to the issue, hearing what is said, answering a request *without defense,* considering and offering alternatives when consent cannot be given.

As mentioned, throughout this procedure the therapist acts as coach. She is the communications facilitator, calls the foul plays, and notes the derailments. Such coaching takes place in an ongoing group or workshop, the group members act as checkers and reporters of the interchange, based on a critical analysis of the "fight style" exposed by the couple. The "fight style" chart* is the instrument used in facilitating critical feedback by the group. Each member of the group is given copies of the chart on which to score each couple's engagement. The group, at the conclusion of a couple's encounter, act as a mirror to the couple. The experience of seeing an intimate relationship objectively acts as a potent impetus to change.

Mind Reading

This is an exercise to see how accurate or inaccurate one is about the perception of another's *being.* It is an exercise in checking out an assumption for reality fit. It starts with a statement: "I think you think. . .". This is followed by a *Check-out:* "True or false?" and requires acceptance of the other's reply as having authenticity when the reply is counter to the assumption made.

Mind-reading check-outs only determine the state of "knowing" or "not knowing" the other at a particular time in living; it has no predictive value. Each assumption one makes of the other must be checked out for reality fit.

Bill of Rights

This is a *declaration* of each partner to the other of basic fundamental rights necessary to one's integrity, to a feeling of self-respect, self-liking and self-worth of the individual—without which one feels enslaved, used, degraded, or trapped. This is a process of information

*See end of chapter

giving, self-assertion, confrontation, limitation, and negotiation in the *implementation* of *rights*.

Autonomous Areas of Living

These are the segmented parts of intimate living in which each partner wants the right of *final decision making*. After discussion, these become defined areas of power in a relationship:

>Work Management
>Home Management
>Money Management
>Disposition of leisure time
>Discipline of children, etc.

Clearing-House

A daily or weekly exercise (pair and family-specific) in emptying the current gunnysack of grievances. This is a specific, negotiated, time-limited, and place-designated encounter to listen to each other's complaints, grievances, and frustrations. This is practice in openness and communication— information giving only. It is not a discussion period. The immediate emotional need may be satisfied just by airing hurts or may be the content of negotiation at a *later designated time*.

Clearing-House is a process of letting the significant other into one's guts—an exercise in open communication.

Expectations Exercise

This involves a confrontation to expose the reality of the roles one partner assigns to the other and to the self. The task is to *tell* what a partner *assumes* the other knows. After the "telling," the information is checked out for "fit" to determine "Can you meet my expectations?". It opens the way for possible negotiations and alternatives in authentic living.

State of the Union Message

This is a periodic review of the relationship by each partner (trouble areas, growth areas, areas of conflict). It is an assessment of past, present and future relationship—where we've been, where we are, and where we are going (goals we hope to attain). It is a confrontation of perceptions of the relationship—a checking out of similarities and differences in awarenesses.

Establishing Belt Lines

A Belt Line is a lethal hurt, provoked by allusion to an unforgiven past sin, or a hurtful labeling such as "drunkard" or "whore." Naming such a pain a Belt Line establishes a process of eliminating poisonous behavior by using the intimate other as an ally for change in order to bring to conscious attention an unconscious behavior. Calling "foul" becomes a signal to the offending partner to immediately back off.

The Hostility Rituals and the Rational Confrontation techniques implement the processes of attaining release from futile hostility, give information, establish limitations of deep hurting, bury the acid of past hurts, define and negotiate current issues, establish individual and interpersonal responsibilities and freedoms, increase authenticity and openness. Maintaining authenticity and openness in a relationship reduces the sabotage of fantasy expectations and makes possible the confrontation of reality issues. To live authentically (with self-respect, self-responsibility, and openness) includes the forgiveness of past sins, the risking of trusting, and the establishment of areas of freedom within togetherness. With a dedication to Self-Care, using ritualized procedures, partners can attain autonomy and intimacy, can differentiate between accommodation which erases the self and accommodation given as a free gift of love which expands the self. They can then enjoy the freedom of independence and the comfort of dependence (being able to lean upon the other when necessary).

Self-erasing accommodation refers to behavior based on such concepts as:

> It's not worth bothering about.
> I *ought* to, therefore I *must*.
> I don't want to rock the boat.
> I don't want to hurt you.

Self-expanding accommodation refers to behavior which clearly says:

> I don't want to go to that ballgame, but I will to please you and I like hearing you want me along.
> I'm not interested sexually, but I'm available because you are dear to me and your wanting me makes me feel loved.

A self-expanding accommodation begins with a statement of authentic being and ends with an act of love—a free gift to the other with no strings attached and completely free of martyrdom.

Explanation of Score Sheet
In this case, the male presented an issue to negotiate for change.

1. Both partners recognized the stated problem as a real issue of discord.

2. The issue was specifically, concisely, and clearly stated.

3. The message given was distorted by the "set" (expectation) of the partner and had to be repeated twice before accurately heard.

4. Sarcasm was used.

5. Past sins were referred to twice before concentrating on the current issue.

6. First reaction was resistance to change. This was followed by commitment to work at change for one week.

REVISED SCORE SHEET—FAIR FIGHT STYLE

*Partners	M	F.				
1. +AUTHENTIC (REAL) ISSUE −PHONY ISSUE	+	+				
2. +SPECIFIC STATEMENT −UNCLEAR MESSAGE	+					
3. +ACCURATE FEEDBACK −INACCURATE FEEDBACK		− ∓				
4. +HUMOR USED AS RELEASE −HUMOR USED TO DEPRECATE	−					
5. +TIME PERSPECTIVE (HERE & NOW) −OLD ISSUES CONTAMINATING PRESENT	+	− ∓				

6. +CHANGE READINESS
   −RESISTANCE & REFUSAL TO
   ACKNOWLEDGE PROBLEM
		∓				

RECOGNITION OF NEGATIVE MANIPULATIONS (check when recognized)						
ANALYSIS: (message interpreted as meaning something else)		X				
DOUBLE-BIND: (I lose if I do & I lose if I don't)						
IDENTITY-DENIAL (being told you don't feel or mean what you say)	X					
DERAILING (bringing in other issues to sidetrack from stated one)		X				
UNCHECKED ASSUMPTIONS (failure to check out a mind-reading)						
OVERLOADING (adding many extras to original request)						

Chapter 3

Self-Care—Process of Self-Validation

The ingestion of the concept of Self-Care carries with it a responsibility: the responsibility for your own actions put on your own shoulders. The concept states "you can direct your own life as opposed to being a victim of circumstances." The concept of Self-Care implicitly states:

> You are the captain of your ship.
> You must test its sea-worthiness by ROCKING THE BOAT (risking authenticity).

The assumption is that only if you are somewhat at peace with yourself (self-accepting—giving yourself the right to goof and taking the responsibility to learn from your goofs), can you release pressure on yourself and others; can you be less judgmental of another and more compassionate of others' foibles, seeing these as separate from you and not necessarily hostile acts against you.

The job of Self-Care focuses on assessing the realities in your living space, determining under what conditions you can best BE, work, and develop. What immediate and long term goals, based on an objective evaluation, can you set as tasks in which to engage? Self-Care means consideration for self *and other* in a relationship. Self-Care is never exploitive of another. It maintains the right of independence, dependence, and interdependence in a significant relationship. The concept of Self-Care poses significant questions:

> What can I do for myself?
> What can I do for you?
> To what purpose?
> At what cost?

Tasks of Self-Caring are very person-specific, pair-specific, and family-specific. The what and how of it are self-assigned responsibilities.

I want to differentiate between being SELFISH and being SELF-CARING.

As defined by *Webster's New World Dictionary*, SELFISH means "Having such regard for one's own interests and advantage that the happiness and welfare of others become of less concern than is considered right or just." Such a self-focus is at the expense of another.

My concept of SELF-CARE is a road to a wedding of who and what I am and who and what I want to be, a realistic assessment of me and my possibilities, a coming to terms with my humanness. It eliminates the measuring scale against which I must pit myself and permits me to set my own norms. It frees me from the pressure of "what will *they* think". This involves the courage taken to present oneself authentically, risking another's displeasure, and realistically assessing one's impact upon a significant other:

> What impact am I making?
> What impact do I want to make?

When these are discordant, what changes in my behavior do I need to make in order to attain a specific goal? Self-Care incorporates work in behavior change to actualize oneself. It embodies a responsibility to consider oneself important in order to commit oneself to *effectively* meet one's own needs without subjugating, exploiting or harming another. This process considers the realistic possibilities of intimate and work relationships. To act "as if" one is important is an effective road to attaining the feeling of importance.

This is the starting point of any productive relationship. It is the process of building self-respect. Only through respecting oneself can respect from another be gained.

The practice of Self-Care frees us from the impotent anger, rage and despair resulting from unfulfilled expectations: the expectation that another's actions will prove or disprove my worth, the expectation that the significant other magically knows or divines my tests of importance in the relationship and as a person.

The practice of Self-Care effectively destroys the need to test and prove one's worth through another's response or actions, thereby releasing the pressure on another to perform to unclear and often unstated scripts.

SOME SPECIFIC SELF-CARE DEFINITIONS

A Self-Care List Presented by a Doctor:

Self-Care means to feel my legitimate power to limit ways of relating to others which are destructive to my self-identity and self-respect and which perpetuate my double-bind behavior.

It means taking necessary risks to hurt feelings of wife, mother, children in order to maintain my self-identity.

It means the right to privacy and not taking the safest way out.

It means sticking to efforts at work to limit the time demands certain patients make on me.

It means to negotiate with my mate the limitation of mutual analysis when it leads to confused attacking.

It means to show my unwillingness to accept labels of being "unfeeling," and to refuse being derailed even if criticized as being closed-minded and authoritarian.

I will limit my mother's accusations of dad before me, even if she feels I'm insensitive and misreading her intent.

I will limit public humiliation from mate and stand up for my feelings and confront her on the spot, even if she and others may get ideas that I'm hypersensitive and insensitive to her feelings.

I will limit the time my colleague ties me up on the telephone explaining his therapy when I want to be sleeping or relaxing.

I will maintain my right to deal with my own situations even at the cost of hurting others' feelings.

I will take action on my right for privacy and distance when I need it.

I'll work on developing discipline to limit verbosity in confronting another and not attempt to soften it afterward or sound apologetic.

I'll develop the discipline to deprive myself of the superior feeling I get from the self-image of being fair, democratic, understanding, patient, sensitive.

I am aware of feelings in me of being insensitive, unfair, not understanding, cold, authoritarian, selfish, undedicated, uncaring, impatient, neurotic, seclusive, engendered as I act at self-care.

In the last two statements this client clearly exposes the *pay-off* of over-accommodation and compliance to others (ideal self-image, and the *cost* of working at change—the pain of conflict between conditioned "oughts" and "shoulds" and reality fit).

Audrey poses four questions and answers them:

WHAT DOES SELF-CARE MEAN TO ME? This is the most important concept I ever learned. It has helped raise my self-esteem immensely. I am convinced if I don't take care of myself, I can't take care of or help anyone else. I owe it to myself to take care of myself.

WHAT LIMITATIONS WILL SELF-CARE PUT ON OTHERS? Sometimes I will have to say "no" when others make a request of me, even if it means someone will be hurt or angry with me.

WHAT FEELINGS ARE ENGENDERED IN ME AS I ACT WITH SELF-CARE? I feel very good about me. I become even more aware of how important this concept is—how self-care is an ongoing process. Much of, or rather most of my guilt about not being "nice," trying to please all the time, is gone. I don't have the need to be loved or liked by *everyone* and I now act because of the way I feel, not because I want to please someone and have them like me—at the cost of erasing myself as a person.

WHAT DISCIPLINE DO I PUT ON ME AS PART OF MY SELF-CARE? I make a more careful effort to listen to what people are asking me to do. I try to be more aware of what I really do want to do and what I don't want to do—what's OK to compromise on and what is not OK to compromise for me—so that I can be honest and give a direct response to someone. When I run into a problem that requires negotiation I think very hard about alternatives or options. I try to discipline myself to be flexible, not rigid. I don't make apologies or excuses for the way I feel or what I do. I am working at not pushing myself too hard at my job and getting more sleep.

To Judd, the meaning of Self-Care is stated as follows:

The actions I take and the conditions that I insist on that make it possible for me to be a fully aware, responsible, outreaching, loving, spontaneous, warm person.

This involves taking responsibility:
to create an environment in which I make impact;
to limit closeness and gain privacy;
to control access to me in the use of my time;
use of my energy;
level of involvement

I must exercise some control over what happens to me socially, economically, intellectually, and psychologically. To this end I will periodically check up on myself and re-evaluate my personal landscape.

A professional woman, head of a mental health institute outlines meaning, work, rights, feelings, and disciplines of Self-Care:

WHAT SELF-CARE MEANS TO ME: Defining to myself the amount of time I need to spend with my mate in order to fulfill my needs. Being able to act as I need to in order to maintain my own integrity without closing myself to avenues of change. Beginning to think about my physical health and deciding which steps I'm prepared to take to insure it.

WHAT LIMITATIONS SELF-CARE MEANS PUTTING ON OTHERS: I will not be disturbed during the time I allot to myself. I will not answer telephones, deal with clients, attend meetings, speak to groups unless I *want* to do that more than anything else. I will not tolerate (will leave the room if I cannot remain disengaged) non-specific criticism. These are neither meaningful nor helpful.

WHAT RIGHTS I TAKE RESPONSIBLE ACTION ON: The right to time—I will make up a schedule each week to let clients and family know when I am available and when I am not. I will work at disengaging from problems I feel are not mine. I will begin to think seriously about my health and to think about what sort of allies I need in order to care for it—particularly in reference to smoking and drinking.

WHAT FEELINGS ARE ENGENDERED IN ME AS I ACT IN SELF-CARE? Very warm and good ones. I have a lot less general resentment of other people and less guilt myself for not meeting the needs of others more frequently.

WHAT DISCIPLINES DO I PUT ON ME AS PART OF MY SELF-CARE: Taking time to make a schedule for work and play each week. The discipline of disengagment—closing my mouth or leaving! The discipline of moderation.

To Beth, Self Care is translated into a person-specific assignment of work and attitude change.

Self-Care items I am working on now:

Allowing *enough time* to do things comfortably so I don't feel pinched and rushed. This includes not overloading my schedule or being unrealistic about the energy and time it takes to do what I want to do or have to do. Being wary of setting my expectations too high so I set it up to feel that I have failed.

Being "proud" of me without deprecating or feeling that I have to explain.

Learning how to say "NO!" to some of my married daughter's impromptu visits and requests—without feeling guilty about "rejecting" her. This includes thinking of her as a woman of some strength, and not as a child.

Making adequate plans to reach out to people I want to be friends with. Take the responsibility of setting dates.

Take many more risks in confrontation with others in expressing my opinion or feelings. My head already knows I am not going to die from doing this, or even being rejected—I would like my stomach to get the message. I am the most important person to please in this area and I need self-validation. This is not an area that needs "understanding" and "rationalization"—in fact, in this area, these two qualities are *outlawed*.

Hopefully, my head and my gut will get more in tune with each other, and I will be more aware of genuine feelings. And conversely, my gut will stop panicking and start believing my head.

To Dick, Self-Care becomes a credo of living:

Self-Care is the realization that my own ecological balance can only be maintained by *me*. Some of my energy, time, and physical resources must be devoted to satisfying *my* needs.

The limitations imposed by my self-care are:
   a. I must eat my major meal of the day at noon or suffer physical discomfort.
   b. I must have at least 6½ hours of sleep a night or suffer de-generating morale.
   c. I must have one night per week in my workshop.
   d. I cannot devote more than three evenings per week to school or civic projects.

I reserve the right to state my real opinion, view, or feeling on any matter regardless of setting. I reserve the right to refuse infringements on my time and energy. I reserve the right to ask other people for help if my needs are not being satisfied.

When I practice Self-Care, I am amazed at how powerful and complete I feel. I experience tremendous waves of energy and enthusiasm.

The disciplines I put on me as part of Self-Care are to practice the eating and sleeping and exercising routines which insure my physical well-being; to say "no" to demands on my time and energy which I have designated as mine, and to verbally establish my value system as part of self-validation.

Janet's person-specific meaning of Self-Care is explicit:

Self-Care is what I need to feel harmony inside myself.

Self-Care involves my giving up part of the day sometimes to get the sleep or distance I need. I need to take nausea-producing pills to keep down a chronic infection. I must exercise when I don't always want to or get flabby.

I take the action of avoiding those who erode my self-concept. I reserve the right to say "no" to requests to community service and to refuse any social invitations. I reserve the right to refuse my children my company when I'm "done in" although I will give them an explanation. I reserve the right to give authentic expression to my views regardless of the company. I reserve the right to travel alone occasionally.

I feel power when I practice Self-Care. Also, sometimes I feel extreme nervousness, but that I can live with because not to practice what I really need is a partial death.

I keep my house neat and I'm on time for appointments because I get very uptight when these things are lax. I try not to overeat as I then feel sick. I sometimes practice at a sport I'm afraid of because the confidence I gain then is worth it.

SELF-CARE IN FAMILIES

In family relations, Self-Care becomes more possible as one becomes more aware of specific irritants and misconstrued messages. The following therapist-couple encounter graphically illustrates a process of gaining clarity.

BETH: My son Ricky had *terrible* stomachaches Thursday and Friday —he's a worrier. I took him to the doctor Friday afternoon, and he couldn't find anything wrong. Then on the weekend they went away. And sure enough—Monday morning, terrible stomach aches! I took him to school anyway, but I went to talk to his teacher, and she just said he shouldn't be so sensitive. But she assured him that if he asked her to go to the bathroom besides recess and lunchtime that she would let him go.

THERAPIST: I'm beginning to hear that this is just part of what's bothering you.

B: Exactly! I love my family, but there's *always* something that I have to do for somebody else. It's not a question of not wanting to take care of them. It's trying to find time for *me* when there are five other people who need my attention. And as the children get older, even though the care element diminishes, it becomes more of an *emotional* drain.

TH: Let's take a look at it this way. Ask yourself first: "What part of the emotional demands do I make deeper by my reaction?" For instance, in the example you gave, what comes across to me is the message that you felt that the stomach aches *were going to recur* instead of feeling that they were actually over and ended. And so you girded yourself for stress in the future—a process that creates stress in the present—so you lose out on the present and lose out on the future by tasting the stress before the event and during the event.

B: I guess I do anticipate trouble a lot.

TH: Yes, I think you do. *(To Ed)* And how did you react in this situation?

ED: I said, "Make him go to school."

TH *(to Ed):* Next time, instead of asking her to make one of the children do something, how about: "I'll take over now. Ricky—or whoever—you will go to school today." Could you have taken over last time?

E: It might have meant my taking him and being late for work, but sure, I could have taken over.

TH: As a rule of thumb, I'd suggest that if it's important enough to issue an order, it's important enough to take care of it yourself.

B: I think you've found my issue! I had to defend myself to Ed when I told him about talking to Ricky's teacher!

TH: Learn to take the course of action that makes sense to you, Beth. If Ed says, "Make him," you can turn to him and say: "If it's that important to you, *you* make him!" Or, you can confront Ed when he orders you to do something and say that you need the freedom to handle it *your* way. There is always an alternative and usually more than one way to go.

E: But I didn't say "Make him" as a command. Beth asked me what I thought she should do, and I simply gave her my opinion!

TH: Now we're into another situation entirely. If I hear Ed, you, Beth, translated an opinion into a command. Examine your behavior in this light, and look at the pressure you put on yourself in this way. If you don't carry out his "order," you feel he'll be waiting to attack you for failing—*you* feel that. According to him, the reality is quite different.

B: How can I change that?

TH: Start by saying to yourself: "This is what Ed wants. Now, *what can I do?*"

NOTE: It is important that *impact* of a message is communicated—"I heard a command," gives a clear message of impact, to be verified or refuted.

A recently-divorced woman and parent reported in a group therapy session her progress on her specific and self-given assignment of Self-Care in relation to family interaction and self-concept as follows:

MARTHA: I really felt proud of myself tonight. I finally controlled my bitterness toward my ex-husband enough so that I didn't lay it on the kids. My daughter (17) picks up her brother (13) from his music teacher's home on Wednesdays so I can come to group. Both children live with me. This morning I was talking to my daughter and I said, "So that I don't have to cook something for you two before I leave, why don't you put something together yourself or go and have dinner with your father?" She said she'd think about it, and I left it there. Instead of fuming or feeling sorry for myself because they might really choose to go to their father, I just went ahead and did some work I had to do. If they were going to stay home for dinner, I figured she'd say so. When she didn't mention it, I didn't ask her—I just got ready to come to group. They left before I did to go to dinner, and I even managed to say, "Good night. Have a good time." Period! No cracks from me! I'm jealous and I know it. I'm alone, and he's not. He has a new wife to back him up. I don't have anyone. I want to use this group to work on my jealousy so I don't keep exploding at the children about their father.

THERAPIST: How do you explode at them?

M: To illustrate, yesterday Bonnie, my daughter, left three pans in the sink that she'd dirtied cooking up something. I started by telling her I wasn't her maid, but then I went into the old song and dance about her father's inconsiderations and the divorce and I escalated into an explosion.

TH: Do you really want to break this pattern?

M: Yes, I do. I don't want Bonnie to be hurt.

TH: Then you need her as an ally.

M: We tried that, but she only did it once.

TH: What did you try?

M: We made a pact the way you taught me. She agreed to give me a cue—"dynamite"—if I started in about her father to her. She said it once. I said, "You're right." I left the room and went to the bedroom and pounded the pillow until I cooled off.

TH: But she didn't do it after that?

M: No, and I didn't remind her.

TH: Then how about renegotiating it on a weekly basis for a while so that you both stay reminded of the pact?

M: Sure, I don't mind. But what can I do to deal with my own problems?

TH: You can start by saying to yourself, "Doing something just for me is OK!" Then the next time you decide not to cook dinner for the kids, how about trying the statement, "I'm doing something for me tonight. You're on your own." The point here is to *teach yourself a new way to put yourself across to your children.* A new way of being for you involves saying out front, "I'm taking off today. I have to get away for awhile and do something for me. It has nothing to do with you children; it is not a rejection of you, or a punishment, or a test. It's an exercise in taking care of myself, in being responsible for myself and not laying it on you." You're learning to give them the message that the bitterness you feel isn't their responsibility—that you don't want them burned by the acid in your guts.

You need to learn to develop a personal Bill of Rights to deal with your own individual wants and desires.

The message you then give is:

I need. . .
I want. . .
I'm going to do. . .
I would like you to. . .

(instead of:)

Why don't you. . .
You ought. . .
You never. . .

Presented as a personal Bill of Rights (freedoms and responsibilities) you change a climate of "poor me" (with the pressure on someone else to perform according to unspecified expectations) to "I am worth doing for" (an implicit and explicit challenge to act). What you are ultimately doing is building self-respect.

These Self-Care tasks are two-way exercises; that is, they are explorations in getting acquainted with oneself and doing for oneself. The specific freedoms are based on the time-readiness of all involved, with the practical assessment that the children are old enough and mature enough to carry out the responsibilities the parental freedom necessitates (getting meals at times, dealing with being alone at times, etc.).

WHAT IF CHANGES AREN'T POSSIBLE IMMEDIATELY

The following confrontation focuses on those difficulties of living that can't be immediately changed and exploring ways and means of meeting current needs.

MIDGE: I'm the breadwinner this year while Kris is back in school and I feel that I have all the heavy load of that without the appreciation that I have seen go to men who carry that load. And Kris and I have gone 'round and 'round on this and I don't know if I expect too much in the way of compensation or support.

THERAPIST: What support would make you feel more comfortable?

M: Well, we've gone over it a lot. I have to drive to work because we live far away. I spend about an hour and a half on the road every-day. I say to myself, "Hey, you're the breadwinner. Why are you driving? When Kris was a breadwinner he never had to drive be-cause we deliberately lived near his place of work."

TH: Let's check out the reality. You and I are huddling now. Is there any possibility of, within the next year, changing that situation? Practically?

M: Probably within the next year.

TH: All right, if we have to wait a year at least, let's take something more current that will relieve pressure on you and support you immediately.

M: Well, I guess it's not living where I work. That's the big bind for me now. I need to stay over a number of nights. I don't like to stay over, I get very tired. To do my job well I really ought to live in the community and I guess I'm saying that we can't do anything about that until next year. I don't know how to relieve that now. Because the load at home isn't too bad.

TH: Well, the idea of a possible move in a year makes you feel better—is that what you're saying?

M: I have very mixed feelings about that, because that's to meet *my* needs. And I have two kids who will be very disturbed if we move and it may not be convenient for Kris to move. And I get in this bind of what can I strongly stand up for and say "I've got to have that in order to continue," and when do I consider other people's needs?

TH: So what I hear is the possibility of excellent practice for a year that will help you make a decision at the end of that time. And the prac-tice I'm talking about is *day by day* to evaluate the stress of the day and what help you need on that day or that week. As a commit-ment to yourself. As practice in taking care of yourself.

M: I don't know what the concretes are. Each day I think of how to do that—weigh the load.

TH: You know your week's schedule more or less, right? You evaluate it, what nit-picking detail of living can Kris take off your shoul-ders or the kids take off your shoulders, or whatever? Clearly assigned—if practical.

M: Yeah. and then I get into something else. I tried to eliminate what I do at night, I seldom go out to speak at night, I try not to have phone calls, I try not to have company, and that gets in Kris' way; you see, he has some needs, too. Because he has some needs to invite guests and entertain guests in our home and I'm saying right now I can't manage all that, I don't feel very good about it.

TH: Keep going. I hear you saying, "I don't feel very good about meeting my own needs and making Kris unhappy."

M: Kris said one of the things he didn't like about me was that I don't enjoy having a lot of people in and entertaining. And I'm saying that I can't swing it now.

TH: Do you want this reinforced as a right?

M: Yes, I would like to feel that it's okay if I can't manage that.

TH: Check it out.

M: I guess I want you to say that it's okay if I can't swing all that right now.

TH: Swing all that what?

M: Having people come and entertain them along with all the rest I'm doing.

TH: For how long? One month, two months, three months, six months, a year?

M: A year.

KRIS: That's okay with me with a provision: if we have people over and throw a party in the yard, I agree to handle the whole damn thing. I can cook.

TH: A conditional acceptance.

K: Oh, let's take that out. It isn't that important, I withdraw that provision.

TH: Wait just a moment, hold it. This mutual accommodation gives me a pain in my rear and acid in your guts!

K: Okay, if I decide I want company and talk it over with you, that we might agree to entertain if I will assume the whole damn load.

M: I'm willing to try that. But I know that I have some trouble letting loose with that. You know, these twenty years I've been at least involved.

TH: The pact is, if I hear it correctly, that you are relieved of the pressure of entertaining. That Kris has the liberty of entertaining on the basis of carrying the whole load. It's his ball of wax.

M: Inviting, buying, shopping?

K: The whole thing.

M: That's great! I like that.

TH: And it's your responsibility to keep out of it.

M: I can do that. It might be hard at points, but not that hard.

TH: Seal that . . . *(The couple embraces enthusiastically.)*

The focus here has been on the immediately possible stress-release to start a *process* of *Self-care* and *decrease* of *pressure*. The following illustrates a process of self-awareness which leads to Self-Care through a group assignment to list aches, gripes, and complaints among intimates. The example deals with unfinished business with a sibling, and also illustrates a group process using a surrogate to work through a problem.

MONA: I have a list of things addressed to a number of different people. As I read them, some of them felt like they were coming through my head and out and I felt almost nothing. And some of them raised my body temperature and some of them brought me close to tears. So what reading my list told me are the places that are hot for me now are the places that I need more cool. These are areas of work for me.

THERAPIST: In the area that's hot for you now, what do you want to deal with first?

M: I think I want to finish what's unfinished with my older sister.

TH: All right, give us background.

M: I have a sister who is two years older than I, unmarried, as I am, and about four years ago she became pregnant and came to live with me and. . .

TH: Still lives with you?

M: No, she lived with me through the pregnancy. And gave the child up for adoption and the statement that's on my list is, "Janet, I resent that you gave my niece away." (Crying) This is still painful to me. The baby girl would have been my niece.

TH: Would you like to tell her directly what you feel?

M: Yes.

TH: Pick your sister.

M: Oh, Barbara, would you be my sister? *(Barbara consents)*

TH: Give your sister her character.

M: You're 37, you're a nurse. Your hair is half-gray. You've got furrows in your forehead almost continuously. You're much smaller than I, smaller and thinner. You're a very serious person, you take life very seriously. You work your tail off. I don't know what you do for fun—I never hear about it. I don't think you've had a date since you were pregnant. I don't know for sure. It seems like your life is very serious. You're two years older than I, you were very important to me growing up. We were very close. (Crying) But that isn't so anymore. And I have a hunch—I know—that the turning point of your closeness is when you were pregnant. We talked about it—tidbits—it gets a bit too painful for you. I still feel unfinished. I feel a little bit shakey, Janet. You are always busy—well, your work is very tiring and you commute an hour each way to work and you do a lot of walking on your job and so you come home exhausted, spending your evenings at home. . .like giving in to your body. Recalling what happened four years ago makes me shakey—

TH: Sink into it . . . go ahead.

M: I feel some sadness, some pain. I feel lost. . .your child that you gave away—sure you gave away your daughter, it must be horrible for you. What's horrible for me is that you gave away my niece and she would be three or four now. So I fantasize, giving her Christmas gifts which I can't do. . .and this is also stirring up in me my own need and wish and want to have a child. I view you as being stupid for having one and giving it away. I feel myself trembling. . . .

TH: Stay with it. . .don't dissipate it. . .sink into it. What's the unfinished business with your sister? "I think you're stupid for giving your baby away?" Did you want it?

M: I think you're stupid for having it in the first place. *(Long pause)* And I resent that you're unwilling to openly deal with it with me.

TH: "And I wonder where the hell you are with it?"

M: Yes.

TH: Ask her.

M: Where are you with this? You know, you named the child Baby Jean, so where are you emotionally with Baby Jean?

BARBARA: You're asking me to tell you about an open, gaping wound. I live with this open, gaping wound. I deal with it in my own way. I work my tail off. I come home so tired at night, I could find jobs closer, but I spend an hour getting home and an hour going, because that uses up some time that I don't have to deal with this. I come home tired—I make sure I come home tired. Fall asleep. You talk about your deprivation, but I'm living with my deprivation daily. Your deprivation is somewhat in the realm of fantasy compared with my deprivation. Because you think of it on Hallowe'en, Christmas, weekends. . .at this point I can only cope with living like this. I can't deal with your feelings about it because I can't deal with my own feelings about it.

M: A lot of what you said must be so with my sister. I would imagine that she'd say that. . .when you say that it's an open, gaping wound, I'm sure there's more pain for you in this. It's more of an unfinished thing for you than it is for me. A scarier issue for you than it is for me. But that doesn't diminish what I feel.

B: I can recognize what you're saying and I think it's true. But I can't cope with your pain.

M: Well, I don't want you to cope with my pain. I merely want to tell you. What I'm saying to you is this issue has separated us and I don't like it. You've been an important person to me when you've been close to me, and I want to get back to that closeness.

TH: Let's huddle for awhile, you and I. Your sister has shut off a topic of communication; not all avenues of communication, but a topic of communication because it's too bloody for her. Realistic? Okay, therefore, what avenues of communication can you open that have nothing to do with the giving away of her child? What would you like to do with your sister? Tell her.

M: So you're saying that this is below her beltline.

TH: Exactly.

M: So this is a topic for me to leave alone?

TH: Right! It's akin to poking a knife through a scab that's hardly formed.

M: I hear you. Janet, you've made it a little clearer to me where you're at with this, and I'll respect that this is a very sore spot for you, and I'll promise you that I'll go around this and leave it untouched.

TH: That's what you won't do! Now tell her what you will do.

M: I'll—this is interesting, I'll be seeing her this weekend, so the timing is right—I'll search in my own mind, with my own creativeness to find other areas where you and I can make contact, that are fun for both of us, that are nourishing for both of us.

TH: Now come up with a suggestion.

M: And I'll come with various ideas. And what I'd like is for you to respond to these ideas, positively or negatively.

B: I think I have to respond first. I would like to *know* that you will leave me alone in this area. I would like to have fun in my life, and I think we could have fun together again, if I know that you will respect my pain area, and not mess around with it. If I knew you would respect my space, then I would be happy to find some fun in life again. And I need your kind of creativity to find fun, because I'm immobilized in that area now. I really do need you, I need your help, but it's hard to ask for it because you might mess with me.

M: I think Janet would say that.

TH: Do you have a direction to go, Mona? Now?

M: Yes, I do.

Double-Bind

The following is an illustration of Self-Care through a self-presentation and reaction to a double-bind within the framework of an on-going group. Some references are to past gripes.

MARGO: You accused me of mothering you, being overly jealous, possessive. . .And yet when I ask you about the good things about me, you like my waiting on you, taking care of you, the attention I give you; so, goddamn you, you put me in a double-bind. I'm damned if I do and damned if I don't.

THERAPIST: Keep going and tell him how you've changed.

M: We've discussed this before.

TH: That's all right—he didn't hear very well.

M: I'll buy that! I like to do things for you. Simply because I like to, not because it's demanded of me. I live to give. And I like to receive. I like to be with you because I find you to be the most delightful person I've ever known. I'm not with you to watch, I'm with you because I enjoy being with you. I enjoy talking to you and I like to listen to you.

TH: And how about the jealousy part?

M: I am jealous, but there was a time when I had reason. I don't think I do anymore and I'm not jealous anymore.

TH: So that's changing. Tell him.

M: You don't believe that I've changed You have a lot of anger about my jealousy and I understand that but I've changed now. Are you still judging me by last year's row? Don't you think I'm capable of change?

JACK: Yes, you're capable of change.

M: But you don't see it, do you?

J: It isn't visible to me.

TH: Do you want information from him? *(Margo nods)* All right, tell her exactly *what* is current that evidences no change. Be specific.

J: You have an expanded egotism. You treat me like a possession.

TH: Let's huddle. First, the labeling: "You have an expanded egotism." This is a category, a label, a cage, a value judgment. Second: "You treat me like a possession." Very, very global. These are statements that make barriers between two people. Now, we could take this same feeling content and take responsibility in meeting needs. When do you feel possessed? Illustrate. We're still huddling, Jack.

J: When she wants me to come and sit beside her, she'll tell me to come and sit beside her. She doesn't ask whether I want to come and sit beside her.

TH: You have no responsibility to say yes or no?

J: Sure. I say no.

TH: So how are you possessed if you say no? She says come sit beside me and you say no. So where and how are you possessed?

J: Well, then she begins her little pouting bit.

TH: And?

J: It makes me feel guilty.

TH: And?

J: I usually give in.

TH: And go and sit beside her?

J: I'll do it in order to keep peace.

TH: So she has no right to pout when she's rejected? If I make a movement in your direction and you say "No way, gal," do you expect me to be happy about it?

J: No.

TH: Is it your job to keep me happy at any expense?

J: At any expense? No, I don't think so

TH: I don't think so either. So I'm sulking, big deal. Do you see what I'm driving at? There are times, many times, when we do openly reject each other. We are in the act of erasing ourselves when we're accommodating just to please the other at our own expense. When we accommodate as a gift of love, say, "No, I don't want to do this, but I'll do it anyway as a gift of love." Then we're not erasing ourselves, we're expanding ourselves beyond ourselves into the needs of another. When we accommodate without love, erasing ourselves, we usually pile up a feeling of antagonism and hate against the person we are accommodating, and I see this operative right here. She is much better off if you don't accommodate her. Then she won't have the acid of your guilt, which is the substance of your anger and hostility against her—which is the substance of your judgment, "You're always on an ego trip, you're so goddamn possessive, you make me do what I don't want to do." She's to blame for all your ills. Do you see the mechanism that you yourself create? Getting off that trip means that you may conceivably hear some crying, you may also manufacture a defense against its impact. And let her cry in peace.

M: I cry as a habit in answer to frustration, hurt, whatever.

TH: I hear you saying, "Crying is a habit of reaction with me under stress, any kind of stress, different kinds of stress. This is my way of being—disregard it. It's not a command for you to do anything, it's just my way of being." Am I hearing correctly? *(Margo nods)* I'll take it one step further. "It is not a mechanism to manipulate you into anything," true or false?

M: I have in the past.

TH: I'm talking about right now. I'm talking about the change that he's not recognizing.

M: Then, no, it isn't a mechanism to manipulate you.

TH: Are you hearing? What do you hear?

J: I'm hearing that her crying is not a way to manipulate me into doing what she wants me to do.

TH: Can you buy that? Rather, let me put it this way. For one week can you dedicate yourself to disregard her crying reactions and do what your guts tell you to do? A freedom bill for one week.

J: I think I've done so in the past to a great degree.

TH: Then how come you feel so possessed?

J: Maybe I haven't done it to enough of a degree?

TH: Possibly. So do you accept the assignment?

J: Yes.

TH: How do you feel about the assignment, Margo?

M: I'm not sure I understand it completely.

TH: How do you understand the assignment, Jack? Explain it to your mate.

J: The assignment is that regardless of what I feel you want to manipulate me to do, that I will do whatever I feel like doing and let you do whatever you feel like doing about it, for one week.

TH: How does that sound to you? Just a new experience of trying out a new tactic of living, for one week. At the end of the week you renegotiate it, either to continue or to be modified according to your experiential learning. Is that accepted? *(Both agree)* Then seal it. *(The couple touch hands)*

M: May I ask one more thing? Would you please throw that line, "expanded egotism" out of your vocabulary? Just let me be proud of you in my own way. Please?

TH: Sounds like the establishment of a beltline. What message are you getting?

J: I'm getting the message that she doesn't like me to use the words "expanded egotism."

TH: All right. Will you throw it out?

Jack: Yes.

TH: So what you are saying is I will honor your beltline. *(Jack nods)* You've established a beltline and he has committed himself to honor it. Seal that. *(The couple embrace)*

Group Comments

BONNIE: There's one concept that I don't understand. If I need a stroke and he gives it, even though he doesn't feel it, because he loves me enough, then if he doesn't do it, I think he doesn't love me enough.

TH: That's a real crazy-maker. You see, what you are now doing is incorporating into your intimate living a scale by which you judge one another. And I'm saying, throw out that scale. A committed relationship frees you to be what you can be. Sometimes we can expand ourselves beyond our guts and sometimes we *can't*. Because I don't see a single angel here. And I know of no human being, no normal human being who can expand himself all the time. It simply means that my capacity for acting over my guts at this point is inoperative—not that you're not important. Am I making sense here?

B: Yes, I hear you.

TH: Any other comments?

EVELYN: What if your spouse's method of validating himself, like Margo's crying, is below the belt for you?

TH: Just a moment. Margo's crying is a release *for her*. If he can't stand crying because, for instance, his mother used it as a weapon to get him to heel and it really triggers his guts, then he has a reconditioning process to go through or other avenues to explore. When she begins to cry he could go into another room and close the door until she's through. He can find other outlets for himself that cut the impact of this trigger reaction. Are you hearing me, Evelyn?

E: Yeah. I'm trying to figure out what my outlets are.

TH: That's right. And you figure until you come up with something. Let your creativity come into play.

E: But you still have a right to say, "Hey, that's below the belt for me?"

TH: Yes. You can say, "Your crying does things to my guts, excuse me, I have to absent myself. This reminds me of a whole crock of shit." You make the statement and exit, or just making the statement can be a release. See what works for you.

PRIVATE TERRITORY

The following negotiation deals with establishing private territory and the power to keep it so.

JUDY: I have an issue.

THERAPIST: See if he will engage you.

J: Chuck, will you engage me in a beef for change? *(Chuck agrees)* The issue is my half of our joint desk. And my demand is: don't put anything on my side.

CHUCK: You don't want me to put anything on your side of our joint desk.

J: Right

TH *(after long pause from Chuck):* What's your resistance?

C: Well, the desk has to serve a large number of purposes. It's used a lot. There are times when I'm doing projects. I built this one as big as it is so that it could be a drafting table.

TH: But you gave her half of it?

C: Yes, I did—I'd build another one if there were room.

TH: Is there wall space for shelves?

C: I've built shelves wherever there is wall space!

TH: You may reject her demand if you choose, or you may accept it on condition that she respect your side or offer a counter proposal.

C *(to Judy):* If I agree to your request, would you be prepared to leave my side of the desk alone and uncluttered? I'm only fishing for information. . .Is it really necessary? The issue of the desk is a good exercise, but if we negotiate it we're liable to get saddled with seeds of frustration.

J: It's not an exercise! It's a legitimate issue with me.

C: The current mess on the desk sounds like the issue—I'd rather deal with that than make a *general rule*.

TH: You're derailing, Chuck. What's the problem?

C: For many years, long before I met her, I dreamed of a desk!

TH: The price we pay for the intimacy we have is a certain amount of freedom surrendered for the commitment to relationship.

C: I designed a desk which was also to serve as a drafting table. There I was with this beautiful space when she came into my life. And I, in a stroke of inspiration, redesigned the desk to accommodate two people. It's rather like a loveseat, if you will. It was all masterfully done. So now what I'm confronted with by this demand is the loss of the drafting table.

TH: Assess the cost to you and reply to Judy's request.

C: I suppose I could do that—not put anything on her side of the desk.

TH: *Will* you do that?

C: Yes. *(To Judy)* I accept your demand for one week, to keep my things off your side of the desk, and then we'll see.

TH: Seal that! *(The couple embrace)*

The week's negotiation is simply to determine in practice how productive this negotiation is. In the course of carrying out the honoring of distinct territory, other alternatives may surface.

BUSINESS COMPLICATIONS

The ensuing confrontations are the problems of a husband and wife who are also business partners.

ELLIS *(to therapist):* I'd like to dialogue with you. You told us that a Musuem List was what you had in your craw and wanted to get out and dispose of. Then my wife came up with ten pages—all of which was current! We never dealt with it all, and I'm worried about it. Were you trying to be kind by not having her read all of it?

THERAPIST: I'm not trying to be kind, just practical. You know I have copies of the lists, and her items are all variations of the same thing. *(To Martha)* Am I right?

MARTHA: That's true. They could all be summarized in two or three items.

TH: So what we do then is take *one* current item that can be dealt with immediately.

E: Then the others either get dealt with one at a time or become irrelevant?

TH: Right. By the way, how did your negotiation about keeping work problems at work go?

E: Great, until today. We'd decided to limit our griping about work to conversations during office hours. We had a bad day today, and she called to vent something. Before she got a chance to discuss her point, though, I told her about the problems I was having.

TH *(to Martha):* Let me see If I got this straight. You called him, and he answered with his problem—which was a business problem. So according to your agreement it was legitimate—but you didn't call him on butting in before you got a chance to vent.

M: Oh, I called him all right. I got furious with him!

TH: When did you get furious?

M: After he told me his problem.

TH: Exactly. What I'm getting at is that you do have an opportunity to say: "I'm first!" But apparently you didn't say it. What I'm talking about is precedence: the chance to say, "Hey, hold your grief until I tell you mine."

M: How can I stop getting snowed under though?

TH: There's no guarantee, but you're sure to get snowed under if you don't yell "Stop!" You can always say, "You can tell me your problems *after* I tell you mine." The emotional reaction builds to an outburst when you don't confront him at the outset and then misread his motive. How do you know he was deliberately trying to snow you under? *(To Ellis)* Were you?

E: Hell, no. I was just full of my own woes and didn't realize what was happening. Incidentally, when I finally heard her story I had to admit mine was minor in comparison.

M: I'll agree to try it. Next time you interrupt, I'll say, "I want my turn first."

E: I could accept that if it wasn't accompanied by an emotional outburst at me.

TH: When the emotions are directed at someone else, can you listen?

E: Sure.

M: If the situation comes up and I call, you agree to try to respect me if I say, "Wait. I want my turn first"?

E: I can as long as you don't attack me for being selfish in the next breath!

M *(to therapist):* I tend to feel put upon. A lot of the Museum List is where I feel he's taking care of himself, first, last, and always!

TH: What comes across to me, Martha, is the message: "You take care of me, because I don't know how." When you don't take care of yourself, of course you're going to be put upon, and then you blame him. Now think of one area where you want to practice taking care of yourself.

M: Crazymaking! I feel when we get together to try to discuss something, he says that I have to make a decision. I accept that, and then he rejects all the answers I propose. For example, there was a meeting yesterday with a distributor, and Ellis promised something that couldn't be delivered. Then he turned around and put it on me: "Deliver!" Everytime I presented a suggestion of how to explain the situation, he'd get angrier and say that wasn't what he wanted. But we couldn't deliver, we really couldn't. So finally we ended up accepting one of the alternatives, but he stomped out furious—it was somehow all my fault.

TH *(to Ellis):* Did you get furious and blame Martha?

E: Yes, I did. She told it pretty much the way it happened.

TH: You do have alternatives—a Vesuvius, for instance.

E: I did that—it was a doozy.

TH: By permission? And time-limited?

E: It was a quickie.

TH: By permission?

E: No.

TH: That's where it stinks!

E: You mean I have to get her permission to sound off about my anger at somebody else? I'm a very ad-lib Vesuviuser. When I start listening to what I'm going to say, then I might not say it.

TH *(to Martha):* There are always alternatives. When he ad libs his Vesuvius, you can disengage by simply saying: "I give you permission to have your Vesuvius." He's insisting that he enjoys his habit of blowing his stack. So I'm suggesting that a different attitude on your part can possibly change the feeling in your guts.

M: But I feel responsible. . .

TH: So you remind yourself, "I'm not responsible for him. I'm only responsible for myself."

E: Yetta, I hear what you're saying, but I really get uptight if I keep these things in me.

TH: I'm not suggesting you keep the things in you. I'm saying that when you *ask permission,* you can have your Vesuvius and not destroy your relationship.

E: But that's not as much fun.

TH: I know. And that's part of the price of a relationship, *you say you want!*

Self-Care in a relationship is a consideration of *both* partners and always involves limitations of freedoms. There is the freedom to vent rage but not the freedom to abuse or exploit the other. To make rage informative as well as cathartic there must be a structure of disengagement from the *rage* of the listening partner. This, hopefully, is accomplished by asking and giving permission to hear the rage and time limiting it. An underlying necessity to achieve this goal is *good will* between the partners.

CAREER PRIORITY

The following exchange establishes the fact that career takes primacy in Mel's life. The relationship is secondary and commitment to it is premature.

ROSE *(to Mel):* A lot of the time yesterday I was feeling like we really didn't belong here together. Our relationship will not be continuing because Mel is leaving the city. We see each other occasionally. I get stuck with knowing that we're different and in different places, in terms of making commitments. We're different ages, have done different things, and, of course, there's a difference in us. I don't know what to do with that. I still don't really accept it. I don't accept that you're leaving, not in my gut.

THERAPIST: So "I'm hurting that you're leaving, and I can't do anything about it. I'm powerless." Is that it?

R: No, I'm not powerless to do something for me. I don't want to stop him from leaving. I want to get to where I can feel okay that we won't be seeing each other, that our needs aren't the same, that I have need for commitment and he really doesn't.

TH: Have you checked this out? *(Rose nods)* Okay, "How do I get rid of the pain? I have a need for commitment and he doesn't, so between us we cannot have a committed relationship." This separation is particularly painful because it might be the end of a relationship. Is that what's eating at you? Okay. That is sad and painful. Was it nice knowing him?

R: Sometimes.

TH: So it wasn't all sugar and spice?

R: No.

TH: Do you expect to go into a convent after he leaves? *(She shakes her head)* Is there a possibility of a committed relationship in the future with someone else? *(Rose nods)* You're young enough with lots of time. One thing my husband tried so hard to teach me is that nobody is indispensable. Only now that he's been dead a long time and since I've made a new life for myself do I know the truth of it. There's no short cut to eliminate pain that I know about. It's just a given. So look for choices and alternatives that will lessen the pain. What can you do for yourself after he leaves?

R: I'll be leaving here and I'll be with other people again.

TH: People you like? *(She nods again)* That will occupy your time productively?

R: I'll be in school to get my degree. I'm not saying that I won't be with other people and that I don't see future relationships.

TH: But "I'm hurting now. . .and I'm also surviving now. I have a program for the immediate future—but I shouldn't be hurting." Is that how it goes inside?

R: Yes, I should understand, but that doesn't alleviate the pain. I want a short-cut out of the pain.

TH: I don't know any, but I know a path, and that is action. Let's hear from Mel.

MEL: I feel a lot of pain. There's a conflict with me between leaving you Rose, and my Bill of Rights which includes continuing with school and doing what I want to do. It's hard for me to let go of you. I have difficulty believing that I'm going to meet somebody who will be anything near like you. I know there won't be anybody exactly like you. . . I have to let go of you to do what I need to do.

TH: Do you want to huddle? *(Mel nods)* The question of commitment came up. I hear you saying, "My Bill of Rights is to pursue my career as I feel; you are very meaningful to me but I need freedom of movement just in case I'm not ready to make a final decision." Am I on the right track?

M. Yes. In terms of commitment I'm saying that I can't make a commitment for a long time, and I'm also saying I don't want to forget you right now, either.

TH: "So let's keep contact while we're still meaningful to each other; that way it is not a separation necessarily. There's the mail, the phone, and possibly an occasional visit." Does that fit? *(Mel nods)* So it sounds like you're looking forward to continuing—not continuous—contact. True or false? *(He indicates true)*. Tell her this.

M: We'll be seeing each other on Wednesdays as long as the group meets and as long as I wish to continue to see you. After that, I don't know.

TH: So let's enjoy the present and let the future take care of itself.

R: You've been doing that, and I've been avoiding it, anticipating the final end. You are now saying it may not end—there's no foretelling. I'll have to live with that.

TH: This sounds like a good place to stop.

This is a reality-facing of what *is*—a coming to terms with the fact of primacy in this relationship is clearly unobtainable, that the future of this relationship is equally uncertain, and that the pain of parting is the cost, perhaps, of mutual self-growth.

HUMILIATING LABELS

The following confrontation became an exercise in Self-Care when Ted imposed—by mutual consent—the outlawing of humiliating labels.

TED: We tried to negotiate a beltline for me a few nights ago, and it didn't work out too well. I don't want Helen to say to me again, "I don't trust you." I don't want her to impugn my honesty. By that I mean I don't want her to accuse me of lying. I feel I'm honest and trustworthy, and I don't want her to say I'm not.

THERAPIST: I hear you saying: "Do not call me untrustworthy and don't call me a liar!" See if she'll listen to that.

T: Will you listen to my beltline.

HELEN: Certainly. I hear you saying that my calling you untrustworthy or accusing you of lying is a beltline. *(To Yetta)* I can eliminate the phrases, but I can't escape the feeling.

TH: Are you saying that you don't trust him and that he *is* a liar?

H: I'm afraid to answer that for fear I'll incriminate myself!

TH: Can you both say and mean: "Your idea of trustworthy and my idea of trustworthy are two different things?" People can deal with a situation without labeling each other in the process. And it can still be an authentic interaction. You can take care of yourself without calling each other names!

H: But I feel it's unfair to ask me to do that! There are just too many times in the past when—

TH: Hold it! Then what I hear you ultimately saying is: "I can't honor your beltline because I don't trust you."

H: Well, no. I can see that saying it and feeling it are different.

TH *(to Ted):* Can you accept that this process modifies behavior, and settle for that?

T: I understand the idea, and I guess I'll have to settle for it. She's not about to change the feeling.

TH: Changing the behavior is the first step. Ask her again.

T: I want you to respect my beltline. Regardless of what you feel, I don't want you to *call* me a liar, and I don't want you to *say* you don't trust me.

H: I can do that.

TH: What have you agreed to do?

H: No matter what, I won't tell Ted I distrust him or accuse him of lying.

The concentration in this confrontation was on pulling out one painfull thorn in this stressed relationship. Hopefully the specific *issues* of distrust will be confronted as problems to resolve as they appear and when they appear.

Each encounter is a specific focus on issues of intimate living. They serve as practice sessions in a process of considering alternative behaviors that more effectively meet specific needs.

The limited negotiations attempt to pinpoint attention to a bit of the current acid that is corroding the relationship. Hopefully, as one immediate stress point in intimate living is transformed into a problem to be resolved through new behavior patterns, the door is opened to deal with other items of stress—one by one, week by week—in emotionally digestible quantities. This becomes a continuing practice in the art of Self-Care.

Chapter 4

Rage, Hurt, and Healing

Hostility rituals are used when needed and when allowed. Need often arises in the process of mutual confrontation on specific issues of discord. They serve to decrease the rage that shuts off the ability to listen and hear the other. This is possible only when there is good will between the confronting partners and a real desire to improve the relationship.

A HOMEWORK ASSIGNMENT

The following encounter starts with a report of a homework assignment that needed reconsideration. The process of confronting unrealistic expectations and different styles of *Being* surfaced the target of a specific rage and opened new possibilities of dealing with the realities of this relationship.

THERAPIST: Bring me up to date.

JIM: We'd negotiated that Betty would reserve two nights a week for us. So the first evening I suggested we play cribbage. It seemed to be a little strained after a while. Then she said, "That's enough. I want to watch TV now." I didn't mind, but the next evening when I wanted her attention, she said: "No go." I want to re-negotiate the commitment this week, and I want her to give it a try. *(To Betty)* I want you to consider very seriously giving me two nights a week completely.

TH: Before we begin to re-negotiate, I want Betty to monologue and give her side of the story.

BETTY: It was a smashing bore. It was tension-filled and uncomfortable. I don't mind playing cribbage and not watching TV. But it's dull. I can read, crochet, and write a publicity release all at the same time while watching TV! I guess I want him to explain what he means by a "complete evening."

TH: Okay, that's a legitimate fishing expedition for information relating to the issue. See if he'll explain.

B: When you say you want me to give you an evening completely, what kind of schedule do you have in mind?

J: I mean the time between the end of supper and eleven o'clock. That includes some time with the children and some time together.

B: I'd be willing to accept one evening a week, if you'll tell me generally what you're planning to do.

TH: I hear the words, but your tone belies them. What's going on?

B: I know. I want to cooperate, but I have a very bad feeling about it. It's so boring—so terribly boring— I can stand it when there are other things happening.

J: You're saying I'm boring? More boring than TV? I feel about that high! *(Showing a distance of one inch with his fingers)* And you're not helping. You have some responsibility in this, too.

TH: Wait a minute! Learn to fight for what you want, and to avoid assigning responsibility. Instead of blaming each other, try figuring out alternatives for action. Fish for information from Betty. For example, "What do you enjoy doing that we can share during this evening together that I want?" *(To Jim)* Do you see the difference between seeking alternatives and laying blame?

J: Sure. It makes sense. I guess what bugs me is I don't feel welcome at home. I'd like to work on that.

TH: Do you like Jim? *(To Betty)*

B: Yes, I like him. I also love him. Sometimes I feel I love him more than I like him. He's so nit-picking.

TH: How about having a Vesuvius about that?

B: He's never had a Vesuvius.

TH: I'm talking about you.

B: I'm afraid of what I'd say. I'm really afraid of what I'd say.

TH: Do you want to risk a Vesuvius anyway?

B: No.

TH: What do you want?

B: I want to be interested in spending an evening a week with him.

TH: That's very unrealistic—to try to force the feeling. If you want to change, you have to work against the feeling—but that doesn't mean that you don't acknowledge the feeling and learn to express it. Saying nice words in an unwilling tone is *not* where it's at!

B: Why can't this be a natural thing, to spend time together and enjoy it?

TH: Because you say you're bored. To change the emotional climate you have to consider alternatives and that does not come naturally.

You *make* it happen by choice.

B *(to Jim as he writes down the previous exchange):* Now you're going to take notes! I'll have a Vesuvius now!

TH: Get permission. *(Jim assents)*

B: Lists! Lists taped to mirrors, pinned to things! You're right! You're not welcome with your God-damned nit-picking lists! The evenings you're not home the kids and I are *relaxed*. We aren't always worrying about how we're acting or what we're supposed to be doing. It's not easy to spend an evening with you. You act like you're guilty for asking me to play cribbage. And then you criticize me for not being enthusiastic. And all the time I get the feeling I'm under your thumb. You're always saying something is going to go wrong! I can't stand your always telling me something's not going to work because I'm going to foul up. I can't do everything your way! I get tense—I can't live the way you live. The way you fold your pajamas—you're super neat! I can't live up to your expectations of what you want me to be.

TH *(to Jim):* What information did you get?

J: That I let all kinds of things come between us. That she has trouble with personal habits of mine—demanding neatness, order, schedules. That's the way she feels!

TH: Of course. We're only talking about information in the sense of messages about the way she feels.

J: But you know, I feel better—at least I think we can do something about that stuff.

TH: So do I. I'd like you both to consider accepting the assignment I'm about to give you. Betty, every time you're given a list or schedule this week, look at it, see what's acceptable to you. Then tear up the list and do it your way. Can you do that?

B: With pleasure!

TH *(to Jim):* What do you enjoy doing with her?

J: Making lists!

TH: That's doing *to* her, not with her.

J: Seriously, what I enjoy is playing games—cards, chess, even checkers. Not as a steady diet, but—

TH: What are you hearing me say?

J: Play chess with her for a week?

TH: How versatile are you? Offer a positive suggestion when you want her attention. Give her an invitation that she can accept or reject. Have alternatives.

J: I don't know how to present it—ahead of time? By appointment?

Tₕ: Come evening—don't plan—just make a suggestion.

J: Before, during, or after supper, she goes over to the TV and is stuck there for the rest of the evening.

Tₕ: Then during any intermission, ask for her attention.

J: I don't think it's going to work.

Tₕ: I hear you asking for guarantees of acceptance, and in intimate living there aren't any. I suggest you take the risk of presenting her with positive statements of need for one week.

J: Okay, I'll try it, but I don't think I can change her.

Tₕ: The homework assignments I've given both you and Betty aren't meant to change the other. They are Self-Care assignments, designed to work against established patterns. The question is: How can *I* change to meet *my* needs more effectively? It is conceivable that a more positive approach by one may elicit a different response from the other. This is a practice session in creatively exploring possible fun time together.

The following encounter demonstrates a person-specific creation of a hostility release ritual by permitting what *is*—but changing its impact—as a prelude to direct communication.

COMMUNICATION PROBLEMS

EUNICE: I want to know how we can keep communicating at times when our immediate needs conflict. Bill controls me by threatening a scene.

THERAPIST: What kind of scene? How does it go?

E: Yelling.

Tₕ: Outside in public, like "If you don't behave I will make a scene?"

E: Yes. Or on our son's birthday, Bill came in and blew up when the guests were all there waiting to yell surprise. I tried to poke him, but he had to have the blow-up. Afterward he related beautifully to the guests. I didn't know what to do. How could I have communicated so it wouldn't have upset Bill and avoided a scene which upset our guests?

Tₕ: Let's phrase it differently. "How can I communicate to stop an untimely blow"—never mind the upset.

E: I'd like to add something else: can I stop an untimely blow and continue communication when we're tense?

BILL: I think the first part of your question is crucial. I don't think you can stop it. If I let myself blow, things work out better afterwards, even if there is some embarrassment.

TH: Let's huddle. Does it matter where you blow as long as you do?

B: Of course, I wouldn't do it in a work situation.

TH: No, no, keep it in intimate living. Naturally you wouldn't do it at work unless you were willing to risk your job. At home, does it matter where you blow?

B: You mean, could I blow somewhere else instead? Yes, I've tried that and it works. I use a tennis racket on a sofa or door.

TH: So when guests are in the living room you could go to an isolated place and blow? *(He nods)* So we have a choice.

B: But suppose we were away from home and I needed to explode—I don't think I could defer it. I've tried before. I can't just *decide* to be mad at a later time.

TH: What other choices do you have? If you come in and there's a house full of company at a time when you're emotionally loaded, could you go straight to the bedroom and use the tennis racket?

B: From what my wife says, I must have a problem keeping things in perspective. I have to be honest and say that I could promise here to realize the extent of my hostility and avoid the guests, but I'm not sure I'd really do it at home the next time.

TH: Okay, so we always talk in terms of alternatives. You can take it any way that makes sense to you. You could say you're having a Vesuvius or translate it into something acceptable to yourself.

E: Not true. I understand how people feel like blowing up. I know it helps clear the air. What concerns me is that you've upset guests who are friends of our son.

TH: Just a moment. These friends have never heard a man blow his stack? Do you think they'd put him down because of blowing?

E: Yes. Some even said they were scared.

TH: How about suggesting to the bothered ones that they discuss it with him. Confront him directly, like: "Your blowing up has a terrific impact on me, it scares hell out of me." You are not responsible for changing him to protect someone else. But you can direct the concerned persons to confront each other. You're saying he just blows with his mouth, right? *(She agrees)* So it's just the verbal blow. Ask yourself another question: what impact does it have on you? Just you—never mind others.

E: If we have a disagreement, I feel that just as I want to get to a point of crucial communication this blow comes and drops the curtain.

Then I can't pursue it. I feel he's won every time.

TH: Let me check something out. *(To Bill)* After you blow, are you relieved? *(He nods)* Are you ready to continue communication? *(He indicates yes)* At that point could you have a better listening ear?

B: Yes *(To Eunice),* but I sense that at that point you don't care to communicate.

E: I sulk.

TH: All right. Are you, Bill, aware of the rising temperature immediately preceeding the blow?

B: No, unfortunately. I think if I were aware of it I would stop it because I don't really want to behave that way.

TH: I'm trying to get a warning system across. *(To Eunice)* Can you see the escalation, the change in temperature?

E: The temperature rises fast, and while it's going it's like a volcano. I've tried to divert it but he says at that point that I'm not facing the issue.

B: I see an effort on your part to stop me as your way of winning an argument. It's a can't-win situation in terms of your stepping in to stop me. I wish I could step in to stop myself.

TH: Now, the information I milked out of both of you is that his blow is not dangerous, just noisy, and you both dislike what is happening. So another way to go is to develop an immunity to noise. That means change the internal dialogue from "I am shamed," to "That's just noise and noise doesn't hurt anyone." The information we have is that when he finishes his blow, his ears are open. So the release preceeds a possible road to communication. The very thing you're asking for. You can turn the inner dialogue into "His blow is a signal to communicate." If the avenue to communication is a hullaballoo of noise, just call it a price to pay. The hell with finding a hostility ritual—you just turn what *is* into a ritual.

E: I'm willing to try. I don't like being controlled by fear of Bill's blowing up.

The expectation that communication in intimate living be rational at all times has no basis in reality. Such an expectation does not permit intimates to be human beings.

A possible inner dialog may be: "I can't get angry at you because you might get hurt; you may not take it well; you may not accept it." These are all the risks we take. If it isn't taken well, if it isn't accepted, you keep at it until you find a productive alternative.

Accept that conflict and anger are okay. Just things with which to deal. They need not be lethal. The structures I've been talking about de-lethalize it.

RAGE—RELEASE

The following illustrates a pair-specific utilization of a rage-release. The partners become allies in dealing with spontaneous rage by allowing the naming of it in the process of ventilating it.

BOB: The last time we were here my assignment was to cut my moody time down and learn to get *permission* for my expressions of anger or hostility.

THERAPIST: Have you carried out the assignment?

ANNE: When he explodes without permission, I just tell him: "You just had an unscheduled hostility release!" Or if I catch it coming on, I ask him: "Do you want my permission to ventilate?"

TH: And I hear that for you the process of telling that—of calling it—helps "de-lethalize" the explosion.

A: It makes it much more bearable and helps me save my sense of dignity somehow. It's easier for me to disengage when I know that he knows that I know it's a ritual!

B: We're learning to signal "foul" when we hit below the belt. We've started to let each other know when we're hurting, and that really helps.

A: The tool we've used most often is the Clearing House. I've found that sometimes it turns out to be another explosion, but on a much reduced scale.

TH: What you're describing is the development and use of a series of tools designed to assure that your aggression and hostility is vented as you go along instead of being allowed to accumulate. I'm delighted with your report.

In this brief report, Anne and Bob have demonstrated the incorporation of the use of productive tools of living in their daily encounters. A new depth in intimate living is being attained through a process of decontamination from the other's emotional acid through such safety valves as ritualizing or labeling a hostility release, through reinforcing the established beltline taboos, through emptying the emotional garbage pail via the Clearing House and through the practice of authentic communication (risking hurting the other to give necessary information). The build up of trust and good-will is apparent.

Note: To establish a beltline:

1. The unabsorbable hurt is designated.

2. A commitment to avoid this hurt is made.

3. A process to implement this avoidance is engaged in—the yelling of *foul* when hurt is the immediate cue to back off, retreat, excuse oneself.

A BELTLINE

The following confrontation begins with background information leading to the establishment of a Beltline.

It demonstrates a fishing expedition into the nature of the relationship. This process uncovers a new reality: commitment to the relationship. It also demonstrates the release effect when a bit of humor is inserted.

RON: Joyce has a revolving exit door to the marriage. We've been married three and a half years and I've had about fifty threats of divorce. That's a crazy-maker for me. I've had about forty threats of suicide *(and a couple of faint attempts at it)*, and recently she's added "I'm going to commit myself to a mental hospital." And that really blows my mind. When she gets into these kinds of spaces, I can't tolerate her threatening me in the relationship. I feel it's blackmail to use this. It gets me really so angry.

THERAPIST*(to Joyce):* Okay, let me check out some information. Do you want a divorce?

JOYCE: Not at the moment.

TH: Is the exit door really closed?

J: He's labeled it our revolving door. I think I can honestly say from what I heard this weekend that it's closed.

TH: The exit door is closed?

J: Yes, because the price is too high for me to pay.

TH: To get out?

J: Right.

TH: Okay. So then when you make a threat like this the feeling is really desperate and may be a manipulative attempt to control, correct?

J: At the moment I really feel at the end of my rope.

TH: Now, are you saying I will honor this beltline about divorce? Because I don't want a divorce and this exit door is closed?

J: Yes.

Tн: The suicide road out of difficulties is final. Let's examine the meaning of the threats. If living is too much of a burden, you can end it, if that's your choice. And it's up to you to decide to use that or not. To *threaten* takes it out of the realm of my person-privilege, my personal right. Do I demand complete control over you or else I'm going to punish you so drastically that you'll never forget it? What is it with you?

J: That price is too high, too.

Tн: Okay. Is that exit door closed?

J: Yes.

Tн: To confine yourself to a mental institution would give you a wonderful rest. No responsibility, no duties, no nothing. And opportunity to meet all kinds of interesting people. So if that's the kind of rest you want, fine! But again, to use that kind of rest as a threat—"I'm going to shame you! The world is going to know that YOU drove your wife crazy!"—again, what's the meaning? Do you want to shame him publicly?

R: That's right where it's at.

Tн *(to Ron):* Your job right now is just to listen. Are these exit doors closed? The threat of suicide, the threat of institutional confinement, and divorce?

J: Yes, because I don't think I belong in any of those.

Tн: I don't either.

J: But I do like the idea of rest. I don't do enough Self-Care.

Tн: Ah! That is our next area of work.

J: One of the things on my museum list is that when we have things to discuss, we don't make time to discuss them.

Tн: We'll deal with that as soon as we finish this. Now your husband has a three-point exit closure. Tell him.

J: I establish a beltline that threats of divorce, suicide, and institutional committing of myself are outlawed because it is too high a price to pay.

Tн: What are you hearing?

R: What I want to hear from Joyce.

Tн: Seal it. *(The couple embrace)*

RIGHT TO RAGE

The right to rage as a Bill of Rights is presented in the following encounter.

WILLO: As I learn to express my own anger to him, I sense that Dick has a hard time accepting that. We don't seem to clear the air when we fight. There always seems to be a kind of heaviness that hangs over. That makes me feel it would have been better if I had kept it to myself or worked it out alone. I feel devastated by that heaviness. We've talked about it, but nothing's been resolved.

THERAPIST: What I hear is "You're not letting me be who I am and I'm not paying the price anymore of peace at any cost." *(Willo is nodding)* So what you are doing is declaring a basic bill of rights: I will yell when I want to. That is not negotiable!

W: That's right. I'm going to express my anger when I feel like it and how I feel like it, to you and to the kids. It may be pretty strong and pretty rotten stuff sometimes, but I'm going to do it. I hope you can accept it.

TH: What have you heard?

DICK: I just heard you make a declarative sentence. Whatever you're going to do, I'll have to handle it. Does this mean that she can come through with a Vesuvius or anything?

TH: No. A Vesuvius is by permission only.

D: Then what about the line saying she's going to say what she wants when she wants to say it, with or without my permission?

TH: She has just declared she will react to a specific issue—one issue at a time—taking care of the immediate hurt as it is felt. A Vesuvius is a whole blow on many issues.

W: I'll ask your permission for a Vesuvius. I'd also like for you to work at accepting it so I don't feel rejected.

TH: Willo, let's huddle. When we have the freedom to be bitches, we cannot reasonably expect acceptance.

W: But if I always feel rejected when I become angry, then I don't feel free to become angry.

TH: Did you say "I'm tired of being a good little girl"? *(She nods)* Then if you're going to be a bad little girl occasionally, that liberty takes with it a certain amount of isolation.

W: What is the difference between isolation and feeling so rejected that you don't feel free to express feelings?

TH: That's what you do to yourself. That's your own evaluation, saying, "I can only be a bitch if you will accept me with all my shit." Now we have to shit. But we don't have to stand there delighting in it or expecting the other person to.

W: I see that. Still, can't we do something about the silences from Dick?

TH: Perhaps you can put a time limit on them. I'll share something with you. My husband used to clam up when he was angry, shutting me out. Finally I'd had it. We negotiated a limit to his clamming up. Because I was important to him and our relationship was most important to him, the negotiation was something like 24 hours of nurturing his pout. In a year, it was decreased to one hour. One hour of permission to sulk—and then to talk, regardless of how he felt.

W: I can see I put him in a bind when I want to express my hostility, then expect him to accept it completely, at the denial of his feelings. Dick, at another time would you be willing to negotiate a time limit for sulking? *(Dick agrees)*

As soon as you change a relationship from one of adversaries in a power struggle to one of authentic confrontation and negotiation of differences as a mutual growth process, you are out of the win/lose arena and into the area of mutual expansion through authentic being. This is a process involving Self-Care, awareness of the other, and enactment of whatever disciplines are necessary to meet common goals.

"As If"

The following is a brief exchange between therapist and client—introducing the concept of "as if" behavior.

GINA: What happens if you have a rage-release which takes place in an out-pouring of upset, which apparently I do. But then, I find, it still bothers me afterward. I haven't gotten over it. A day later I can hear myself, and I'll say, "Well, shut up!" but I'm not done, I'm still mad about it. What if one rage-release is unsatisfying?

THERAPIST: That's why you have your idiosyncratic rage-release always handy—your solo performance, always at your fingertips to use. Okay, your mate says, "You can have a Vesuvius. Address me now, for three minutes and that's it." And after three minutes you are still loaded—you hardly got the top content out: then you disappear and continue by yourself.

G: Or even continue the next day.

TH: That's always a possibility. "May I continue at a later time?"

G: Or the next day I'm still sore? All right, but I've said it, so shouldn't I be done?

TH: You see, this is exactly what I mean when I talk about the importance of programming behavior over feeling. Okay, your guts are still churning, you still want to break his neck or break dishes or do something. You're still angry. It's not out in spite of all the releases. Nevertheless, you act *"as if"* you are not angry and the productive action, done consistently and persistently, may pull a feeling up by the bootstraps. Eventually there might be a congruence. What I'm emphasizing is that the productive behavior is a programmed affair and need not be stymied or sabotaged by what you feel.

DIALOGUE HELPS

The following illustrates the arriving at a focus on the specific areas of concern through the process of a dialogue.

CARLA: Yetta, there's something that I need to discuss, but I'm not sure whether it's an issue or not.

THERAPIST: Why not dialogue with me first and we'll try to determine that.

C: It's what I call Tim's negativism—his pessimistic outlook. He's building a building out back for a studio and he's afraid it won't meet the building inspector's approval. So he's constantly complaining about it or worried something will trip him up. Everything that comes up, he takes a black view. We buy something, and it breaks, so I say, "Take it back and exchange it." Immediately, he says, "They won't take it back!"

TH: If you're tired of hearing him gripe, you have at least one alternative I can think of. How about limiting his expression of gripes to the daily clearing house?

TIM: We've already tried to negotiate this, and I have a problem with it.

TH: Okay, let's you and I dialogue now while Carla listens.

T. We negotiated that I refrain from voicing complaints about the building or any other problems last week. No exceptions were made. I rapidly became aware that I objected to the idea of not being able to discuss my fears and apprehensions.

TH: Are you saying, "This negotiation has pinned me against the wall, and I can't stand it?"

T: At first, yes, that's what I felt, but then I realized my voicing things wouldn't really change the situation. However, your idea of saving things up for clearing house seems against the principle of *not* bottling things up and releasing them—*blah*—but rather dealing with them in small doses. I concede Carla's point that it's tiresome to listen to all that. But I don't like the idea of bottling it up and saving it for a certain time. I'd like to release my frustrations and fears to something else—then Carla wouldn't have to hear them at all.

TH: Suppose she wants to hear them—in a clearing house?

T: Carla, would you be upset about hearing about the building in a clearing house?

C: No, I wouldn't. And I'd much prefer it to your releasing it on some inanimate object, and my not hearing about it at all!

T: Yetta, by the time the clearing house arrives, I may have been able to put far from my mind my fears about the building. Do I have to dredge them up again?

TH: You don't *have* to do anything that's not meaningful. What's the most productive approach for you?

T: Well, in the case of the building, the agony arrives with the waiting for an inspector at the time things are all set to go. I need to release it at that time.

TH: Then ask for *your* need—to release your concern when this happens—in the form of a Vesuvius. Ask her to disengage, and respect the time-limit she sets.

T: Good. Is there another motion on the floor we need to clear up first?

C: That we have a clearing house every day, and that you can speak about your frustration then, *if you still feel upset at that time.*

T: Can we seal that first?

C: You want a kiss maybe?

T: I don't want a kick in the teeth. *(They hug and kiss)* Now, may I *have* a Vesuvius about the building inspector when I get upset?

C: Yes, if you understand that you ask permission, and I can say yes or no depending on my feelings at the time.

I see the above negotiation as a four-way win: Tim was given the freedom to react spontaneously *(within the framework of the Vesuvius hostility ritual)* and the optional use of the clearing house for any left-over resentments or frustrations.

Carla obtained the means to limit Tim's negative impact and at the same time initiated a procedure to get information she wanted. Also, upon Carla's refusing Tim's request for a Vesuvius, Tim retained the option of working out his frustration idiosyncratically.

HAIRCUTS

This encounter was a prelude to step-by-step dealing with the areas of conflict in the relationship. The way was cleared to deal with facts—not imaginings.

THERAPIST: Who is ready to work?

EDNA: You go ahead. I know you've got a beef. Why don't you start?

TH: I want to teach you a technique of confronting one another. Please avoid "why don't you" questions in these situations. It puts your partner on the spot.

HAROLD: That's exactly right! I want to give Edna a haircut.

TH: Will you accept a haircut at this time, Edna? *(She consents)* Since you're the one who's getting the dressing down, you're the one who time-limits it. How long do you want to give him?

E: I'm not sure how much I can take. Let's start with a minute—if I can take more, I'll extend the time.

H: Okay. Somebody time me. Edna, I resent the way you read my mind. Tonight was a perfect example! You said: "I know you've got a beef." You don't know because you didn't ask me! *Stop reading my mind.* I hate it when you do that; it bugs the hell out of me. And most of the time you're wrong anyway! That's all I wanted to say—and I feel better for having said it.

TH: Fine. Now if there's anything in the haircut that needs to be discussed, make an appointment and do so at a later time. Don't escalate the anger at this point.

H: Now what do I do? I've never given a haircut before.

TH: You have an option. If you're still angry at her, if you want to punish her, you can put her in the doghouse. Then she'll have to seek her release by negotiating a suitable penance. Do you want to punish her further?

H: No, I'm satisfied with the haircut.

TH: All right. Then do either of you want to make an appointment to discuss anything related to the haircut?

E: I do. I was told last week that my parents weren't the crux of our problem and that he had beefs of his own he wanted to deal with. That's why I said what I did.

TH: Are you saying you didn't deserve the haircut?

E: Well, no, not exactly. I do read his mind at times.

TH: Then the substance of the haircut was accurate, despite your memories of the conversation last week.

E: I guess so. Yes, I accept it.

The following illustrates the emergence of a new awareness through the process of engaging in a haircut.

The spewing out of an old grievance opened the way to a new clarity: Wanda's responsibility for and to herself. This was a change from seeing herself as a victim of her husband's short-sightedness and fear to seeing herself as one *choosing* to take the responsibility of *her own* decisions.

WANDA: I have some unfinished business to attend to. I have a daughter who gave up a child for adoption. This was some time ago. She wasn't home, but in a distant city. My husband at that time felt that it would be completely inappropriate for me to be with her; that it would be a threat to his job, his position. This is a gaping wound because there's a grandchild out there, a piece of me and a piece of her. I can remember my own tears, my anger and frustration at my husband and my anger at myself for not defying him.

THERAPIST: Do you want to deal with that now? *(She agrees)* Pick a surrogate husband from the group and ask permission to give him a haircut on this one thing.

WANDA: Bob, would you act as the surrogate and allow me to give you a haircut? *(He consents)* How long do you think you can stand my hysteria?

BOB: Let's try one minute with a possibility of going longer.

W: Thank you. I am still furious that you could think your job, your position in the community was more important than our daughter—that it was necessary to send her away when she belonged with us, that you were so afraid of gossip and what people would say you wouldn't even let me go to Albany to be with her. I think that was less than human. It put me through the ringer and prevented me from doing what I felt I wanted to do for my daughter. I think I was a shit to accept your decision, and I'm angry about that. I still think you should have given me the freedom without putting it in the context of the safety of your job, the economic security of the family. You didn't let me be a mother and you didn't let me be a woman. Granted, I have some responsibilities for that, but it somehow got put on an economic basis which immobilized me. It seems to me that if you had been willing to acknowledge that we were both in the same leaky boat we might have found a solution. But you kept walking out of the room, and the day that baby was born, you never came near me. You got the telegram that she was in the hospital with a social worker, and I was left alone in that big empty house to deal with it myself. I could have used some help. You didn't share your pain with me, either. You couldn't let yourself down enough to share it with me so we could cry together. That to me is just not a whole human being. I resent that! I want some wholeness. That's it.

TH: Is the husband still living with you? *(She indicates he is not)* Then this is past business. How does it feel getting it out of your system?

W: It felt good. I just realized where my anger really was—not at my daughter, not at giving up the child, but at my former husband and what a shit he was!

TH: All right, What did you learn from this experience? I hear you saying *this can't happen to me again;* no man will be able to influence me this way.

W: I don't think it would happen again.

TH: Do you dedicate yourself to the proposition that I will not ever permit *myself* to be violated? That's an exercise in *self*-validation.

W: There is something that is blocking me. I tend to take responsibility for other people's feelings and try to smooth things over when I sense conflict.

TH: Who are you taking responsibility for? Erasing yourself is a hell of a price to pay for peace.

W: It's a terrible price to pay for it.

TH: Is it worth it? *(Wanda shakes her head)* Then your assignment for next week—to be re-negotiated ad infinitum—is "I am taking care of myself. I will not violate my own guts at the price of peace." Accepted?

W: Yes.

TH: That means your guts are going to churn plenty in the process of change.

W: I'm used to that.

The following encounter begins with a rage-release. The content of the rage surfaces important information regarding need for limited power in the specifics of maintaining a home and the establishment of a beltline—the power to outlaw criticism for a limited time on a specific issue.

KATHY: May I have a Vesuvius? I'd like three minutes.

STAN: I think a minute would be more reasonable.

K: What happens if I don't get it all out in a minute?

THERAPIST: Try and see what happens.

K: I'm so mad! You're so stingy! You're tight with money, tight with

your feelings—*you ignore me*. It's so sad. I feel I work at this relationship and you just sit there. And now you're mad at me because
you wouldn't take care of the painters. And that's it!

TH: I hear a whole area of autonomy that you haven't negotiated. Its
process and *power* I want to deal with—mutually established. Do
you want the management and upkeep of the house to be your area
of autonomy?

K: Yes, but there are things he has more knowledge of. I asked him to
contact these house-painting people for me, he knows about that
particular type of work. And there's something else. The house is
torn up, and I don't want to put it back together before the painters
come. He keeps bugging me to do something about the mess.
Well, I can put the house back in some semblance of order until
the painters come, if he won't *criticize* it until *after* the painters are
finished.

TH: Are you saying, "Until we get a painter, don't expect it to look the
way we like it, until a week after the painting is done?" *(Kathy
agrees)* Learn to establish autonomy within a certain specified
economic limitation, take the power to do what you need. You
have power you're not using and you're blaming him for having
reservations afterwards and not hearing what you want. You have
the power to run your house the best way you can at the time you
can.

K: Does that mean without comments or criticism?

TH: You get in trouble by asking that he like everything you do.

K: I do as much as I do as a gift of love. I do more than I want to do. I
need his approval, and I am hurt by his criticism.

TH: Now I hear you saying, "I keep the home more clean and more
orderly than I ordinarily would and I want you to appreciate that."
Are you saying with this partial gift of love, this extra effort, "I
don't want *any* criticism. I'm establishing this as a *beltline?*"

K: Yes! Stan, I want this as a beltline. I keep the house nearer your
standards than mine. My *beltline* demand is not to criticize my
housekeeping. Will you honor my beltline?

STAN: Yes, for one week I'll give it a try.

TH: Stan, you are giving Kathy the power *this week* to say "Foul! Outlawed!" whenever she hears a criticism of the house, and that's
your cue to shut up.

In this stressed relationship one small step at a time is taken. A week
free from criticism may be the emotional vitamin pill necessary to support building more understanding of differences as problems to solve.

The complaints "You're tight with money, tight with your feelings—you ignore me" are postponed for separate consideration until a *time readiness* to deal with it is productively possible.

Practice in carrying out specific negotiations validates in action the power and rights mates give each other. This opens the road to eliminate one by one the issues that cause alienation through further processes of confrontation and negotiation.

PICKBONE

A *Pickbone* is the delightful emotional alchemy that may turn acid into honey. When there is good will between intimates, this becomes a challenge to creativity. When a search is made into the particulars of discord (acid) and a realization that a particular discordant behavior is not going to be changed, *labeling* the behavior a *pickbone* may be a freedom road to *be;* a method of disengaging one's ego from the discordant behavior, and a means of eliminating such judgmental attitudes as:

"This is silly!"
"This is not rational!"
"This is not right!"

My classic illustration is my husband's underwear. Each night he would drop his shorts, shirt and socks on the bedroom floor wherever he was. Each morning he would pick them up and put them in the clothes hamper. And I would fume, "What an annoying behavior! Am I supposed to walk over that pile, around it or pick it up myself! You know I'm offended. What does it take to put that in the clothes hamper now instead of tomorrow?" My internal dialogue was, "You're getting back at me for something" or, "You are deliberately showing me who is boss" or, "You don't give a damn about me." I realized the danger of these inner dialogues and exposed them. The response shook me to my toes as I saw the scene through my husband's eyes. *He* was fighting for the right to do things his way. He was resisting *my manipulations* to do things *my way*— and his way was not necessarily a hostile act against me, a deprecation of my worth or evidence that he didn't care about me. The moment my ego got disengaged from his behavior we both became free: he to do things his way and I to grumble about it, bitch about it, dramatize it—each knowing that my responses were not demands for change on his part but a joyous release on my part, by mutual consent and understanding. So options were now opened to me:

I could pick up the underwear if so desired; *I* could lecture on man's ir-rationality; *I* could ostentatiously wade through the underwear to my side of the bed, etc., and my husband thoroughly enjoyed my perfor-mances and so did I. We had turned acid into honey by labeling an item of discord a pickbone—giving him the right to *be* and me the right to bitch about it.

In a workshop on Self-Care, one of the paired participants turned a current issue of deep conflict into a pickbone. He was urging that she get pregnant and have a third child. She was insisting that two children were enough and that she was satisfied with the size of their family. To him, another child meant extra security and proof of worth in the rela-tionship. To her, it was an unacceptable demand to reproduce— a vio-lation of her *personhood,* a taking away of her *right* to a decision about her own body.

He further clarified the meaning of his wanting another child. He came from a large, closely knit family. He enjoyed the family get-togethers and to him, three children were already a compromise on his desire to have six children.

She clarified that to meet her goals in life (wanting a career and time to work at it) as well as being a responsible mother, she had to put a limit on the child bearing.

He, appreciating her career goals and acknowledging the advantages of two paychecks for their mutual ease and comfort in living, agreed to make campaigning for a third child a pickbone. This now was recog-nized not as a *demand* to reproduce, but a right to express. Now the same campaign goes on, but with a different impact. He misses no op-portunity at family and friend get-togethers to put an infant in her arms and coo over it and remark on its loveliness and ask "Wouldn't you love to take it home?"—an act she thoroughly enjoys and responds with a smiling "No."

Chapter 5

Close-up on the Inventory of Corrosives (Museum): Ammunition for Destruction or Dynamite to Defuse

At this point, I believe it would be useful to examine the Museum more closely. We know it is an Inventory of Corrosives in Intimacy (I.C.I.)—a list of accumulated and hoarded grievances in a relationship between significant others covering the period of the relationship. The contents, when unresolved, maintain distance and alienation between individuals. These usually hidden sources of pain fester until they infect the entire relationship. Like acid, these items eat away at feelings of intimacy.

The purpose of listing such grievances, aches, and pains is to focus awareness of the erosions in a relationship—to surface the alienating emotional ingredients in order to deal with them more productively.

These grievances represent the raw material which is used to teach the process of negotiation by consent. They also serve as a focused history of the relationship: from the items that an individual lists, I can often see the direction the relationship has taken, without extensive interviewing or involved stories. Sometimes the expression of an old grievance reveals a new reality. What once was felt as painful has lost its sting, and some items, when voiced, can be finally forgiven for good. The contents of these lists may also reveal beltlines, items that cause such intense pain that they need to be avoided completely for the time being. I.C.I lists also reveal unforgiven "sins" and hidden role-expectations. Sometimes the partner is startled to learn that what he views as an innocent habit is seen by his partner as totally unacceptable behavior. And finally, the lists spotlight issues of conflict that need to be negotiated—areas of concern that can be resolved by systematic behavioral change.

The Inventory of Corrosives is created in order to be buried—

hopefully without resurrection. This represents weeks, months, or years of committed work to change the emotional climate of a relationship. The focus is on learned processes of confrontation and negotiation, of adopting new attitudes and behaviors and careful reinforcement of the more productive behaviors. Productive changes in the relationship are emphasized. Unabsorbable hurts are outlawed. Punishment for past sins which are no longer committed is terminated. Issues of conflict are negotiated. Undisclosed role-expectations are verbalized—and checked for reality "fit." The disposition of each item on the list is a formalized, learned, and practical procedure based on a mutual desire to *learn* and *do* differently in a committed relationship.

The step-by-step procedure of dealing with the contents of the I.C.I. is dependent upon the emotional climate of the individuals in their relationship. If the emotional disaffection is great and trust and good will are minimal, it is often more productive to focus on one minor irritant and start a process of pragmatic negotiation.

When judged productive, the content of the I.C.I. may be used as a subject matter for a hostility release ritual. This is dependent on the emotional readiness or "fit" of the individuals concerned.

In all cases, the original I.C.I. lists are composed in private. Each partner is instructed that this is a person-specific task and definitely is not a team task. Neither is to confer with the other or share or disclose the contents. These lists very often are time-bombs that need to be defused with discretion, caution, and care—according to the emotional climate and ability of the partners to absorb and deal with them. Dumping the entire contents of an I.C.I. on one another may result in emotional indigestion and further alienation. The therapist, as coach, is a necessary third party to this step-by-step confrontation.

When good will and a dedication to the relationship are apparent and verified between partners—the procedure of dealing with the I.C.I. may be as follows (partners always have the option to modify, alter, or institute alternative ways to dispose of the contents of this emotional garbage pail):

Each partner takes a turn reading the list to the other, with the therapist acting as coach. The object is information-giving only—exposing one's impact on the other. The obligation of the partner is to listen in silence except where more clarification is desired.

Each partner analyzes his own list—giving more detailed information of the content:

1. Exposing items that are no longer a concern—"This doesn't bother

me any more." This statement may reveal a growth process in the relationship that may show a greater tolerance for the other's specific behavior, or it may reveal a change in behavior of the partner—also revealing impact of the other.

2. Burying and forgiving incidents of hurts that are past. These items are given a "burial ceremony," incorporating renunciation of their use as partner-punishing weapons and reinforcing attitudes of forgiveness.

3. Discovering and disclosing a beltline hurt.

4. Listing negotiable grievances in hierarchical order.

5. Determining pickbone areas (a particular annoyance habitually repeated with no change required).

6. Discovering possible areas of autonomy and power.

7. Disclosing need to establish a bill of rights.

8. Making an appointment to deal with a specific item.

There is no single rule or procedure for the disposition of the contents of the Inventory of Corrosives. This is person-and-pair-specific. The procedure is interrupted at any accepted point—to be continued at a mutually-designated time. The process can start at the most hurtful point or the least stressful point of discord. The object is to clarify "turn-offs," to uncover "under the carpet sweepings" (those items not worth bothering about, but nevertheless hoarded as hostile ammunition for retaliatory behavior), to cease endless punishment for past crimes and to recondition alienating behaviors.

The I.C.I. is focused on the concerns of intimacy:

PRIMACY   Do I have major importance in your life? Am I significant to you?

POWER   Do I have the right of final decision-making in a specific area of living? Do I have impact on you?

SOCIAL BOUNDARIES   Whom do we include and whom do we exclude? Are we in agreement? Are your friends my friends and *must* they be?

ROLE EXPECTATIONS   Am I living up to your expectations and are you living up to mine? Are we aware of these expectations? What is fantasy and what is reality "fit?"

SEX   Do we use this aspect of living to enjoy and deepen intimacy, or do we abuse it—giving or withholding as reward or punishment?

Can we communicate expectations and needs or is this a secret area of living?

DISTANCE   Does your need for separateness or recharging conflict with my need for closeness? Can this be negotiated?

TRUST   Can I rely on you to be authentic, to communicate gut-level feelings—to take the risk of hurting and being hurt when communicating vulnerability? Can I rely on you not to use my confidences against me?

IDENTITY   Do I see you as you perceive yourself and is your perception of me my perception of me? Can we accept each other as we are or must we strive to live up to each other's fantasies of what we *should* be or *ought* to be?

The following were specifics from the contents of I.C.I.s gleaned from the lists of seventy-three participants,* presented to the author at various Fight Training groups and week-end workshops throughout the country. Of the 32 male and 41 female I.C.I, lists, the following is a composite sampling of *similarities* between the male and female complaints and grievances.

COMPOSITE I.C.I. LISTS

MALE	FEMALE
You don't lift up my ego enough.	You sit in judgment of me instead of being compassionate.
You don't follow through after you announce a decision to act or after you start something.	I resent your starting something and never finishing it as you promised you would.
I resent your yelling at the kids for minor things.	I hate it when you lose your temper with the kids over nothing.
You interfere when I'm disciplining the children.	I resent your interfering when I'm disciplining the children.
You don't say thanks when I help clean the house. You just say, ''You missed a spot.''	I resent your comments about my housekeeping like: ''There's a cobweb on the bookshelves, and it's been there for a week.''
You get on your high horse about many things I do which don't offend you when someone else does them!	You're very critical of my physical appearance and behavior when we're with your associates.

*Research analysis on the I.C.I. inventories by Catherine Bond.

You won't listen to me unless I say what you want to hear.

You don't pay attention when I talk to you.
You don't respond when I tell you about an experience that upsets me.

You avoid argument at all cost.

I resent your getting involved with another man. That was a *beltline* for me.

It makes me furious when you impose your "I know better" attitude on me by calling me stupid.

Being sarcastic, and accusing me of lacking a sense of humor if I object.

I resent your not wanting to listen when I want to talk with you.

You don't listen to me; you don't hear me.
It makes me angry when I express my feelings about a particularly meaningful (to me) situation, and you don't respond.

You cannot express anger and get upset when I do.

I bitterly resent your never taking into consideration that I would be deeply hurt by your publicizing your affair.

Calling me stupid—and when you do this to the kids, I cringe.

Being too sarcastic.

The following list represents a sampling of grievances categorized and designated for possible initial disposition.

GRIEVANCE	CATEGORY	INITIAL DISPOSITION
I resent your putting the children before me.	Primacy	"Mindreading" exercise.
I feel trapped—caged.	Power	Declaration of "Bill of Rights."
I resent your everlasting need to get in with the "right" people.	Social Boundaries	Possible Vesuvius followed by negotiation for change.
You're not giving me enough love and affection.	Role-Expectations	Fight for change.
I resent your turning me off or putting me down sexually.	Sex	Possible Beltline negotiation.
I need a certain amount of space at times so that I can give. You're crowding me.	Distance	Fight for change.

| I resent your accusations about extra-curricular sex. | Trust | "As if" trust exercise. |
| You don't accept me as I am. | Defense of self-identity | Reality confrontation and validation of self. |

The 73 inventories of corrosives presented by 32 males and 41 females listed a total of 484 items of discord: 178 from the males and 306 from the females. A careful analysis of the contents of these lists suggests that although the women reported more grievances than men, the men reported their grievances more globally and less specifically than the women. "You nag!" was a common male complaint as opposed to a female's more specific, "I resent your pointing out cobwebs I missed in cleaning house when I was busy doing your report!" Another factor in the discrepancy between numbers of complaints may be the reluctance of males generally to verbalize complaints—judging this as a possible sign of weakness. The most striking conclusion of the analysis was the similarity between the men's and women's complaints.

Complaints regarding unmet *expectations* were the heaviest of all those included in this pilot study. There were 188 items that dealt with unmet expectations: 116 from women; 72 from men. The items included in this category touched on all the dimensions of intimacy, but the focus of the gripes was on their lack in the intimate other, with the implied or stated judgment that this quality *should* be present. This category of unmet *expectations* was further divided into:

Complaints About Your Not Having Met My Expectations and
Complaints About Your Putting Your Expectations on Me.

(Either you have in some way not met my expectations of you as a "person in role" (wife, husband, mother, father, lover, provider, housekeeper), or I resent your bugging me about some expectation of yours that I haven't met).

Of the two subdivisions, it would seem that the major source of Corrosives in Intimacy are harbored judgments of how the other *should* behave in the relationship. Men and women both mentioned many expectations of the other (men 56, women 98). These complaints were further broken down into:

Pair-Specific and Person-Specific Expectations (Male 33; Female 52)
Dissimilar Interests and Priorities (Male 2; Female 6)
Complaints Related to Time Expectations (Male 5; Female 3)

Complaints about Parenting Expectations (Male 8; Female 19)
Complaints about Household Expectations (Male 8; Female 17)
Only in the category of complaints about procrastination and lateness
(Time Expectations) did the men's complaints outnumber the women's.
In the areas of parenting and household expectations, the women's
items outnumbered the men's by more than two to one.

PAIR-SPECIFIC and PERSON-SPECIFIC EXPECTATIONS

MALE	FEMALE
You are too independent. You don't take care of me properly. I resent your helpless tears; you should be stronger.	You're too passive. I resent your male chauvinism. I resent your alliance on outside authorities—you should be stronger.

DISSIMILAR INTERESTS AND PRIORITIES

MALE	FEMALE
Your interests and priorities are not the same as mine You didn't enjoy the trip I planned for us—that hurt.	I resent your making light of *my* work and not being more involved. I resent your wanting peace rather than involvement with me.

COMPLAINTS RELATED TO TIME COMMITMENTS

MALE	FEMALE
You wait until the last minute to do something instead of organizing your time.	I resent your never being on time.
I resent getting to a dinner engagement one hour late.	I can never depend on you for getting home on time—dinner is always delayed and often ruined.
You're never ready when I am.	You have no sense of time when you get started on a project.

COMPLAINTS ABOUT PARENTING EXPECTATIONS

MALE	FEMALE
I resent your dumping your excess hostility on the kids.	I resent your unrealistic punishment of the kids.

You are sometimes very, very sarcastic to the kids and it bothers me.

You intimidate your children with too much pressure when they don't respond to your liking.

You interfere when I'm disciplining the kids.

I resent your lack of cooperation in the disciplining of the children.

I could hit you when you chew me out in front of the children.

I hate your correcting me in front of the kids and causing them to lose respect for me.

COMPLAINTS ABOUT HOUSEHOLD EXPECTATIONS

MALE

I resent your accumulating and saving all that junk!

You're a messy housekeeper, you're too disorganized.

I resent your insistence that I participate in every decision to do something around the house.

FEMALE

I resent your leaving the house in a mess when you go off to work.

I resent your comments about my housekeeping—I feel "put down."

I resent feeling I'm imposing on you when I ask what you want done in the house—you live here, too!

Evident in this group of *expectations* corrosives is the absence of clearly-stated role expectations of significant partners:

What do I expect of me and what do I expect of you?
What do you expect of you and what do you expect of me?
What are the specific differences and can we negotiate them?

Another problem disclosed is how individuals saw one another as extensions of themselves: "When you act offensively or make a fool of yourself, I am shamed." The question here is: to what extent am I able to disengage from my intimate other in specific situations? Here the question of separateness, tolerance of differences, and autonomy of action are considerations with which to deal.

COMMUNICATION COMPLAINTS

Complaints about the corrosive effect of the partner's communication style in the relationship made up the second heaviest category in the analysis of this pilot study. In many instances, this category overshadowed the entire list. What is taught in Fight Training (Conflict Management) is a new communication system that can be used to build a relationship in a more realistic and constructive manner.

Communication complaints fell into seven areas:

General complaints:	Male-14	Female-30
Complaints about indirect communication patterns	Male- 5	Female- 1
Complaints about styles of dealing with anger	Male- 4	Female- 4
Beltline reminders	Male- 4	Female- 4
Deprecating via labeling	Male- 6	Female-12
Hostility under the guise of humor	Male- 1	Female-12
Threats (verbal)	Male- 5	Female- 5

The total number of complaints in the category of Communication was 105: Male 39, Female 66.

GENERAL COMMUNICATION COMPLAINTS

MALE

You won't listen to me unless I say what you want to hear. You won't even give me ten minutes of your time when I get home to talk about my concerns.

It makes me fighting mad when you counter what I'm saying before hearing me out.

Your "why" questions always put me on the defense. I hate your always wanting to know the "why" of everything I do.

FEMALE

I resent your not wanting to listen when I want to talk with you.

I resent your judging and starting to punish me without hearing me out.

When I want to clarify things and ask you questions, you take this as a criticism.

INDIRECT COMMUNICATION

MALE

You don't communicate directly.

You are unable to stick to a subject.

FEMALE

I resent your not giving me clear messages about what you want.

I resent your telling me about previous involvements in such a fragmented, evasive way that I feel you are trying to hide something from me.

Engaging me in a deep conversation as I'm about to leave for work makes me furious.

In this subdivision the total response is represented: only one female complaint recorded as against four male complaints.

COMPLAINTS ABOUT STYLES OF DEALING WITH ANGER

Male	Female
You avoid argument at all cost.	You cannot express anger and get upset when I do.
You refuse to fight to a conclusion. You want to make up before the issue is resolved.	I don't get enough information about what I do that displeases you. You don't say what you're angry about.

BELTLINE REMINDERS

Male	Female
I resent your getting involved with another man. That was a beltline for me.	I bitterly resent your never taking into consideration that I would be deeply hurt by your publicizing your affair.
Stop saying I drink too much—I'm sick of hearing it!	I resent your crying constantly about something I did seventeen years ago.

DEPRECIATING THE OTHER VIA LABELING

Male	Female
You make me out as the COP or the VILLAIN in every situation.	I resent your showing your anger at me by calling me WOMAN when you're upset.

It makes me furious when you impose your "I know better" attitude on me by calling me STUPID.

Stop telling me I'm COLD and RIGID.

Calling me STUPID—and when you do this to the kids, I cringe!

Stop calling me a HIPPIE.

HOSTILITY UNDER THE GUISE OF HUMOR

MALE	FEMALE
Being sarcastic and accusing me of lacking a sense of humor enrages me.	I hate your "funny" sarcasm.
	I dislike your laughing at me, not with me.
	You make it difficult to tell serious talk from teasing.
	I hate it when you make jokes about my intelligence.

In this pilot group of 73 participants the use of humor for the purpose of hostility release is almost exclusively a female complaint. Only one man complained of his partner's "humorous" sarcasm, while twelve women listed complaints in this category. Three of the twelve complained about their partner's habit of "not taking them seriously," a convenient way to ignore or deny impact.

THREATS

MALE	FEMALE
You threaten to turn me into the Army if I leave.	You always threaten to leave if I get upset or demand you change in any way.
You threaten to commit suicide if I leave.	I resent your leaving me rather than trying to change, and your threatening me with a messy divorce.
You threatened to kick me in the balls the last time you got angry, and to flush my camera down the toilet!	

One of the first steps in the work of decreasing alienation between partners is the outlawing of the most lethal weapons wielded against each other: threat of leaving (ending the relationship), threat of suicide, threat of gross physical and emotional harm. Outlawing such threats can only be done by mutual consent based on a time-committed resolve to work at building a more productive relationship.

Illustrations of complaints and grievances relating to the specific concerns of intimacy:

POWER, PRIMACY, DISTANCE, SOCIAL BOUNDARIES, SEX, TRUST

POWER

MALE	FEMALE
I need to be in control, and you keep challenging me.	I resent your dominating me.
I hate your high horse didactics about every fucking subject, and your insistence that I damn well better agree!	I resent you when you feel there's only one way to do things—your way.
You solicit allies from among the family to help overwhelm me in an argument.	Other people influence you more than I do, and I resent it.
You established a joint bank account and health insurance without consulting me beforehand.	I resent your borrowing money on your signature to buy office equipment and not asking me if I agreed nor telling me afterwards.

Key questions in the area of power relate to "who is boss" and "does there need to be a boss;" "you must agree with me or I feel rejected or put down." Can differences be tolerated as differences and not as proof of unimportance? Using family members as allies against the partner in a power struggle is a major engagement in alienating partners and family. Control of money is a key issue in determining the power balance in a relationship. All these items of discord are negotiable—provided the bases of minimal good will and commitment to the relationship are existent.

PRIMACY

MALE	FEMALE
You loved your fucking mother more than you loved me. That really hurt.	I'm still resenting your not telling your family that you loved me, and that you wanted them to treat me with your love in mind.
You never consider what's important to me—only what matters to you and the children.	I resent your putting the children before me.
Too often you won't let anything interfere with your school work.	I resent your thinking that your job is more important than mine.

In a paired relationship, making time for children, work, and in-laws in a manner that gives each realistic dimensions and enhances, enlarges, and deepens the paired relationship is a major task in the work of productive intimacy.

DISTANCE

MALE	FEMALE
You're too dependent on me. I resent your asking for affection when I don't feel in the mood to give it, and then pouting when I turn away.	You're too dependent on me. I feel rejected when you refuse to kiss or hold me when I ask.
I dislike your withdrawing from me and getting quiet when we have a fight.	I resent your leaving the house for long periods of time when you're mad, when that's just the time I need you to stay around.

Individual differences in readiness to engage the other or need to disengage from the other when used and interpreted as rejection of one partner by the other becomes a process of accumulating acid in the relationship. When accepted as personal differentiation one from the other, then specific needs can be negotiated as a problem to solve without ego involvement.

SOCIAL BOUNDARIES

MALE	FEMALE
You don't take enough initiative in social engagements.	I wish you would take more responsibility in our social life.
I need more time away from people than you do. Your constant interest in socializing is a drag.	You seldom take me out.
Your rejection of my relationships with others burns me.	You drive away my friends with your snide remarks about me.

SEX

MALE	FEMALE
I resent that there is not enough sex activity.	You talk too much about sex and do too little.
I resent your expecting me to respond sexually when I'm tired.	I resent it when you try to turn me on in the morning when I want to sleep.
When I am interested in sex and you are aware but not interested, you attempt to ignore my interest.	I resent your not being intuitive about my sexual desires and getting angry when I instruct you.

Clearly this is an area where mutual expectations have not been shared and discussed for reality "fit."

TRUST

MALE	FEMALE
I was furious when I realized you'd taken our savings for a trip after you'd told me it was a gift from your family.	I can't trust you—you lie and cheat and you're dishonest.
I resent your being possessive, pouty, and unreasonably jealous.	You're ridiculously jealous.
I resent your accusations about extra-curricular sex.	I resent your attentions to other women.

The first listed complaint in this illustration (of each partner) was in reference to dishonoring a value system—the value of a committed word was violated—"I can't trust you to be open with me." The next listed complaints disclosed distrust of one another's primacy or exclusiveness in the relationship. Jealousy is conceivably a manifestation of distrust of the partner, of insecurity in the relationship, and of deprecation of the self: seeing other male-female relationships as a threat to one's own primacy or exclusiveness.

CRAZYMAKING GAMES

Closely related to the area of Communication are patterns of behavior designated as "crazymaking." Many of the crazymaking patterns could as easily be grouped under miscommunication, but their peculiarly destructive quality is highlighted by this classification.

Manipulative Behavior

MALE	FEMALE
Trying to manipulate me to get what you want instead of confronting me directly.	I don't like your con game—when you try to make me do something without my realizing what you're trying to do.
	I hate it when you make me do your dirty work:
	Meeting your mother at the airport and giving her bad news. Handling bill collectors. Lying to people for you. Telling former friends they offended you, and you never want to see them again.

Denial of Identity and/or Reality

MALE	FEMALE
It infuriates me when you tell me I do not feel the way I say I feel.	You tell me how I feel about something but don't listen to me.
I resent your saying that we have never had anything when for years we've owned our own home, had two cars, and sent our kids to private schools.	

I resent your monopolizing conversations; saying things for me.

Stop saying "I don't believe you" when I try to tell you what I believe.

Don't interrupt me and then tell me I can't express myself.

I get mad when you shut me up in public. Either I say something your way or you won't let me say anything.

Unchecked Assumptions

MALE	FEMALE

When you park the car on the new grass, I feel you are doing something to refute me.

When you argue with me in front of others, I feel you are doing it to cut me down.

When you got pregnant, twice, while using contraceptives, I felt deliberately burdened by you subconsciously.

You assume how I feel about something without asking me.

I resent your saying that you didn't go somewhere because of me, when you didn't bother to check out whether I minded or not if you went.
I resent your assumptions that I'd be happier with someone else; that I hate your business.

Analysis

MALE	FEMALE

I resent that you take my feeling depressed as a personal affront that *must mean* I'm upset with you.

When I'm feeling good about something I resent your explaining to me "why!"

I resent your analyzing my motives for helping others as either guilt or self-gratification!

I resent your *questioning my motives* for deciding not to have children.

Blamemanship

MALE	FEMALE

I resent your agreeing to something when pressured, and then resenting it and blaming me for your decision.

I resent your saying my illness is
my fault.

I resent your saying that I'm the
one who has problems in our relationship—that if I'd get myself
straightened out we'd both be okay.

Set-Ups

MALE	FEMALE
	Asking for information and then cutting me off as soon as I begin with "Just answer 'yes' or 'no'." Then you probe further, sarcastically, after I answer "yes" or "no."
	Pushing me to get angry at times and then resenting it when I do. I resent your asking me for my ideas and thoughts only to put them down.
	Pushing me to have sex with other men so you could feel justified having sex with other women.

Double-Messages ("Yes, but . . .") and
Double-Binds ("I'm damned if I do and damned if I don't")

MALE	FEMALE
I resent your telling me to call you when I know I'm going to be late getting home and then giving me hell when I do by accusing me of not considering you important enough, and calling me names.	You give me and the children double messages, and it's driving us crazy! You make decisions and then countermand them in the next breath.
	I resent it when you look so needy and say: "I wanted to take you out tonight, but . . ."
	I resent your saying you don't tell me you love me because of your fear of needing me.

Basic factors in all crazymaking communications are entrapment and
collusion. The subject or victim must be "hooked" into the engagement. As soon as one partner realizes what the other is doing: ma-
nipulating, denying identity, mind-reading, analyzing, blaming,
setting-up (to strike down), double-binding—the game can be stopped
by calling it and disengaging from it, rather than defending, arguing,

and explaining untenable positions. Just as it takes two to engage in disruptive behavior, so does it take two to make behavior more constructive. An awareness of behavior patterns is essential and a commitment to change that which is destructive is basic. The procedure of instigating change is always pair and person specific.

Crazymaking communications have the effect of painting ourselves and each other into corners difficult to get out of and going deeper and deeper into frustration. When recognized through such explicit complaints as previously outlined, we have the basis upon which to back up and make another start. In some cases making a specific negotiation for change; in others, developing the capacity to listen long enough to get a clear message; in all cases calling a halt to the process of crazymaking and concentrating on individual issues and specifics as opposed to global condemnations. Risk taking is obligatory in such a commitment to change, risking trust that what is said IS WHAT IS MEANT in spite of doubts—ACTING "AS IF" YOU DON'T DOUBT in order to validate a commitment to change. This becomes an exercise in overcoming the possible sabotage of one's own guts. Acting as you don't feel in order to attain a growth-producing relationship becomes an exercise in self-expansion and in deepening intimacy.

This pilot study of 73 Inventories of Corrosives in Intimacy makes readily apparent the need for intimate partners to educate one another, i.e., "When I'm hurting I want you to listen. I want emotional support—not a lecture on what I should have done." This is a communication of specific need and specific limitation.

The silent partners—the hoarders of grievances, male or female—on closer examination and follow-up were negatively interpreting their mate's messages, receiving distorted information that was not intended. The message given became contaminated by the acid in the guts of the receiver—working as a "set" to receive what was *expected* and not that which was sent—a process of actually hearing only what one expects to hear.

Many couples are unaware of how they "turn each other off." A frequent specific complaint is: "When I do express what I feel, she (or he) takes it as a criticism or blames me for feeling the way I do—so what's the use?" This is a psychological dynamic of male and female input to provoke alienation.

A closer examination of interpersonal relationships also reveals a series of meta-messages underlying the "what" of the information given, such as, "I so seldom get a chance to talk to you that I have to get it all out at one sitting,''—while the partner feels overwhelmed and overloaded; or "I want you to know I'm around and pay attention to me—and I feel ashamed to ask directly,''—putting the mate into the untenable position of guessing the meaning of specific actions.

In fight-phobic individuals, often behind the refusal to say what angers one is the oft-stated remark, "You ought to know what angers me''—the additional assumption wedded to this so-called fact is ''. . . therefore you are deliberately doing this to make me mad,'' or "You don't care about me.'' A basic premise in this therapeutic communication system is TAKE RESPONSIBILITY FOR DISCLOSING ALL "OUGHTS" AND "SHOULDS" AND CHECK OUT VERBALLY ALL ASSUMPTIONS. Risk being authentic—giving straight messages, taking responsibility for self, negotiating differences, living around what can't be changed, and designating freedoms and limitations.

The following are illustrations of various uses of the I.C.I. by partners in conflict:

Husband's Inventory of Corrosives:

GRIEVANCES	ANALYSIS AND DISPOSITION
I resented your continual arguments over money	Essentially resolved—disengaged.
I resented your continual arguments over how to raise the children.	No longer an issue—the children are grown and out of the house.
I resented your criticism of my smoking, my drinking, and how I keep my expense account.	No longer an issue—disengaged.
I resent your criticism of my work schedule.	Negotiation for change.
You don't accept me as I am.	Defense of self-identity.
You want me to live up to your expectations.	Declaration of Bill of Rights.
You say you are interested in my work but you don't act like it.	Trust establishment.
I resent your interrupting and answering for me.	Negotiation for change.
I resent your continual battling; I can't handle disagreements.	Practice in confrontation and aggressive self-care and work at overcoming fight-phobic characteristics.
I feel like a stranger to you.	Disclose mutual expectations.

I feel put down.

I feel trapped.

Negotiation for change.

Establish areas of autonomy and distance.

The Wife's Inventory of Corrosives

GRIEVANCES	ANALYSIS AND DISPOSITION
Your refusal to face conflict drives me up the wall.	Focus on one specific issue at a time as a negotiation issue.
You don't understand me or allow me to have my own feelings.	Defense of self-identity.
You lie to me and constantly change stories.	Trust-formation.
I resent your other women; I feel threatened and hurt.	Coming to terms with what is or possible negotiation for change.
You changed your value system, mine remains the same, but you won't talk about it, you run away and find pleasure elsewhere.	Confrontation of differences.
I'm panicky about your asking for a divorce, even though you said you'd give this marriage another try.	Work at staying in the present.
It hurts when you tell me about your other woman, and then you resent it when I don't respond to your overtures when I'm hurting.	Confront conflicting messages and establish beltline.

By mutual consent this couple agreed that they were emotionally separated and estranged but not enraged with each other, that there was enough good-will existent to work at the relationship, that they could each—at this moment in time—tolerate hearing each other's complete list of grievances.

From a mutual presentation of grievances it readily became apparent that the wife was totally unaware of the increasing disaffection of her husband in the marriage relationship. Differences were dealt with by withdrawal from conflict by the husband. Each was unaware of the other's emotional reality. A beginning of authentic presentation was made by a respectful listening to each other's list of corrosives.

A "HOT" I.C.I.

In the following verbatim account of another style of dealing with the

Inventory of Corrosives the emotional atmosphere between the partners was electric with hostility. Snide remarks belittling each other's integrity preceded the following exchange:

LEAH: Would you like to listen to my Inventory?

PAUL: Would I like to or will I? *(Belligerently)*

L: All right! WILL YOU listen to my list? *(Exasperatedly)*

THERAPIST: Just a moment. I want to clarify something. An Inventory of Corrosives includes aches, gripes, and complaints that you have with the other which you have not satisfactorily explored to date. It is meant to provide us with a program of action, a direction. It is *not* intended to be wielded as a weapon, or used to stir up a hornet's nest of hostility. Based on your initial exchange, I want to use my prerogative as therapist and ask that we deal with this particular Inventory by concentrating only on one item. Pick that issue which is most painful at this particular time.

L: All right. My first item is the fury I feel when we're having a fight and you walk out on me.

TH: Let's dialogue. *(In this procedure the mate, Paul, is obligated to act as listener only; since no defense, explanation or inclusion is permitted, a more attentive ear is possible.)*

I hear this as a current issue, and I'm wondering if you want to make it the subject of a negotiation for change. It represents a frustration with your partner's fight style that may be resolvable. Do you agree?

L: Yes. I feel that fits very well. I'd like that. Paul, will you engage in a negotiation for change?

P: Yes!

L: I want you to see an issue through and not leave the house when we've been arguing and take off.

P: This is a compound issue—

TH: Don't evaluate the request—don't explain—just repeat her demand verbatim at this point. If you're evaluating the message, you often don't hear it so well.

P: Okay. I hear you saying that you want me to stay with an issue until we've both finished negotiating it, and not to leave the house.

L: That's correct.

P *(to Therapist):* Let's dialogue about this.

TH: Fine. Leah, it is now your job to just listen attentively.

P: One of my ways of releasing rage is to get in the car and drive. And when I cool off I come home. And I don't run away from the problem when I leave. I use the time away to think about the issue. It's important to me to be able to absent myself at times to do that.

TH: Obviously, Leah hasn't heard your purpose clearly in the past. How about announcing your choice of this option just the way you would any ritualized rage-release. In the same way we get permission for a Vesuvius, you could, possibly, get permission for your absence—as long as you would be willing to put an announced time-limit on it. When your anger has reached the boiling point, signal Leah. We all need the safety valve of being able to call a halt to a heated fight for a length of time *within a twenty-four hour limit.* See if Leah will agree to the use of a signal to clue her into your need for the argument to stop for a specified length of time.

P: I think I can try it her way, if I can call a halt and she'll stop. *(To Leah)* I'll agree to try for one week not to leave the house when we get in an argument, if you will agree to respect my signal when I need the argument to stop. I want you to stop talking on the issue if I call "time out."

L: I hear you agreeing to stay in the house as long as I stop at a signal from you and not continue talking.

TH: Hold it! Did you mean no conversation at all?

P: No, I didn't. I only meant that conversation *on the issue* would cease for a specified length of time.

TH *(to Leah):* Can you feed that back?

L: Can I dialogue with you for a minute?

TH: Does it have to do with this issue?

L: Yes, it does. He left on Thanksgiving and he returned the next day!

TH: You're dealing with what he *did,* not with what he plans to do.

L: But he usually does leave!

TH: What did he just say? Are you willing to try a new style of behavior for one week? *(Leah nods)* Then repeat the final message.

L *(to Paul):* You're willing to try staying in the house and not leaving when we have an argument, if I will stop when you give me the signal.

TH: And what's the signal?

P: "Time out."

L: If you call "time out," the argument stops for a specified length of time, not to exceed twenty-four hours.

P: That's right.

L: I accept.

TH: Seal that commitment. *(The pair embrace)*

In my opinion, a reading of the total museum list at one sitting in this instance was inadvisable—based on an assessment of the participants' lack of ability to absorb this information without the danger of escalated rage inciting immediate counterattack. The relationship was adjudged too tenuous to be so bombarded. The immediate realistic concern was to take one thorn out of a many-thorned relationship to partially ease an over-all tensed and stressed relationship.

The fact that this couple was able to embrace upon concluding a first attempt at cooperatively looking at an issue in order to solve a problem is a dramatic illustration of the deescalation of rage and the creation of a bonding effect in the process of a "negotiation for change."

The Wife's Side

The following deals only with the wife's list of corrosives to which the husband took issue. Each method of presentation of grievances is person-and pair-specific as well as the procedure in dealing with information given.

Jean(*to Bruce*): May I read my list to you?

Bruce: Okay

1· You hide your feelings. I resent your control of yourself, me, and the kids. I resent your rigidity. I resent your withdrawing and shutting me out. I resent your not dealing openly with our relationship. I resent feeling put down, blocked, and annihilated by your words. I resent your deviousness and secretiveness. I resent your acting out. I resent that I don't know I'm important in your life, you don't let me know. I resent being your mother and you're not working completely through your mother hang-up. I resent your taking extra work-loads as a punishment when I displease you. I resent your coldness—your not showing me and the kids physical warmth and compassion. I resent your fixed schedule and lack of spontaneity. I resent your clenched jaw and steely eyes. I resent your being influenced by outside authorities you admire and by being controlled by them. I resent your excesses—getting drunk and over-working. I resent your assumptions and mind reading, and I resent my fear of you.

B: I feel shitty! I have a really shitty feeling in my guts.

Therapist: What do you do about it. How can you get rid of the shitty feeling?

B: Not take responsibility for it?

TH: Take responsibility for your own self-care—acknowledging the feeling is the first step. Doing something about it is the next step. What in Jean's list hurts you the most—makes you feel the shittiest?

B: My being devious and secret.

TH: All right, now we're huddling. Are you devious and secretive?

B: I don't think so.

TH: Give Jean that information.

B: My being devious and secretive is an unfair accusation because it's not true.

TH: Do you believe him?

J: I guess I believe that what he's saying is true. I believe that he believes that he's not secretive and devious.

TH: Are you willing to take the *risk of trusting* him to be what he says he is?

J: Yes, I admit I could be wrong.

TH: Then cross that item from your list.

J: I'm glad to do so.

TH *(to Bruce):* What's the next strong ache?

B: My being rigid and not spontaneous.

TH: What about that? We're huddling now.

B: I think I've made a big change in this area.

TH: Fine, tell Jean the changes you have made in this area—specifically.

B: Jean, I feel that I have been less rigid and more spontaneous in the last year or two. I demand less of you, of the children, and even of myself at work.

TH: Do you recognize that, Jean?

J: Yeah, I do think he's less rigid.

TH: So there has been an advance. What I am sensing, Bruce, is that you want this recognized. Is that so?

B: Yes, I would like a little stroke on my change. I accept all her shit—let her pile it up on me and never hear I do anything right.

TH: What I hear you asking for now is some emotional nourishment that can conceivably go like this: "Jean, look at me every day and once a day tell me what you like about me." Does that make sense to you?

B: I like it!

TH: Ask Jean if she will engage you in a negotiation for change.

B: Jean, will you negotiate with me? *(Jean agrees)* Would you be willing to . . . .

TH: Try the feeling of stating exactly what *you WANT*.

B: I want you to tell me something nice about me once a day.

J: You are telling me you want me once a day to say something nice to you.

B: Correct.

J: I think I like that.

TH: You like that—then you are accepting it?

J: Once a day I will say something nice about him.

TH: And renegotiate it at the end of each week to check on performance—reinforce it and hopefully make it a new pattern of living. Seal that commitment. *(After couple hug)* How do you feel, Bruce?

B: Considerably less shitty!

In this encounter between Bruce and Jean, the impact of Jean's Inventory of Corrosives was heavy—and distance-making. Immediate dealing with strong hurts and possible misconceptions, accepting the possibility of misjudgment, taking the courage to confront, make it possible to negotiate differences on a more rational basis.

Chapter 6

Separation of Power and Self-Presentation

SEPARATION OF POWER

A Bill of Rights and Areas of Autonomy are statements of power in a relationship. As mentioned, the bill of rights is a reference to a basic need of one individual in order to guarantee personal integrity, around which another is asked to live in order to maintain a bonding relationship. An area of autonomy is a statement of power in a relationship— subject to *mutual acceptance* and negotiation—in which each gives to the other the power of *final* decision-making in defined areas of living. A bill of rights—*non-negotiable power*—is a declarative statement of personhood. An area of autonomy is negotiable. It is separation of power in a committed relationship by mutual consent. In operation, it is a process: of discussion, viewing alternatives and choices, and allowing power of final decision-making in one's area of autonomy.

A declaration of a bill of rights sets the basic *currently* non-negotiable realities of an individual's being, upon which it is possible to build and maintain a relationship with a significant other. It is self presentation, giving information about what is essential to one's integrity. It sets the boundaries and limitations of togetherness—very person-specific—and keeps open an area of freedom separate from the intimate other. This declaration does not eliminate the possibility of change. What is necessary to one's self-esteem today may not be important tomorrow. The type and manner of change evolves out of the realities of a significant ongoing relationship.

Recognition of a bill of rights may *emerge* through the process of an interrelationship in intimacy—surfacing some vital new awareness of self and its significance and impact on the partner—bringing to light much needed information. A bill of rights that involves *demands* on another may be ammunition that has to be defused, or point out problem areas to deal with, or sometimes such demands become the trigger that blows up the relationship.

New Awareness Through a Hostility Ritual

The following encounter, with the therapist acting as communications facilitator, illustrates a new awareness as well as the use of a hostility ritual and a negotiation for change.

Wanda: I have an item from the past I want to deal with.

Therapist: Ask permission first.

W: Bud, can I discuss the time you said you didn't want me to run for president in front of my club?

Bud: Sure, but I don't know what we'll be able to do about it.

Th: We have several options for dealing with museum items. Let's hear hers first and then discuss the possibilities.

W: You humiliated me in front of my friends. You were drunk, and you told me in front of everybody that you didn't want me to run for office in my community organization. I was really hurt and resentful. You didn't give me any warning, and I felt embarrassed—I didn't know what to say. I don't ever want to hurt about it again.

Th: How can you prevent that? What alternatives can you propose? Painful memories can be erased gradually by constructive acts in the present. Determine the degree of impact this behavior has on you. Two possibilities come to my mind: to establish a beltline or engage in a beef for change. Does this make sense to you?

W: It's a beltline. I couldn't stand for him to do it again!

B: I can commit myself to discussing what I want her to do or not to do in private, but I won't pretend to like something she does that I don't approve of.

Th: Hold it. Let's backtrack and find out exactly what Wanda wants to outlaw.

W: I don't want you to publicly order me not to do something like run for office, or to announce that you don't approve of something I'm going to do in the way you did.

B: I hear you saying that you outlaw my saying I don't want you to do something like run for office in front of other people.

W: Yes, and if you're asked how you feel about it, you can say how you feel but not as if it's an order to me to stop.

B: And if I don't like something and someone asks me about it, I can say how I feel as long as it doesn't sound like I'm telling you that you can't do it.

W: That's exactly what I want.

B *(to Therapist):* That's what I heard. But I don't think that's what she means.

Tн: Go with her exact words for the moment. Save the mind-reading for another time. This is a beltline and it's being outlawed in the terms of the person who is hurting.

B: Then I can honor your beltline and not publicly say you can't do something you want to do.

W: I have a beef for change that's related to this.

Tн:You also have the information from previous discussions of this matter that you do not have his cooperation. If you run for office, you have to organize the entire thing yourself. Is it worth it to go it alone?

W: That's where my beef for change comes in. It's worth it as long as he doesn't actively work against me.

B: I'll engage you in a beef on that issue.

W: Bud, I want you to agree that you will not actively work against me while I run for president.

B: I hear your demand as being that I not actively interfere in your campaign for president.

W: That's correct.

B: I will not actively oppose it. But I will resist passively, because I don't want you to do it.

Tн: Is that acceptable to you, Wanda?

W: Yes, except that now I realize I'm dealing with an item on my bill of rights!

Tн: Bud, will you hear Wanda's statement of her right? *(Bud agrees)*

W: Part of my bill of rights is that I be able to select an activity such as running for office. I demand the right to run for an office in a function outside the home if I choose to. Will you accept that?

Tн: Wanda, you are making a statement of identity. You don't have to justify it. It's non-negotiable. Bud is simply asked to hear your bill of rights. It would be beautiful if he honors it, but whether he honors it or not, that's *your* bill of rights. Let it go at that, and pick up specific points of contention when they arise. *(To entire group)* Establishing a behavior as a bill of rights establishes a right the other is asked to acknowledge or live around. Passive resistance may be desisting from doing favors that will facilitate Wanda's presidential responsibilities.

W: I guess I'm just pissed off because he keeps bringing up the accusation that I neglect the house and family to do this.

Tн: Wait a minute, Wanda. Do you want a Vesuvius? *(She nods)* Then ask permission!

W: Bud, can I Vesuvius—just for thirty seconds—on this?

B: I guess I can stand thirty seconds' worth.

W *(she stands and meditates for several seconds):* I resent the way you keep dragging up this accusation. Every time I want to do something, you always accuse me of neglecting the house and the family. That's not true any more. At one time it was, but not now! I do take care of my house and family first! I organize my time well, and I don't want to hear you accusing me that I don't. Why don't you trust me?

Tн: Wait a minute, Wanda. That's one of those immediately unanswerable questions. If you want him to trust you, prove his misgivings unfounded. Enjoy the challenge of showing him how wrong he is.

B: She's right about my worrying about the time she spends outside the home.

Tн *(to group):* May I fish for information? I want to show you one way to clarify what's bothering you.

B: Sure, go ahead.

Tн *(begins dialogue with Bud):* How do you see Wanda's outside interests?

B: I do think she's overcommitted to community activities. I think she overdoes it; she's anemic, and she tends to start vaginal bleeding too easily. And our sex life suffers. Then she's gone so much that I feel isolated at home. I'd like her to spend some time with me, too!

Tн: How about having a beef for change with her? How many nights a week would you like her to spend exclusively with you?

B: Wanda, will you engage me in a beef for change? *(She agrees)* I'd like you to give me two evenings a week.

W: I hear you saying that you want me to give you two evenings a week.

B: That's right. Will you do it?

W: You may have two nights a week. I didn't realize you were feeling that isolated.

Tн: Seal that negotiation. *(Couple embraces)*

This last beef is an example of love and intimacy expectations. We need to learn to express our needs directly.

This series of interchanges illustrates the process of getting at more meaning and awareness of what we do and what we want. The couple started at one surface and progressed to another depth.

A museum item designated as a beltline was found to be a bill of rights item.

His protest became a fight for change based on a recognized need for inclusion in her life apart from outside interests.

The following brief exchange illustrates another instance in which the experience of discord pinpoints an area in living established as a bill of rights.

BEN: I'd like to dialogue with you about something I want to outlaw.

THERAPIST *(to Kate):* In a dialogue, your responsibility is simply to listen without comment—as non-defensively as possible. You are just getting information.

B: Since 1965 I've been getting told that I devote more time to my business than I do to my family. Every time we have a problem, Kate blames the business. She keeps harping on that. I feel that that's a cop-out. The fact that I'm very involved in business is not the cause of all our problems. In the future I want to outlaw any reference to my business as the cause of our problems.

TH *(to Kate):* What did you hear?

KATE: He wants me to stop blaming the business when I have a gripe.

TH *(to Ben):* Now, there are several ways we can go with this. You can declare it a beltline, or you can declare your work an area of autonomy—that is, I don't want to be blamed for something it is my responsibility to do. Or you can include it in your bill of rights: "I have the right to determine hours of work according to the needs of the business, and I demand that you respect this."

B: I think it's part of my bill of rights.

TH: All right. Then see if Kate will respect this.

B: Kate, my working as much as I do is my right, and I want you to respect this and stop using it as an attack.

K: I hear you declaring your workload your right to establish, and I hear you telling me not to blame work for our problems.

B: That's right.

K: I won't use it as a cause of an issue, but I reserve the right to Vesuvius now and then about it.

In this confrontation, both partners came out with power—he declared his work hours non-negotiable, his sole responsibility and right to determine; her conditional acknowledgment of this right gave her the freedom, within the boundaries of a specific hostility ritual (Vesuvius) to ventilate her feelings.

The following are specific declarations of bills of rights.

"A" BILL OF RIGHTS—FEMALE

1. The right to decide and act on what I need for my career in terms of getting training, supplies, practical experience.
2. The right to control and spend my money (inherited and earned), being responsible for my own expenses plus half of the household expenses.
3. The right to get my needs for affection and intimacy met in the marriage as far as possible, but outside when necessary.
4. The right to live in an atmosphere where I feel that each adult interacts with other family members appreciatively and affirmatively more often than critically and negatively.

Items 1 and 2 are declarations of power and responsibility in two specific areas of living: career and financial, taking control over both.

Item 3 is a declaration of the right to include others in her intimate living. This may or may not become a value system clash with her partner. It is sometimes necessary to break a relationship when one's basic stated needs are in non negotiable conflict with a different value system. When one demands exclusivity (intimacy with the mate only) and the other demands variety (intimate relations with others) as basic rights, the irreconcilable differences that result may put an end to the relationship.

Item 4 relates to family members and assumes good will and understanding. The atmosphere (demanded as a right) is the result of teamwork meshing ideally—a long, hard investment of work in family intimacy is necessary before one can hope to approximate this ideal. It may be that "A" is asking for her diploma before taking her course of study which is to work in relationship-building.

One's bill of rights has to be tested for reality fit and timeliness.

"B" BILL OF RIGHTS

1. Right to privacy.
2. Right to decide regarding time and money commitments, regarding my professional areas.

These two simple statements may be accepted and honored basics in a relationship. The details of the *meaning* of the "right to privacy," however, have to be clearly spelled out.

In regard to money commitments, a problem arises. Does this conflict with the other's expectations? What specifically are the limitations or are none allowed? Clarification is essential. Basically "B" is establishing areas of separateness in intimacy.

"C" BILL OF RIGHTS—FEMALE

1. I have the right to excel in my profession and in areas of special interest.
2. I have the right to take the time necessary for my optimal development in these areas.
3. I have the right to fail in some areas or to be totally disinterested in some things.
4. I have the right to maintain my autonomy by continued use of my maiden name and by not participating in a community property arrangement.
5. I have the right to not bear another child and to make decisions regarding my body.
6. I have the right to vacation alone if I choose.
7. I demand the right not to have to make decisions for my husband.
8. I have the right to privacy in a geographic area (room) from which I can exclude others.

In items 1, 2, 3, 4, and 5, "C" is stating her right to competitiveness in outside interests—for power and significance as a separate person—apart from her mate.

Items 6, 7, and 8 are declarations of areas of freedom in family relations.

Over and over again, the question is posed: what price are you willing to pay to validate a bill of rights? When partners' value systems are not in conflict, the price for validating a bill of rights may be minimal. When partners' value systems are fundamentally incongruent, separation may be the price to pay for validation of a bill of rights.

"X" BILL OF RIGHTS—MALE

1. I take the freedom to make my own decision as to the choice of activities I want to get involved in.

2. I want to take the freedom to make this decision without expressed or implied criticism.
3. I would like the freedom to change the yard design, buy and put in new plantings, take out existing plants, and encouragement to make my own mistakes unhindered.

In item 1, "X" clearly states he will decide what interest pursuits he will follow.

In item 2, he is demanding another freedom from criticism as a *right*. In asking that no criticism be expressed or implied, he is asking for total acceptance, a rare possibility. A more realistic approach may be a negotiation to limit expression of criticism from the mate in a specific area of power.

Item 3 needs clarification. As a bill of rights statement, the landscaping becomes "X's" unchallenged area of power from which the mate is excluded; the price she pays in order to maintain closeness in the relationship.

When "X" adds "encouragement to make my own mistakes unhindered" to his bill of rights, he is asking for *help* in maintaining his bill of rights. Indeed, that would be beautiful and would add an extra bonus to the joy of living, but a bill of rights is that item of freedom in a relationship essential to *one's own* integrity as a person. It is not a request of another to meet one's needs. It is a stated responsibility to meet one's own basic needs.

Two men present the following bill of rights:

"Y " BILL OF RIGHTS

1. I have the right to practice my profession as I feel best for it and my health.
2. I have the right to participate and attend golf and sports events.

"Y" makes two non-ambivalent statements establishing power and autonomy in two defined areas of living.

"Z " BILL OF RIGHTS

1. I have a right to have friends, male or female, outside the marriage.
2. I have a right to find and do work that is fulfilling to me. I choose to limit this right by consulting my wife in those situations where she has indicated that this is her desire.

3. I have a right to spend money for reasonable professional and ongoing educational expenses.

The basis of "Z's" commitment to an intimate relationship is his declaration against exclusiveness in intimacy.

His second item includes consideration of his wife when exercise of his right to pursue and do fulfilling work creates special situations. This becomes a self-limiting exercise in utilizing power.

Item 3 may be too global. Boundaries may need to be set (within a particular financial framework) in order to realistically implement this right.

A couple presents the following bill of rights and areas of autonomy.

EVE

Rights:
1. To have a hobby which may be useless.

2. To avoid being overworked.

3. To have a voice in the choice of social entertainments, especially in regard to work-related acquaintances and escorthood.

4. To have an occasional vacation alone with my husband.

5. To have a few days by myself.

6. To have recreation.

ADAM

Rights:
1. Must have 2 hrs. privacy on any day exposed to kids.

2. Right to rest when I feel overworked.

3. Right to seek self-realization in career.

4. Right to an identity I can respect.

5. Right to do nothing when it isn't harmful.

6. Right to choose my own friends.

7. Right to my own political opinions

8. Right to a voice in all major decisions regarding my children.

9. Right to sexual gratification.

10. Right to a voice in all major expenditures.

11. Right to some personal allowance.

12. Right to a place at home where I can work undisturbed.

Autonomy:

1. Career and how to run it.

2. Wardrobe and grooming.

3. My relationship with my relatives and pre-marital friends.

4. Books I read.

5. Political and religious beliefs.

6. Child care arrangements if I am solely responsible.

7. Housework arrangements for that part of house maintenance that's mine.

8. Areas of the house which are my own.

Items 1, 2, 5, and 6 of Eve's bill of rights are person-specific and have to do with Self-Care.

Items 3 and 4 have to do with the relationship with her husband. When the mate's action is involved in an area of power we want, we have the problem of establishing this by mutual consent through a process of negotiation.

All areas of autonomy are powers we opt for, and are implemented by authentic acceptance of the right of one to say "butt out!" to the other when this is encroached upon.

Autonomy:

1. House operation: mechanical functioning of house & yard.

2. Paying of bills.

3. Mechanical functioning of cars.

4. Choice of new car.

5. Purchase of tools.

(Emotional & Political:)

6. Who I will donate money to.

7. Who I will meet at house with (not party or overnight).

8. Child care.

(Career)

9. Where best job is

10. Associates with whom to socialize.

Items 1, 2, 3, 5, 6, 7, 11, 12 in Adam's bill of rights deal with the specifics of the meaning of personal integrity. Implementing this creates Item 4, a self respecting identity.

Items 8, 9, and 10 need further clarification, a process of confrontation, communication, and negotiation.

Adam's areas of autonomy need Eve's cooperation to implement.

The following statements of rights surface problems this couple must face.

FEMALE

Rights:
1. I have a right to request time for discussion of concerns & differences.

MALE

Rights:
1. Right to self-respect in role in the family unit, to lead, not subjugate my wishes to those of my wife.

2. Right to discuss & to be a part of decisions with the children's plans & their discipline.

3. Right to develop myself & my interests even if they differ from interests of my husband and family.

4. Right to set my own pace and timing without parental reminders & control.

5. Right to equal recognition and importance as the female part of a partnership.

6. Right for time and privacy with my children.

7. Right to set priorities in my educational & professional striving.

8. Right to be me, not role or image.

9. Right to plan social activities for us, if you're willing to go, as well as participate in, if I wish, those you plan.

(No areas of autonomy)

2. To plan and enforce the family financial planning & major expenditure guidelines with consideration for wishes and needs of the family.

3. To privacy when I request it, up to 1 hour a day.

4. To pursue personal interests in sailing, flying, civic affairs, without major interference with planned family. To fly up to 2 hrs. a week; to sail one weekend out of each three; to stop for cocktails with office gang once a week for 2 hrs.

5. Right to affectionate and loving response (in bed) a minimum of 2 or 3 times a week with lovemaking; plus an affectionate acknowledgement of my strokes (smile, touch, words).

6. Right to equal authority in guidance and discipline of my wife's children, without interruption and opposition from my wife.

7. Right to a mutually-agreed level of social life with friends on a planned basis.

8. Right to pursue, as a goal, peace, love, and harmony in my home.

Autonomy:
Financial: blocks budgeted for household, recreation, schooling.

Sailing: 1 out of 3 weekends, family day sailing, cruising, or racing.

Equal responsibility and authority to manage the children without interference from their mother.

When one demands the right to "lead" (Male #1) there must be someone subservient to be led.

Obviously, in this bill of rights, there is a head-on clash with the mate's bill of rights (Female #5)—the "right to *equal* recognition and importance in a *partnership*."

A bill of rights that requires a specific set of responses from the mate (Male #5) may be the ingredient of a master-slave relationship—or the impetus to explore avenues to fulfillment through a process of mutual input.

In the following couple's bill of rights, the matter of the husband's sexual freedom is clearly established. The wife puts a definite limitation of encroachment on her stated power area.

FEMALE	MALE
Rights:	*Rights:*
I have the right to refuse to share my household items and equipment with any other woman with whom my husband is sexually intimate.	1. To discover and meet my own needs.
	2. To have other continuing relationships which may be sexual outside marriage.
	3. To change or leave my employment for school or other reasons.
	4. To allocate my time (free time) as I wish.
	5. To go on vacation with another woman.

There is no ambivalence in Elsa's declaration of rights:

I will visit with or entertain at least every two months, four sets of long time friends.

I will not listen to, TV-view, or be a spectator to sports games.

I will listen to mostly classical, Baroque, folk, Dixieland, opera, choral or ethnic music.

I will not spend more than one evening per every two months with people I consider boring.

I will eat out in a good restaurant approximately once per week.

I will have a housekeeper to maintain the house and do chores.

I will have a 24-hr. answering service.

I will have a part-time secretary/bookkeeper.

I will not go to great lengths and personal effort to entertain friends, but would rather spend more money than effort.

I will continue my endeavors to expand my practice locally and non-locally.

I will travel in my practice at least once per month for a weekend and frequently twice a month.

I will not have more than one person smoking in my house at one time no matter how many people are present.

I will not go to crowded, smokey night clubs or parties.

I will not exclude people from my association on the basis of race or social position.

I will make at least one trip out of the country per year.

I will spend Christmas eve with my parents and sister and brother-in-law. This could be *with* my husband's family as well—in fact, I would prefer a joint family get-together.

I will be an equal partner in any marriage.

I will go to the theater at least once every two months.

I will take part in any political activity I wish.

I will live at the beach in hot climates.

Elsa's position in a relationship is clearly stated:

Her social interests and intentions;

Her personal interests and disinterests;

Her personal care—at home and professionally;

Her explicit restrictions on others;

Her recreational needs;

Her status in her marriage;

Her politics.

She gives her mate relevant information. She knows where she stands. The limitations he has to deal with are apparent.

A BILL OF RIGHTS IS RECOGNIZED

The following illustrates the recognition of a bill of rights emerging from experiential impasses.

BRAD: I want to tell you about a typical problem that we encounter every time I relate something that happens at the office. I said one of the girls is going to work part-time until after exams, and she said, "What you really mean is she's not going to be at work Wednesday or Monday." Then she said, "I never had a job where

I could take off whenever I darn well pleased!'' It didn't go any-where from there, because I didn't take it up. But I hate to tell her anything about the office because I only get negative responses like that. What can I do?

TH: Your office and your discussing it could be the subject of a beef for change, or it could be an area of autonomy, or it could even be an item in your bill of rights. But before you decide how to deal with it, let me get Doris' view of the week.

DORIS: I thought I'd been nice about it. I didn't mean the remark about her taking off as a put-down. I said I'd never had a boss who was that good to me. I meant it to praise him!

TH: You may have misheard her statement. When you told the story, you related her remarks as criticisms of yourself.

B: That's true. I took her remark as a put-down—that I'm not running my office right.

TH: Then maybe you should establish running your office as a bill of rights: "I run my business my way, and my office is my con-cern." You then get the freedom to do as you please, but you don't get the opportunity to discuss things with her.

D: That's just fine with me. His office is a museum piece. I don't want to hear any more about it!

TH: Wait a minute. Brad, do you want to establish the conduct of your office as a bill of rights? *(Brad nods)* Then ask her if she will re-spect your request.

B: Doris, I want you to respect my office and its conduct as my area of power—my bill of rights.

TH: Feedback what you hear, Doris, before you reply.

D: I hear you say your office is an area of power—your bill of rights.

B: That's right.

TH: All right, can you live around that?

D: Yes, but I have a request—that you bring home the check-book with the balance each week so I know what's going on, so I know how much I can spend.

TH: Wait a moment. Do I hear you saying you really do want to know what's going on at the office?

D: I don't really care about that as long as I know how much money we have.

JOE: I think you're a phony!

TH: Just a minute. I object very much to that label "phony" or any label. Labelling builds a cage and confines a person in it, present-ing a categorized view only. It's a smokescreen hiding the prog-ress that's been made. Give Doris information that Doris can use *productively*. A put-down won't accomplish that.

J: Okay. I just have trouble believing Doris.

CORA: I think Doris is in a double-bind. She needs to know, but she can't handle the information. I think she's competing with the girls in the office.

TH: Check that mind-reading out.

C: Are you competing with the girls in the office?

D: You're right. I'm a jealous person. I'm jealous as hell. I stay with the children at home, and he's down there enjoying himself.

TH: Brad, do you hear what Doris is saying about the motivation for her remarks about your nurse?

B: She's saying she feels jealous, not that she meant it as a put-down.

TH: Right. And how about you, Doris? What have you learned?

D: I just realized what my jealousy did to me, what message I was giv-ing out that I didn't mean to—and I really don't know how to take care of myself.

TH: All right. Then your assignment next week is to find something you really want to negotiate for yourself alone. A gift for you. Bring the news next week.

D: What about Brad's bill of rights item?

TH: What about it?

D: I guess I don't really have to see the books, as long as he lets me know the balance.

TH: How does that sit with you, Brad?

B: Fine. I don't discuss the office, and she doesn't ask, except to bring home the bank balance each Friday.

TH: Is that what you understood, Doris?

D: Yes.

TH: Seal that. *(The couple tentatively embrace)*

In this illustration, I remind the group of the guidelines of group feedback: refraining from making value judgments, checking out per-ceptions, and responding to impact.

AUTONOMY

The following negotiation establishes Fred's work hours as his area of *autonomy*.

FRED: I have to dialogue on this. It involves the feeling I have that I don't get credit from Betty for *working*—day-to-day, eight-to-five work. Instead, I experience a lot of pressure from Betty about not getting home earlier. I feel I really work hard at spending as much time as possible with her. I leave for the office at the last minute. I have lunch with her every day. But what I get continually, I feel, is *blame*—the message that my law practice isn't really work for me. I get pressured by this. Sometimes I have stuff to do after work; all of us in the office are over-worked. But I actually get to feeling anxious if I stay to do it. When I go home even twenty minutes late, Betty is upset. I feel the job's a necessity, and the time I spend there is not unreasonable.

THERAPIST: Fine. Then the question is: how could you use the time you have more efficiently to decrease the pressure?

F: I can do that, but I need Betty to remove *her* pressure.

TH: All of you need to learn to assess—first alone and then together—what issues are non-negotiable between you. *(To Fred)* Determine clearly that time at your work is non-negotiable, if that is so—that removes it as an area of competition. Then budget your own time for your own greatest comfort. What I'm suggesting is a statement of this as an area of autonomy: "I take responsibility for determining my workload. Trust me that this is legitimate."

BETTY: That's the problem. I can't trust him. He's always getting involved in something!

TH: Just a moment. *(To Fred)* Were you referring to any other specific situation than the need for an occasional twenty-minute delay when you want to catch up on some paperwork after office hours?

F: No.

TH *(to Betty):* He's talking right now about a twenty-minute delay. You seem to be talking about much more than that.

B: There are some strong feelings underlying this. I know it's irrational, but I feel he's running away from me. First he's going into a specialty training. Then he gets "gung ho" and wants to take psychodrama. Who knows what would happen if I just really let go—for a week or a month. Maybe he wouldn't keep running away from me.

Th: Betty, I hear you say that the nature of his job is such that he could be away 24 hours a day. But the reality is that he's usually home in the evenings. Right? *(She nods)* It's not the issue then that's causing you such pain, but what you forsee in the future. You're building a nightmare for yourself.

B: I'm constantly panicked he'll pile up one thing after another. If I don't keep pounding, I'm afraid it'll get out of hand.

Th: Yet we always talk in terms of *limitations* and freedoms, Betty. It's never an either/or.

F: I want to say something here. When I first started in practice, I admit that I did over-extend myself. But the only extra-professional thing I'm involved in now is the specialty training. That takes up one week-night. *(To Betty)* And I thought we'd agreed that after June nothing will be done without including you and with your permission.

B: I really don't believe you—but if we put it into the legitimate fight style, I know you'll honor it.

Th: All right, then. Do it!

B: Will you engage me in a beef right now?

F: I want to very much.

B: I want you to commit yourself to keeping your extra-professional activities limited to one night a week—whether I'm involved or not.

F: I hear you asking me to limit my outside professional activities to one night a week—whether you're involved or not.

B: Thank you for listening. Will you do it?

F: I'm willing to try it until June, and to re-negotiate it weekly if you wish.

B: You'll try it until June with a weekly re-commitment if I wish. *(He accepts her feedback as accurate and the commitment is sealed with enthusiasm.)*

A recurrent theme between couples is: my job comes first which the mate reads ". . . at my expense." The man's orientation is "If my job doesn't come first, the family is in economic trouble." In our society the man usually carries the economic load, although this is rapidly changing. His image of masculinity and stability is often wedded to his job. The blunt truth is: the job (in many cases) must come first. That doesn't mean the mate is second in importance. When a woman competes with her man's job, she creates a very unhappy kind of competition—a testing of incompatible areas of power.

In reality, the exercise of a bill of rights and areas of autonomy is practice in the art of Self-Care. It is also a process of deepening awareness of self in a relationship.

Chapter 7

"AS-IF" TRUST

DOING AND RISKING

The only way I know to build trust is *to act as if you are trusting*. That means taking the risk of disappointment, betrayal, disillusionment, and pain. It may be the means of making a relationship meaningful and lasting, or it may be the means of breaking the relationship. There is a potential possibility of intimacy or alienation. To trust means to be willing to gamble that the other is trustworthy. But to my way of thinking, "as-if" trust is well worth the risk. In reality, I see nothing to lose, because you either make possible something worthwhile between you or find that nothing worthwhile was possible. Trusting does not guarantee trustworthinesss.

The kinds of negotiations involved in "as-if" trust depend on the specific areas of distrustfulness involved. Before we can successfully act as if we trust another, we often need to work on our trust in ourselves. Many of my initial exercises in *as-if trust* are exercises in *Self-Care;* people need to learn to take responsibility for their own personal well-being before they can begin to practice trusting their partners. Building a solid emotional base of your own worth by taking responsibility for Self-Care eliminates the possibility of falling apart in case trust of another is misplaced. Your own structure stands secure in spite of hurt.

Validating intimate reality is possible only in a climate of trust, born of the self and of the other. Otherwise you may find yourself shadowboxing—fighting unrealistic fears instead of negotiating realistic conflicts. An "as-if" exercise in trusting is a process by which a human being experiences extending himself beyond the limits of his ego-centered concern for self-protection. It is an exercise in greater self-awareness as well as often being an "out front" (by consent) reality test

113

of the partner's reliability. When you practice Self-Care and "as-if" trust, you practice doing what you feel you "don't want to do" because you recognize that this is something you *need* to do in order to attain a relationship you want. As a result you create greater personal power and greater self-control. You become responsible for your own choice of direction, for trusting—not blindly, but thoughtfully and willfully.

BUILDING TRUST

The following engagement considers "as-if" behavior as a possible road to building trust. Here, a couple in conflict disclose a key issue.

POLLY: I don't trust you. I'm always afraid my words will be twisted.

LES: Nothing I say is *enough!* Can you understand how I feel threatened when you say that?

THERAPIST *(to Polly):* When you become aware of the impact of your distrust, you will see the importance of *as-if* behavior. Once you have decided that your relationship with Les is worth maintaining and improving, then you are faced with a commitment to taking risks. To take the risk of trusting, you undertake to act *as if* you trust in spite of how you feel. This may very well be the productive road to building trust.

P: I know that, but in the past my words have been changed when the time came to honor a commitment. I'm afraid that when the time comes again, he'll renege. I really think I'd feel better if we signed a formal pact!

TH: Les, what do you think of that idea?

L: I'll sign anything she puts in front of me if it'll help—but I feel *shitty* about it! *(To Polly)* I'm sick of having to prove things! It's not my goddamned impact on you; it's your goddamned insecurity!

TH: I sense that what you are reacting to is not Polly's words but your interpretation of their meaning—taking this as another test you have to meet—instead of seeing the proposal as a means of implementing agreed-upon behavior. Does this make sense to you? *(Les agrees)* It may be productive to write down the agreements. It's too easy for them to get distorted otherwise. How about the following format:

1. You each write out the negotiation as you understood it at the conclusion of the fight for change.
2. You compare the statements as a mutual check on the negotiation made, and change the wording until it's acceptable to both of you. *(To Les)* Does that violate your guts?

L: I'm willing, but I have a counter-suggestion: I'll get two little notebooks. When we make an agreement, the one who gets the commitment will write it down and the other will initial it.

TH *(to Polly):* Is that agreeable? *(She nods)* What have you negotiated?

P: That Les will get us each a notebook, and when we have a fight for change the one with the commitment writes it down and the other one initials it.

TH: Seal that.

P: I don't feel very 'sealy'.

L: Does that mean, "I don't trust you?"

P: What I meant is that I feel raw inside—I don't feel very affectionate.

L: Here I give her exactly what she wants, and I'm not getting what I want in return!

TH: Ask for what you want.

L: Would it be fair for me in the future to only agree to something if she'll trust what I say?

TH: The suggestion you made about the notebooks is the first step in building that kind of trust. What happened just now is a misinterpretation of the meaning of Polly's statement "I don't feel sealy." You heard this as a lack of trust—as a lack of appreciation of your work to improve this relationship. As I see it, Polly was only making a statement of emotional content that needs much new input to change, both on her part and on yours.

P: What can I do to help me feel more loving? We've had an unresolved fight before coming here and old grievances are alive in me—I feel enraged!

TH: At the moment you can ask for an opportunity to have a Vesuvius to relieve the anger, if he'll permit it. Ask him.

L: I'll allow you a minute.

P *(she stands and meditates briefly):* I hate your guts! *I can't stand you!* Here we've been fighting just before coming here for an hour— over what? Over our two extra lousy basketball tickets that you gave your tennis partner and his wife. You know they've insulted me and I don't want to go to basketball games with them. You're worried about hurting your tennis partner's feelings, and I've been hurting for the past four years with their insults! I don't believe you really care. He admits his wife was insulting to me and you disregard it. I'd say, "Your wife can't treat my wife that way— get lost!" and I wouldn't give him our complimentary tickets for sure!

TH: How do you feel?

P: Terrible. I could go on and on, but I don't think it'll help.

TH: One thing that might help is if you consider that your tests of love are unrealistic. Your expectations of proof of love need careful examination. Also, when the use of a ritual does not result in some de-escalation of rage and hurt, then we discard the use of the ritual. At this point, verbalizing your rage over the tickets seems to have the impact of reinforcing the hurt; therefore, I suggest that for one week discussion of this past hurt be outlawed. Do each agree to this? *(Both agree)* Each of you would have a better time with each other if you'd start dealing with each other's limitations.

P: I don't ask for much, I really don't. I've held back from asking for what I wanted since childhood.

TH: Do I also hear, "So when I do ask, you'd better give it to me?"

P: No!

TH: Fine. Then let's stop—right now—with your agreement. I want to hear the group's reactions.

GROUP MEMBER

KATE: Is that what I do to Bud when I make those demands that he love me the way I want him to?

TH: Ask Bud.

BUD: When you insist it must be your way or no way I feel trapped and I get just as resentful as Les does!

TH: This is a good example of how others mirror our own behavior and can teach us the affect we have. When you find a dialogue is beginning to escalate in intensity and that you're both losing perspective on the issue, stop! Call a moratorium on the discussion. Later, find out how you got on the merry-go-round of accusations, and then determine how you can get off the next time it happens. Some guidelines:
1. Decide what cues you both will initiate to help you stop the old process of escalation.
2. Negotiate the agreed-upon cues in a fight for change.
3. Both feedback the negotiation as a formal pact before trying it for a time-limited period.
4. Set a date when you'll review the effectiveness of the cues as reminders to "stop!"

NOTE: In a private session with Polly we dealt with the content of her emotional world, value system, and expectations. The Fight Training System is limited to the use of its own tools to effect change. Supplemental private therapy sessions deal with in-depth treatment of emotional content and meaning.

CHECKING OUT EXPECTATIONS

The following shows a progression from "I don't believe you" to checking out expectations to reality possibilities.

MITCH: Thursday night we decided that we were tired and were going to stay home for the evening. Someone called and invited us to join them at the movies. Betty and I picked up extension phones simultaneously and, in the course of the conversation, I heard her say to me, "Well, what do you think, Honey, should we go to the movie?" In other words, she put me in a position—I felt that she put me in a position—of making the decision when she already knew where I was that particular evening.

THERAPIST: This was an assumption. Check it out.

MITCH: I assumed you knew where I was at. True or false?

BETTY: False.

M: Okay. *(Laughs)* I don't believe that it was false.

TH: Hold it—this is very important. Betty said "false." What you just did was, in reality, a big crazy-maker. "I don't believe you" denies her trustworthiness.

M: Okay.

TH: In order to build trust, you take the risk of accepting the answer given as the answer that is correct. When Betty says your assumption is false, that comes to you like a bomb—"How could you not see what was so apparent to me?" We can't read each other's emotional climate, no matter how apparent it may seem. She said "false." And I am saying when your assumption is checked out like that, you buy it—no matter what you feel.

M: I agree. I'm sorry, but that's not the real issue. I had stated earlier in the evening what my situation was and, I'm sure, one of Betty's gripes is that I'm not very flexible as far as certain situations are concerned.

B: How very true!

M: The point I'm trying to make is that it really didn't have anything to do with whether or not her assumption was correct. I resented the fact that I had another person on the telephone at the time and that she was putting me into the position of saying yes or no. I resented that. I thought she should have said to the individual, "I'll talk about it with him and we'll call you back." I don't like it when she puts me into the position of making the decision on the spot without talking to me about it.

TH: Mitch, let's you and I confer. Did you want to go or didn't you want to go?

M: No, I didn't want to go.

TH: So you knew exactly what position you were in—"I didn't want to go." What's wrong in saying, "The answer is no. I don't want to go?"

M: I did say it. That's what bothers me.

TH: What's so bothersome about being in the position of saying no?

M: It's one of my problems. I have a lot of trouble with that!

TH: As I see it, the power to say no and mean it frees you to *be,* to take care of yourself. You don't give your mate the job of mind reading you—"You ought to know what I feel about this, so therefore, make the right decision. And if you don't make the right decision, you're not considering me, you're not sensitive to me." This is passing the buck. Does this fit?

M: It fits. But I feel she knows me well enough not to put me on the spot.

TH: Right at that sentence—that's where we all get into trouble. He or she knows me well enough to understand this and act upon it. That's an illusion—a fantasy. You will *never* know each other that well. I have yet to meet people who know each other that well. We may occasionally win (*Oh, you think this? Yes, I do. Or I anticipated this and it happened*) but that is a rarity. You cannot bank on it. So your job is to say your noes. And Betty's job is to be herself. And be as sensitive to each other as you can be. But you'll never be as you *ought to be.* When you say what you perceive, you are giving information, and you're clearing the way to check it out. Add one sentence: "This is what I perceive; is it accurate?" And accept the answer as being the other person's truth, not yours. And go from there.

M: I have no justification for my resentment?

TH: None whatsoever, when the justification is based on an impossible expectation.

B: How about my justification for being upset with him for two days because of his resentment towards me?

TH: That's retaliation and you're each being unrealistic. You see, again you're faced with alternatives, like: "I don't accept the blame for your resentment. You're putting something on me that doesn't belong there." There are other ways of dealing with resentment than sulking for two days.

B: I think I did say that but I just never felt finished about it.

TH: If I'm tuned into your guts right now, this might be a possible alternative: "And I'd like to have a Vesuvius or give you a haircut on it. Will you permit me?"

B: I did it, but I didn't ask for permission.

TH: That phrase, "May I?" or "Will you permit it?" is a bridge to the other person. It's an acknowledgment of mutual rights, permission to be different, to see things differently and keep the relationship. So I give you a haircut because I am angry with you.

B: If permission isn't given, then you have the right to use your own rage-release?

TH: Exactly.

B: But I can release it and yet it's not going to change him and it's still going to bug me.

TH: Has this encounter changed or added anything? Does hearing Mitch acknowledge his unrealistic expectations of your mind-reading abilities help at all?

B (to Mitch): Somehow I don't really believe that you heard it, that you were being honest when you said you see those things in yourself.

TH: All right. Mitch, were you being honest when you said, "Yeah, I see this in me. It's a fault I have to deal with?"

M: Yes, I was being honest.

TH: Tell her directly.

M: I was being honest.

TH: Will you take the risk of believing him?

B: Okay.

TH: What we have is *possibly* a start in a new perception of a relationship and a possibly changed behavior in dealing with it. A first step to change has been taken.

LEFTOVERS FROM THE PAST

The following illustrates how the experiences of the past can spoil the taste of related experiences to come.

It highlights insights into other selves (group members) as they personally recognize and relate common behavior patterns.

RALPH: There's still something hazy about the question of entertaining friends. The thing is that before, either you have told me we would go ahead and entertain so and so—

THERAPIST: Okay, this is just background information to which we listen. This is a monologue. Go on.

R: —And then it goes on and on and on, until I push you to be specific about the invitation that hasn't been issued all this time. I haven't said this before about the Smiths, but there have been other people. I ask, could we have them over a week from now or two weeks from now, or whatever. Then there is some tension and nothing happens. So last night when you said, or you agreed, "Okay, no problem, I'll invite them over," I really had a problem and it isn't all your fault. I really don't believe you'll do it because of a comment that you made about Mrs. Smith that indicated to me that you don't care to get together with them. I suppose it's that one comment that you made that makes me skeptical. So could I check that out first?

TH: Sure. Am I drawing the right conclusion that this comment means that you won't carry out your commitment? That's the question? *(Ralph nods)* Ask her directly.

R: Are you going to invite the Smiths even though you don't care to get together with them?

EDNA: In my initial relationship with her, I didn't feel that we could be friends. However, I would like to please you and my wish to please you and entertain is more important than my not wanting to become close with Mrs. Smith; so when it came across straight that this is what you wanted, I made that choice.

TH *(to Ralph):* What did you hear?

R: I heard your willingness to please me and entertain who I want is more important than how you feel toward Mrs. Smith. I guess then, where I'm at is—

TH: Do you believe her?

R: I don't believe her. She says that now, in this setting, and maybe she will go through with it, but I have hurts from past experiences when she's said, "Let me know who you want to entertain and we'll work it out." I've let her know who I want and once in a while it's been worked out, but if it isn't her friend or if she doesn't feel positive about the situation, she's unwilling to take the risk.

TH: What did she just tell you?

R: She told me that her willingness to please me is greater than her risk of being uncomfortable.

TH: And she has committed within the next month to issue an invitation and carry though this social engagement, did you not, Edna? *(Edna agrees)* The original commitment stands. Now, what I hear you say is that the content of my museum is spoiling the taste of what has just happened. And I am saying bury your museum and live in the present. Do you believe what she said?

R: I believe she'll entertain the Smiths within the next month.

TH: Okay, on what basis?

R: Only because it's in front of this whole damn group and she knows damn well she better follow through this time. I guess that's partly my hang-up. I have trouble believing her because I'm so damn mad about the number of times we've negotiated and then she's wiggled out of it.

KEITH: I heard you and Edna say I will entertain Mrs. Smith, I am not committing myself to become a friend of hers.

E: But I am not going to enjoy it as much as I would enjoy entertaining someone else, and I expect him to tolerate my not enjoying it as much as I might.

K: I hear Ralph saying not only should you entertain her but you should enjoy it and you should be friendly and become friends.

TH: Check it out with Ralph.

R: That's incorrect.

K: So you don't want her to be friends.

R: I don't *expect* her to be friends. I wish she would entertain the Smiths.

FRED: I put myself in your place, and when I say what you're saying now, I find that when it really comes down to it, I really don't want to entertain the Smiths. I just want my wife to do something that she doesn't want to do to please me. And really when it comes down to the date, I'll feel awfully damned uneasy about having people here when I know they don't get along at all with my wife. And I'm mixed up in my own mind as to what I really want.

R: You're very perceptive. Because as I was sitting here—

F: Yeah, because if I can sabotage it enough, she'll back out and I can blame it on her.

R: As I was sitting here I was wondering, "Do I really want that?" I really like him, we've had some good sharing times and maybe there's something that will happen in our social life and we'll get along even better. But I know that I have sabotaged Edna in the past. And there's something there which I'm not able to clarify in the battle of wills.

BILL: Sounds like you want to control Edna, and even if there are things you don't really want that badly, you're still going to win.

E: We entertain a lot of people, but there are specific ones I care less about, and I feel you've used this to punish me, to have something to hold against me.

TH: I'd like to interrupt this. This kind of nasty game can go on only if both play. Anyone can stop it. And the way to stop it is to take the surface message: "I want you to entertain my friends, you always only entertain your own, and you don't listen to me." To take him up on it and say, "Look, I don't like this female very well, but you're important to me so I will be a gracious hostess. I will issue the invitation, I will engage in the social activity and I will carry it through," answers the request. After the "happening" you may finally come up with "What the hell did I bring them over here for?"

R: That's a very good point. I'll catch me. . .in my dirty game.

TH: Exactly.

A new dimension of "as if" trust has emerged. This may well be a possible road to uncover another layer of relationship meaning. When the carrying out of a commitment makes one aware that the stated issue was not the "real" problem one is more directly led to facing underlying realities, in this case exposing our "dirty games."

Chapter 8

Identity: As an Individual and in a Relationship

WHO AND WHAT AM I? AND WHO SAYS

A frequently frustrating impasse arises when one intimate says to another, "You don't mean that," or "You don't feel that," or "You really *can* do that." The one making the judgment assumes omnipotence—a God-like power of knowing exactly what is. The one receiving the judgment is either put in a quandary of self-doubt or in a position of having to fight for identity and understanding of self by the other.

In the statement, "That's not like you," we have a denial of the self by another.

In the statement, "I'm not myself today," we have a denial of oneself by oneself—a negation of the assessed undesirable behavior as being a part of a total wholeness of a person.

A way out of such an impasse, as I see it, is:

First, to *recognize* that one's identity is being denied (by self or other);

Second, to *refuse* such denial by confrontation and self assertion;

Third, to *deal with* the reality as it affects the self and the relationship. This may be a job of just a statement of BEING, a negotiati   c differences, a setting of limitations, or a reassessment of self by ' porating strengths and weaknesses as part of the wholeness of a

A DEEPENING AWARENESS

The following illustrates a process of development from one concern to another - a process of deepening awareness of self in a relationship and attaining clarity through direct and specific communication.

124   *Self-Care*

JOAN: I want to extend Dan's homework assignment. I want to teach him how to approach me. I want *more* likes and dislikes from him.

THERAPIST: Check out whether he was withholding reactions.

J *(to Dan):* Was there anything I did or didn't do that you didn't say?

DAN: No, I don't think so.

J: *(to Yetta):* I want more reactions anyway. Now what do I do?

TH: How about asking for a specific time for some response for a week and see how it works?

J: Okay. Dan, will you accept a revised assignment? I want you to look at me every day long enough until you find something to say *about me.*

D: I'm willing to do that.

TH: As I see it, Joan wants to know, "What's my impact on you? Give me some feedback about my being."

D: I accept the assignment, but I also want to deal with Joan's museum this week. We were involved with mine last time.

TH: Fine. Joan choose an item you want to deal with.

J: Your mother is rude and critical of me, and you've never supported me or defended me.

D: I assume you want me to be more helpful in this area. Is that it?

J: Yes.

TH: You're giving him an impossible job. When his mother is talking, only you know what *you're feeling.*

J: Are you saying I have to fight my own battles with her? She overpowers me.

TH: Then how about asking for support right then and there in front of her. I'm not speaking to the question of feeling now, but to the question of action.

J *(to Dan):* Would you mind if I did that?

D: I'd be more than willing to help if you'll let me know when you want me to.

TH: Good! Seal that. *(The pair exchange a kiss)*

J: I want to establish a beltline. It's funny. I want feedback about how I come across, and I want help when I think your mother's attacking me, but I *don't* want you to tell me: *"You can do it"* when I've determined *I can't!* I feel I know what I can and can't do now, and I'm convinced that math and sewing are not my things! I want you to believe me when I tell you what I can and can't do.

TH: I hear this as a fight for identity. The beltline message is: "Don't tread on this sensitive area of my identity by telling me I can do something when I know differently.''

J: Exactly. Dan, will you respect my beltline?

D: I won't try to tell you that you can do math or sewing, but I need to hear loud and clear if there are any other areas included in this.

J: Then how about agreeing to believe me when I tell you whatever I can or can't do? No further discussion necessary. Just take my word for it.

D: I hear you wanting me to trust your evaluation of your own abilities, and I can respect that.

TH: Wonderful. Seal it! *(The pair hug)* This negotiation moved from a simple beltline to a beef for change without difficulty. This is a good illustration of what I mean by ingesting a process. When the rules of a system interfere with a good interaction, you forget the rules. When there is a mutual feeling of trust and mutual agreement, you can proceed without worrying about exact formats.

The course that you're taking is a many-faceted trip in interpersonal relating. When we talk about fighting, we're talking about clearly communicating in a productive way about such factors as identity and roles, about issues of conflict, about all the many parameters of intimacy. The purpose of the relationship then becomes that of self and other-nurturing. When you accept an assignment, that means you recognize that as a growth pattern you want to try. That *you* want to try. I take no responsibility for your lives. I have enough to do with my own.

SELF-IDENTIFICATION

A clarification of differences in *self-identification* is clearly set forth in the dialogue between Martha & Jeff. This is followed by a negotiation—the *right* to do things differently.

MARTHA: I have a beef. Jeff doesn't take care of himself, especially when he drives.

THERAPIST: Explain what Self-Care means to you when he's driving. Give Jeff the basic information upon which you base your judgment.

M: It upsets me when he sits there and lets others go ahead of him, even when it's not their turn. I suppose I want him to take the right of way when it is his.

TH: I hear you interpreting *his way* as lack of Self-Care. Check it out.

M *(to Jeff):* I see your neglecting to take the right of way as lack of Self-Care. How does it seem to you?

JEFF: When we're in the automobile, I drive calmly and carefully. *It doesn't bother me* if someone gets ahead of me in traffic or at a stop sign. I'd rather be safe than sorry.

TH: What I hear you say is, "As far as the automobile driving goes, I'm using my judgment. Back off!"

J: Yes, I go when I'm ready to go.

TH *(to Martha):* What are you hearing?

M: He doesn't care!

TH: That's not what he said. He's saying that he doesn't see himself as being put down, but as a careful driver without ego involvement. *You're* saying, "You're wrong. My perception is the right one."

M: I can't help it. He does let people in front of him all the time.

TH: Hold it. The *fact* is not at issue. Your *interpretation* of the fact as being a put-down is the issue. If you want to take the idea of behavior modification seriously, you'll have to give up that notion that you "can't help it." You *can* help it. You can drive, or you can watch him drive and program yourself not to interfere, or you can entertain the truth of what you're being told—that letting cars get ahead is not an insult—BUT *YOU* CAN'T CHANGE HIM.

M: Okay, I can accept that, but can't I comment?

TH: The information Jeff's giving you is, "This is *my* territory." That means if you want to comment, you're going to have to negotiate your way to do it.

M: But how do I stop bugging him when he's driving?

TH: What key word will you accept to clue you that you're doing it?

M: I'd stop if he'd just tell me to shut up.

TH: Are you telling him, "I give you permission to use the key words, 'Shut up,' and I will honor that message?"

M: I'll try it for a week anyway.

J: If you can accept my telling you to shut up when you and I are in the car and I'm driving, I'd be delighted!

M: Only when it has to do with my commenting on how you drive.

J: The only time you bug me is when you start on that.

TH: All right. What have you agreed to try for a week?

M: That when I start to criticize Jeff's driving, he'll tell me to shut up and I'll stop.

Tʜ *(to Jeff):* Is that your understanding of it?

J: Yes, I'm to use the cue to stop her only when she's talking about my driving.

Tʜ: Fine. Seal that. *(They embrace)*

M: This business of letting others go ahead of him extends into other areas, too. Can I dialogue with you about it?

J: Sure.

M: When we go to the market, I see you being taken advantage of. People push ahead of you at counters and at the check stand. True or false?

J: It's true that people get ahead of me, but false that they're taking advantage of me. Normally, when I go to the store, I like to dilly-dally. I enjoy looking around. If *you're* in a hurry, I want you to tell me that you're in a hurry. Otherwise I don't want to hear about how slow I am or what I'm doing.

Tʜ: Can you feed that back?

M: You said that if we're in a market and you're dilly-dallying around— and if I want you to hurry, I should tell you.

J: That's not it. I said, "If *you're* in a hurry, I want you to admit it first."

M *(to Yetta):* That's so funny. When I'm in the market. I can't wait to get out! Today I went to the store alone, and it was such a relief. I went right to the section and got what I wanted and was out of there in ten minutes.

Tʜ: Maybe that's the more realistic solution. But you do have another option now. You can tell him when *you're* in a hurry and he'll speed up.

M *(to Jeff):* I hear you offering to hurry if I'll accept responsibility for wanting to hurry as my thing. Is that it?

J: You tell me you want to hurry, and I'll cooperate. But no side remarks about me!

M: Agreed.

Differences in perception of *what is* are clearly demonstrated in this confrontation. How *I* see things must be checked out against how *you* see the same thing. This is always a subjective reaction and very person-specific depending upon one's own value system and ego strength.

A VESUVIUS HELPS

The following deals with a process of communicating the meaning of actions which appear sabotaging to one partner and to the other partner as realistically necessary and productive. It demonstrates the use of a Vesuvius to clear the way to negotiation and clarification. It establishes responsibility for Self-Care and decision-making. It establishes separateness—the right "to do it my way, not your way." It opens doors to consideration of alternatives.

STAN: We've had bad vibes between us for the last two weeks. Part of it is Mazy's physical incapacitation. I feel I can't approach her on some of the things that are bothering me, and I'm concerned that she's not taking proper care of herself.

THERAPIST: What do you mean?

S: Well, it's what I call "not practicing Mazy conservation."

TH: Do you want a beef for change on this?

S: Yes. Mazy, may I engage you in a fight about your Self-Care?

MAZY: I'm not sure. I'm doing what the doctor said I could do. I've rested every day. I haven't done housework or outside work. He told me to get up every day and walk—to do the exercises.

S: May I state what I understand to be what the doctor told you?

M: Yes.

S: I understood that he said he'd give your back another week—that you're supposed to be in bed this week. Then he'd decide on the spinal fusion.

M: He said he'd give it another week, but he didn't tell me to stay in bed. He said to stay down as much as I could. I can't be an invalid! I have to keep walking.

TH *(to Mazy, observing facial and body movements):* I see pressure building. Take advantage of the tools you have to deal with this frustration.

M *(to Therapist):* But I don't think it's fair to unload all this on him.

TH: It's not a question of fair; it's a question of need. Do you need to let off steam?

M: I guess I do!

TH: Then ask him to hear you.

M: Stan, will you listen to my Vesuvius?

S: I will as long as we get back later to my issue. You can have as long as you need.

M (loud and clearly): I'll go nuts if I stay in bed all the time! I need to get up once in a while just to stay limber! Besides you haven't been much help. For the last month I might as well have been in the house by myself. You were really "down" and you hardly spoke. I know things are difficult at your work, and that you're under a lot of pressure. But even when I asked you to discuss it with me, you wouldn't. You constantly tell me I mother you, and that I tell you how to do things. But you're the one who accuses me of not doing what I'm supposed to! You make me sound like an ogress or something, and I'm not! There are things I don't like, and I probably never will. But when I mention something like that, you keep saying I'm being negative. I'm stuck home alone all day, and when you come home you won't talk to me and you don't want to hear what I have to say!

TH: Have you asked for what *you* wanted? That he get off his depressed kick and talk to you?

M: I assumed that he knows what he's doing.

TH: And you didn't want to make a demand on him?

M: I know. I have a hard time with that.

TH: You both do. How about trying now?

M: I think the main thing right now is this back business.

TH: See if he'll engage you.

S: Since that was my original issue, I'd be happy to.

M: I want you to trust me with this back business. I'm not ready to jump into surgery. I can't see at my age going through that when there's no guarantee it'll work anyway. Trust me to do what's right for me—and not to overdo at home.

S: I hear you asking me to let you decide what's best in the care of your back and not to push the operation.

M: That's exactly it.

S: I know you have a nervous disposition and hate to lie still, but I can't help feeling you're not giving yourself a break. I find it difficult to let you follow your own intuition when I see that as going against the doctor's advice.

TH: If I hear Mazy, she's saying, "I'm following the doctor's advice, and I must keep moving somewhat. I demand the right to determine what is or isn't appropriate behavior in this."

M: Yes! *That's the point.* It's *my* back after all!

S: I can accept this for one week, but I want to discuss it again after you see the doctor.

M: I'll discuss it, and you can even monologue about it if you need to, but I like Yetta's suggestion that this issue is part of my bill of rights and should be respected as such!

The above illustrates much acid content underlying the stated problem. It also discloses an awareness of a bill of rights emerging from the process of communicating and negotiating differences in perceptions and meaning of behavior.

I AND US

Consideration of how we were, where we are, and where we are going forms an assessment of the relationship. Perceptions of what is may be fantasy or reality.

A confrontation is necessary to determine whether or not my assessment of myself and the other in the relationship is congruent with my partner's view. Is one blissfully unaware of the other's frustrations and restrictions and does awareness of these come as an unpleasant surprise? Are my perceptions your perceptions?

In the presentation of the past, present, and future assessment of the state of their union, George and Alice agree that changes have taken place, old roles no longer fit, new conflicts now are being faced and there is a mutual acknowledgement that the union is worth working for.

PAST

ALICE

I had dedicated myself to two roles: as a wife I must serve, defend and protect my husband; as a mother I must serve my children and sacrifice myself to them. In the struggle to serve others, I lost a sense of my own identity and made myself totally dependent on my husband. Gradually I was aware of the result and found myself with a reservoir of unresolved anger—masking hurt at the loss of my separate identity. I built up manipulative behavior to compensate.

GEORGE

In our marriage, I was the breadwinner and Alice took care of the home. Even though I took considerable interest in and gave much time to the children, their care was her responsibility. The basic theme of our relationship: what was good for me and my career was good for Alice. Her success was dependent upon my success.

Therapist's Comments: Her rigid role-assignment built a cage around her. When the bars of the cage became too restricting, she began the process of pulling them asunder. His role was comfortable. It had no bars to confine him and no opposition to confront.

PRESENT

ALICE

Now I am more self-assertive in meeting my own needs and less willing to be totally dependent. I am still not sure of the parameters of my freedom and there is still that unresolved reservoir of anger at letting myself disappear. I am less willing to cover for what I believe is his responsibility and I am more open about my feelings, defying his decisions when they differ from mine. I'm still manipulative and covertly hostile. Our commitment to the relationship, not to divorce, frees me to take risks.

GEORGE

The children are grown and away from home. Professionally, we are co-therapists. Our success is dependent upon the success of both of us as a team and each of us as individuals. The basic theme of our relationship: we are equals as seen from the man's perspective—it is the man who knows, says I. Oh, no, says Alice, I know, too! We are going through the throes of the independence/dependence discovery but with love.

Therapist's Comment: Alice is clearly aware of the work she has to do with herself and the series of shocks the relationship will have to sustain as she becomes more and more self-assertive and self-caring. He recognizes the threat to his supremacy as well as the delight and mutual growth of a partnership.

FUTURE

ALICE

I foresee our relationship as stable and permanent, incorporating growth and autonomy for each of us. I look forward to an exciting and more fulfilling relationship.

GEORGE

We shall continue to be co-workers. We shall continue to love each other, and we shall have clarified our independence/dependence struggle. I will have become more open to Alice's autonomy and also more assertive of my own. Alice will have become more comfortable with her newly asserted freedom. The boundary contacts between us as a couple—professionally and personally—will be more impactful.

Therapist's Comments: Each foresees the future together. Each recognizes continuing struggles for independece, interdependence, and dependence as growth processes leading to enrichment—individually and in the relationship.

STATE OF THE UNION MESSAGES/PERCEPTIONS

BEFORE, DURING, AND AFTER THERAPY

POLLY

Five years ago was the most crucial period of my 26-year marriage to Howard. He was 66; I was 63. The gap between us was dangerously widening—a new development in our formerly compatible relationship. I tried but failed to rekindle his former zest for mingling with others. I came on strong—his ring-master, flinging orders at him, needling him for reactions. He retreated into silent hostility, stoically maintaining our marriage was a "good one." I couldn't accept his new way of being: "Let me rest on my past laurels." I struggled to hold on to my still-alive enthusiasm; found it dwindling as his apathy persisted. His attention was focused on *me* and *my* interests; he showed little inclination to develop his own interests. I felt suffocated by the "emotional island" we were stranded on. I took one last step, the decision to go into therapy, hoping to avert what I'd been weighing—divorce. I imagined Howard's unhappiness was as acute as my own.

HOWARD

After 26 years of a beautiful relationship with my wife, Polly, *I* thought I had it made. Then came my awakening! Polly told me that she was unhappy with our relationship and suggested, or rather *insisted,* that we seek help. Reluctantly, I agreed.

Therapist's Comments: Obviously he and she were living in two totally different emotional worlds. She was close to the breaking point and he was comfortable and secure in his fantasy of the relationship.

DURING THERAPY

POLLY

Yetta Bernhard conducted our first experience with therapy of any kind—a 24-hour, non-stop, group therapy marathon. I was almost devastated by the cold probe for details of my personal problems by the other participants after I blurted out a self-conscious summary of my relationship with my husband. Throughout feedback of how the group saw us (which I interpreted as a series of mocking put-downs of us and our marriage) I clung to Yetta's eyes. She was aware of my terror and shock at hearing how Howard and I appeared to others. I was numbed into silence for about 22 of the 24 hours, unable to handle what seemed to me the facial and verbal violence. My lifetime control over tears left me. During later private sessions Howard and I had with our therapist, she woke me up to how I had contributed to the deterioration of our marriage; how I could change my behavior to regain a degree of our prior relationship and form a new one with Howard. Her last words are deeply implanted in my head. "*Your* marriage has no exit door—by mutual commitment—you both have a big investment in it. Enjoy your dividends!"

HOWARD

With a sinking sort of feeling in the pit of my stomach, I became a participant (with 14 or 15 others) in a 24-hour marathon confrontation led by Yetta Bernhard. I resented her deflating my ego. To me, it was a frightening, bitter, yet exciting and stimulating experience. I came away shattered and in doubt as to whether it bettered or worsened our relationship. After a few private sessions with Yetta (and a few group sessions with other couples) I left with a feeling that Polly and I had found a new basis on which to better our relationship.

Therapist's Comments: In this case, there was a mutual agreement that there would be *no divorce* (no "exit" to the marriage), that differences were to be negotiated, changed or lived-around—that there was a *mutual* commitment to the relationship and the realization that there would be storms with which to contend.

Each partner in this marriage risked exposure to the miniature world of the group and felt the pain of the shattering of their own self-images.

How they saw themselves was not how they came across to the outside world. A fantasy of self-concept and relationship was exposed to the reality of objective (unemotionally-involved) feedback.

Through the pain of letting go of a fantasy, new realities emerged. Ways to do differently were explored and tentatively tasted. Each acknowledged responsibility for the impasse they experienced and drew upon their own courage and intelligence to grow out of the impasse.

AFTER THERAPY

POLLY

My scars of self-discovery have healed. They only ache a little when I slip back into a *temporary* ring-master role. Yetta introduced me into the realities of my husband's world—and I saw a new man. Howard and I are on a perpetual treasure hunt—I've discovered all kinds of new "goodies" in him, including *sex*. When Yetta asked if Howard and I would care to add comments about our therapy experience for inclusion in her book, I unhesitatingly said, "Yes, *I'd* love to; however, I'll have to check with the 'Master' as to *his* decision!"

HOWARD

Five years after my EXPERIENCE, I'm still asking myself if it really helped us to a better understanding of each other's needs. There are times during which I'm *very* doubtful if it did. Most of the time, though, I *know* it has helped, and I'm very grateful to Yetta for guiding me to a "door that has no exit."

Therapist's Comments: The differing personalities of Polly and Howard are readily apparent in their presentations. It is conceivable that this couple has found a new balance in their relationship. Her high-flying and delightful enthusiasm and zest for living are beautifully harnessed by his earthbound, but not confining foothold.

Chapter 9

Children, Friends, and Other Relationships

A common scene today is the varied styles of family living—the after-effects of divorce, the part-time father or mother, problems of visitation rights and expectations. Each brings specific conflicts. When conflicts become specific problems to solve, we begin the process of more fruit-ful living.

Giving and accepting becomes more possible realistically when good will is built between intimate partners, as illustrated in the following encounter.

GIVING AND ACCEPTING

EDITH: Because of the fight training my entire life has changed. Our sex life is better. Everything is just great! We have a clearing house every day. Our whole marriage is on a sounder basis. And I've learned where I was responsible for my past failures. I wouldn't accept any of the blame before. This is my third marriage. I actually drove my husbands away. Archie made me come to this group. Now when I get mad I feel free to shout for an hour. I have marvelous conversations with myself about what I'm going to do to whom—and then it's all over. What I want to do tonight is give Archie a gift of love. I thought it would please him to invite his son to dinner. I have a reservation about that, though, because he used to visit us once in a while and I had nothing but problems. He doesn't live with us, and his table manners are digusting.

THERAPIST: Just a minute. *(To Archie)* I want to hear how you see it.

ARCHIE: He's pretty careless.

TH *(to Edith):* Paint me a verbal picture of what you mean.

E: He won't use a napkin. He lowers his head and slurps the food into his mouth. He eats with his elbows on the table—and he makes *noises* when he eats.

135

TH: I hear you saying that you feel you should invite him to dinner, but his table manners make you climb the wall.

E: That's true, but I'd be willing to invite him once a week for Archie's sake. I don't like his not feeling welcome in his father's home.

TH: All right, then. Make a commitment to change—a voluntary gift.

E *(to Archie)*.: Will you listen to a commitment on my part? I'd like to have Ralph over for dinner one night when you're home early.

A: You're telling me you are willing to have Ralph over for dinner sometime when I'm home early. *(Long pause)*

TH: You're hesitating to answer, Archie. What's the matter?

A: It's more important to me that I maintain a warm, loving feeling with my son than go the table manners route at this time.

TH: If that's where it's at, outlaw picking at his behavior. Tell Edith you like her commitment if she can refrain from criticizing Ralph.

A *(to Edith):* I'd like to try the dinner if you can accept the boy *in toto*—no criticism. *(Edith feeds back verbatim)*

TH *(to Edith):* Now you have several options: 1) accept his condition; 2) rescind your initial offer; or 3) try it for one week and then re-negotiate. *(They both agree to try the third option)* As you understand it, what's your commitment?

E: To invite Ralph to dinner wholeheartedly, and to accept his behavior during the entire time with no comments—no looks of disapproval, etc.

TH: How do you feel about that, Archie?

A: That sounds great! *(They seal their commitment)*

The commitment is clear. The acutal working at it will determine its reality. Edith has assigned to herself a strenuous task in working over and beyond the disgust she feels at her stepson's table manners. This is a job of disciplined behavior in order to honor another's goal (closer relationship between father and son).

The home can be an excellent learning laboratory for children in preparation for meeting the larger world outside. When a child learns that he can go so far with father and much farther with mother, that people are different, he is preparing to deal with person-specific realities. When parents "honor" each other's idiosyncratic behavior, they are modeling respect for differences and productive ways to cope with them.

A LEARNING LABORATORY

JEFF: I have a beef. Norma, will you engage me? *(She agrees)* When I am disciplining or handling a problem with Mary, I would like you to butt out.

NORMA: If you are disciplining Mary you do not want me to interfere. *(Jeff nods)* But we have two children—

TH: Wait. You deal only with his beef—you do not change or add to your partner's issue.

N: In that case, I agree that when you're disciplining Mary, I will not interfere.

TH: What we're trying to do is establish a process of listening. I'm trying to *separate* your own concept of the problem from your partner's message. *(To Norma)* You look troubled. Now, if you wish, you can give the background of what is disturbing you.

N: He's always telling me I was much too hard on Mary at an early age—smacking her hands and stuff like that. He said I was too strict. John *(the three-year-old)* gets into the living room. We have a white couch, and the living room is off-limits. Sometimes Jeff asks John to leave, and he doesn't. If I speak to him though, he knows I mean it and he leaves.

TH: Now you have a beef for change. Do you want permission to intervene in the situation of the living room when John doesn't listen to his father?

N: Yes. Jeff, will you engage me in a beef for change? *(Jeff agrees)* When John does something I feel is not right and you tell him to stop—and he doesn't—may I make him carry out your command?

J *(to therapist):* The problem is that I'm not tough enough with the kids for Norma, and I think she's too harsh.

TH: You have an alternative. You make John do what you want him to do—your way—and she won't have reason to butt in.

J: All right I can accept your demand in the specific case of the living room. When he's in the living room, if I don't get him out in a minute or so, you may interfere.

N *(feeds back Jeff's acceptance, then. . .):* When I'm dealing with John, I would like you to just stay clear.

J: I can agree to that, with conditions. I don't like the way you physically punish the children. When you spank them, I sometimes cringe, and in those instances I won't butt out.

N: I don't know what you're talking about.

TH *(to Jeff):* Let's dialogue. Has Norma ever physically harmed the children—raised welts, broken bones, been dangerous and cruel?

J: Oh, no!

TH: Then you are saying that her punishment is not physically harmful to the children but too forceful for you. Norma is not a child abuser?

J: Definitely not!

TH: In that case, I'm asking you now to take a risk. I'm suggesting you accept Norma's demand for one week. When you find your son being hit harder than you think he should be hit, just say: "This is what I mean." Period. Just give her the information, so she'll know what you're talking about.

J: For one week?

TH: For one week only, with the option to re-negotiate.

J: I can agree to that.

N: You say that like you really resent doing it.

TH: Just a moment! You got a basic agreement in a sensitive area. Now you want him to agree in a tone of voice that you approve of. I say that's a little too much to ask, realistically. In a commitment to work at a different way of handling a problem, we are going against a familiar pattern. That in itself may be an irritant. To add the extra burden of hiding such affect may be a possible sabotage to effective change. For this week, attend only to the words and behavior, not the tone and facial expressions. This makes possible the freedom to *be* resentful about a change of behavior that your intellect tells you is more productive and to your mutual advantage.

The following encounter illustrates the process of stumbling from one awareness to another and finally focusing on whom we include and exclude in our social relations.

One Awareness Can Lead to Another

THERAPIST: Maude, you look upset. What's going on?

MAUDE: We have no social life. It distresses me. We invite people I like, but he can't stand them. He's bored all evening!

TH: You expressed this as *your* need. Then you learn to take care of yourself. Do you want him to be a gracious host to guests you invite for your own enjoyment?

HARRY: Wait a minute. I am a gracious host! I doubt that our guests even suspect that I'm not delighted with them.

Tн *(to Maude):* Is that how you see it?

M: Oh yes, he really does behave graciously to our guests.

Tн: Then what's the problem?

M: I feel that he needs to have a social life that he enjoys, too.

Tн: Are you saying that you know better than he does what he needs and wants? Look, what I'm driving at isn't the thing itself, but what you're making of it. You're turning roses into poison ivy. You can get good and depressed if you keep telling yourself "This isn't right. It's not the way it's supposed to be. It's got to be meaningful to him the way it's meaningful to me." Why not re-translate his behavior into positive terms. He's a gracious host as a gift to you. Translate it as a gift—a stroke of love! When you talk about "my idea of building a life" or "the right kind of social life" you get too global. You need to deal with the specifics of what is.

M: But good friends have always been a part of my life. When I have good friends, he's touchy about them. He resents them.

Tн: That's an assumption. Check it out.

M: Do you resent my friends?

H: Some of them. *(To therapist)* May I give an example? Last weekend we were invited to visit a friend of hers. It was a miserable weekend. I don't like the woman anyway, and she was so sarcastic to Maude it made me sick! I don't like to see her shit on—that's not my idea of friendship.

Tн: Are you saying "You can have your friends, but don't involve me with some of them?" *(He nods)* See if Maude will respect that request.

H: Maude, I'll tell you the friends I don't want to be involved with, and I'd appreciate it if you'd maintain your friendship with them separately.

M: I'll agree to that. *(To therapist)* Can I dialogue with you again?

Tн: Seal your commitment first. *(They kiss)*

M: The trouble is that I'm always the one who initiates the social engagements, and I'm tired of it.

Tн: Do you want a beef for change on that issue?

M: Yes, I do. *(To Harry)* Will you engage me in a beef for change? *(Harry agrees)* I want you to initiate one social engagement this week with another couple of your choice.

H: I hear you saying that you want me to initiate a social engagement with another couple during the next week. *(Maude indicates the feedback is accurate)* I can't just call up somebody and invite them to do something out of the blue.

M: Why not?

TH: Give feedback first, then avoid that "why" again.

M: You said that you can't do that "out of the blue."

H: That's right.

TH: Harry, is that "can't" or "won't?"

H: I guess it's that I won't. It really bothers me to call someone like that.

TH: Then put it in those terms.

H: Okay. Maude, what I'm really saying is that I'm going to deny your demand for change. I don't want to do it.

TH: Are you also saying, "I'm really vulnerable when it comes to initiating social contacts. That's a very uncomfortable area for me?"

H: Yes, that's true.

TH *(to Maude):* Did you hear him?

M: Sure. He won't try it.

TH: Do you understand his feelings? *(Maude nods)* Now the question is: "Can you tolerate him *as he is* in this respect—because *at the moment* this is a non-negotiable issue?"

M: I suppose I'll have to.

TH: We're back to the original situation. The responsibility for a social life is solely on your shoulders because you're the one who wants it. But we've learned something in the process:

1. Often the initial complaint is just a start in a process of communication that uncovers a more immediately pertinent and significant issue. In this case we went from the issue of acceptable friends to the issue of initiating social engagements.

2. The exposure of *differences* and specific *resistances,* that is, "I don't need friends the way you do" and "I don't want to do it" (in reference to the request to initiate a social contact) clarifies areas of future confrontation and insures that the issue remains real.

To Maude this first appeared as a negation of *her* and then as an imposition on her at always having to arrange social occasions. With the new information a change in attitude becomes possible—from resentment of him to caring for self. The change to "This is *my* need (social contact) and it is my responsibility to meet it," changes the focus of the problem and removes a barrier in the relationship. What you have now is a shift to the right and responsibility of self-assertion and Self-Care, which can ultimately be enriching to the relationship.

The following detailed series of encounters illustrates the many uses of group members:

as respectful listeners to ventilation of anger;

as mirrors to feed back impact and individual understanding of anger content;

as surrogate authority figures in the absence of the real person—a simulated "dry run" in practice of a necessary behavior;

as active participants in creating new experiences;

as supporters in needed change—interacting and identifying;

as mutual growth stimulators.

"My Boss Is Not Meeting My Needs"

EARL: I'm very angry at my supervisor and feel frustrated. She heads our physiotherapy department. I have a thing about authority figures—especially females—and I have a hard time putting my anger into words. I don't know what to do about it.

THERAPIST: I suggest you pick a surrogate supervisor from this group and use her to practice a direct confrontation. Does this fit your need?

E: Yes, and I pick Ethel. *(To Ethel)* Would you act as my supervisor? *(She agrees and sits in front of him. Earl begins in a whining tone)* I don't like your stinginess with compliments. You never say anything nice. Can't you tell me I do something right? Why do you have to be so cold? I'm really angry at how lousy I feel when I leave our conferences. I wish you'd check things out with me— what I want to do in a case. I'm sick and tired of your superior attitude. You're always right! *(Then softly, to Therapist)* Oh, boy, I'm putting it all on her! She's really an excellent supervisor. I can't get close to her and I want to relate more personally to her.

TH: All right, now we've moved from "what you are" to "what I want." And what you want is now the starting point of our work. Keep addressing your supervisor.

E: I want you to respect me. Specifically, I want you to compliment me on the good things I do and I know I do good things.

TH: Let's huddle. What are the good things that you do?

E: Well, I think I'm a pretty good physiotherapist. I'm doing an internship and I've got a lot to learn, but I think I'm a good learner and I think I work hard at my job.

TH: Tell her your perception of you and see if it agrees with her perception of you.

E: My perception of myself is that I'm working hard at being a good physiotherapist, and as a matter of fact, I do a good job right now. I have a lot more to learn. Right now I think I function very adequately. How do you see me?

TH: What do you want? An evaluation of strengths and weaknesses?

E: Yes. *(To Surrogate Supervisor, hereafter known as S.S.)* I guess it's very important to me that you be honest with me, that I know where I stand with you, whether you do feel good about me or not. Whether you do like me or not. This is the ambiguity, the big question mark that is bothersome for me. I want you to be straight with me. I think I present myself as thin-skinned and I would like you to disregard my looking hurt.

TH: Okay. Now let's huddle again. We're beginning to hit pay-dirt. You say: "I'm thin-skinned and my thin-skinnedness possibly makes my supervisor tread on eggs with me about criticism. So I don't know where I stand and I want to grow in the position and I do value her opinion." Did I hear you accurately?

E: Yes, and I don't like floating in thin air sometimes, not knowing where I stand.

TH: Exactly. So a specific request, as: "I want a critical evaluation of my strengths and weaknesses, would you give it to me? And disregard the fact that I can be hurt. I will be hurt, but I guarantee you that I will survive. I really want to know this in order to grow in my job, which I respect." Is that where it's at?

E: Yeah, and as I hear you say that I'm aware of wanting that and at the same time, not wanting that, being afraid of the hurt.

TH: Both true, nevertheless, in spite of the fact that you're afraid and would much prefer the answer be only a positive evaluation, you're going to get some critical comments since you admit there's still lots to learn. It must be in the same package. So, are you willing to take the risk of being hurt which this particular encounter will guarantee?

E *(nodding his head affirmatively):* Knowing where I stand, being able to trust that she's telling me the whole truth all the time, I think I can live with that.

TH: Okay, present this to your supervisor in such a way that will make it easy for her to do so.

E *(to S.S.):* I'm aware of giving you some nonverbal facial cues: that I'm delicate and that I have thin-skin, that I can be hurt easily.

I'm now getting in touch with the fact that it is far worse for me to be off in space, not knowing where I stand with you, and I do want to know where I stand with you, and both the good and the bad. What I'd like from you specifically is to be straight with me all the time, whether it's good or whether it's bad. I don't want just negative things, I want some strokes, too; but I feel the critical evaluation will help me grow.

S. S.: I'm not sure you mean it when you say you want me to be honest with you.

E: I'm feeling that's really what I want right now—that you come on straight with me.

S. S.: You're ready to look at both the good and bad?

E: Yes. I think what's in my head is worse than what you could tell me.

S. S.: I suspect that's true. I guess I still have some hesitation because I'm not convinced you really mean it, that you really want to go through with it. Can you say it in a way that makes me feel sure that's really what you do want? That you do want a real picture of yourself as you are now.

E: I don't know how I can convince you.

S. S.: Well, when you say, for example, "I don't want it all negative, I want it positive, too," that casts a doubt in my mind.

E: I don't want a "kick me" sort of thing.

S. S.: Why would it be?

Tн: Let's huddle. Earl, you're hedging. I hear you say, "When you knock me down, be sure that I'm picked up." The information you're giving is, "I'm very fragile." Is this the information you want to give?

E: I want to get away from that. I want to get away from the fragile thing.

Tн: All right. Then take the risk—this is a *business relationship,* right? That's a different cup of tea from an *intimate relationship*–and even there we have to take risks. *(Earl nods thoughtfully)* In one sentence, put it to your supervisor straight: "I would like a frank critical evaluation of my strengths and weaknesses." Period! Does this fit?

E: Right. *(To S.S.)* I would like a frank appraisal of my strengths and weaknesses.

S.S.: I think I could do that.

Tн *(to Earl):* When? Set an appointment for it.

E: I'd like this done once a week on Wednesdays between 4:30 and 6:00. That is our regular time together once a week.

Tʜ: Now, what I see is a possible acceptance of a commitment to present this sentence to your supervisor as a starting point of communication. *(Earl nods emphatically)* Are you making a commitment to yourself?

E: Yes, I'll do that this Wednesday.

Tʜ: Okay.

E: I just had a frightening thought. This Wednesday the field representative from the county is coming to check with the supervisor. This has nothing to do with the commitment of Wednesday, but there's a lot of fright about what my supervisor will say about me to the field representative.

Tʜ: And you will see your supervisor after the field representative's visit?

E: Right, so I'm going to walk in with a lot of not-okay feelings because I'll probably have decided that she said bad things about me; then I won't feel comfortable. I think I'm now saying, "Don't give me any pain, rejection, or critical comments."

Tʜ: All right. We've gotten beyond that to the risk of a confrontation that says, "I want a critical evaluation from you of my strengths and weaknesses at our conference period once a week." Now you're saying that you'll be especially uptight wondering what she's saying to this liason person or vice versa. I am saying, very coldly, so suffer! There is no way out of this dilemma other than action. When you take the responsibility and the courage and the intelligence to carry out your commitment, you are *beginning* to build the structure of self-confidence, self-worth, and self-respect. And this process is painful. That's why I say, so *suffer the pain of growth.* Suffering is a normal, natural part of living—it is a given. It's not something that should not be, it's something that *is,* and cannot be erased. "I do only what makes me happy" is a most unrealistic, fantastic expectation of what living is all about. There is no accomplishment without a price. And the price is usually a pain of some sort. You have the responsibility to determine whether the growth is worth the investment of pain. With this in mind, does the commitment still stand?

E *(sighing):* Yes, Let me mention something that's been happening while I've been working here. For some reason, there's this voice in my head that says, "You have to say the right thing."

Tʜ: Tell me, what's the right thing?

E: I have no idea.

Tʜ: Neither do I.

E: I'm very aware of having the need to be approved and the fear of dis-approval.

TH: Welcome to the human race! Would you like to work on this very common problem? *(Earl nods)* I have an immediate assignment. Pick five people in this room and ask them to give you a one sentence negative evaluation of you. *(A few laugh)* You look upset—are you?

E: Yes.

TH: Nevertheless, do you want to act on the assignment? *(Earl agrees)* Then do so!

E: Fred, would you give me a negative evaluation in one sentence?

F: You don't make much impact!

E: Janet?

JANET: I think you are a phony!

E: Karl?

KARL: You're a disappointment; you look strong and act weak.

E: Mary, would you give me a one sentence negative evaluation?

M: I react negatively to your being so dependent on strokes from women.

E: Bea?

BEA: You have a frozen face. You are a marshmellow.

E: One sentence only, please! *(Group applauds and cheers)*

TH: In one short lesson you find a different way of being. Instead of the helpless poor little boy who asks, "Be gentle with me," you say *"One sentence only, please!"*—and that to a very powerful woman! In other words, who the hell are you conning, Earl?

E: That's what my anger is all about—the conning I do!

TH: Exactly, and primarily of yourself. You say, "I need the strokes," and, "They are never enough." But you don't need them to survive and you know very well how to limit, *but not out in front.* Right?

E: Beautiful! And I'm realizing I'm stand-offish. I'm only good if I am better than someone else. I can only shine at someone else's expense. This is a frightening reality for me from years ago—a good example of that is when I could only run a race if I stayed ahead. If I got behind, then I lost all my will power. I might as well forget about it. What made me win races is if I stayed ahead and that's frightening to me right now.

TH: That puts an unbearable burden on you.

E: Yeah. I'd like to be able to enjoy running whether I'm in front or in the middle.

TH: All right, can we start with Berne's statement "I'm okay." Can you convince yourself of this, "I'm okay, if I win the race or lose the race; I don't have to be on top in order to approve of myself?"

E: I can *say* that, Yetta. It will be harder to put it into action.

TH: I know. So the first approach is in your work—that's where you started with a request for a critical evaluation of strengths and weaknesses to get a more objective picture of yourself. *(Earl indicates the closure is completed)* To group members: Any comments as this relates to you—your own self-conning, the facade you maintain that sabotages your growth?

D: I identify quite a bit with Earl's situation. Mine is very similar in terms of my boss never giving positive strokes; he just will not do it. And yet, something is bugging him, so then I get up the courage to do what Ed has been assigned to do and ask for a critical evaluation of my work. Then he gives me the negative—what's wrong—and that's helpful. Some of it is true, and some of it I don't want! Then I kind of hint that I need the positive strokes, too,—you know, "How about this or that?" which I know is done damn well. So after all is said and done, I still am somewhat thin-skinned, as Earl, and I'm afraid to go in and do this again. If I feel strongly about something, I'll go in again, but there's still this avoidance. And it's still my thin-skinnedness.

TH: Okay, Dick, could you accept the same assignment as Earl and ask your supervisor for a critical analysis of your strengths and weaknesses or the positive and negative aspects of the job? Or, if you did a real good job that you're proud of and are not getting any recognition for, say—depending on your courage—"I think this job is is pretty good. What's your perception of it?"

D: I've done that and I got a low-level, unenthusiastic, "Okay."

TH: You got a low-leveled, unenthusiastic okay. And this is exactly the difference between unrealistic expectations in an office that might be very realistic at home. In your nest, you can say *(where there is good will)* "Hey, Honey, I need some strokes. I want comfort on this or I want appreciation about that. Look what I've done. Do you like it? Tell me so." You see, this is what you can do in intimacy. To expect that on the job is a bit unrealistic. You are transferring a need to where it is liable to be inapplicable and inappropriate—depending on the type of boss you have.

D: It's unrealistic, I'll buy that, because I have convinced myself that my boss is just never going to give me a compliment. But then, my problem is my frustration. I go around avoiding—

TH: Dick, hold it. You could only go along very frustrated if the attitude, the inner-dialogue is, "It could be different. He *should* be different." When the inner dialogue is changed to "This is the way it is PERIOD. The *ought-to-be-perfection* doesn't exit,"— such an inner-dialogue opens the way to other alternatives, as: "How can I give *myself* strokes?"

D: This is true. Yet I guess a lot of it deals with my past—my dad's critical attitude which frustrated the hell out of me.

TH: You have to keep reminding yourself that you are no longer a helpless child and your boss is not your dad. This persistent desire for, I hesitate to use the word need—only an infant needs this kind of tender loving care in order to survive—you put yourself into an infant position when you speak of this as a need.

E: You see, that's what scares me. I don't even have the kind of supervisor Dick is talking about. I have a supervisor who gives me all kinds of strokes, and is a very warm person. Even to the extent where we'll be walking down to the car and she'll put her arm around me. You know, that's unusual and my tremendous hunger for strokes scares me.

TH: Are you telling me "I have an insatiable hunger for strokes—I am a bottomless pit?"

E: Yeah, or I'm an infant.

TH: How does this fit? "I don't have to reinforce the infantile in me. Furthermore, although I feel like an infant, I'm going to act like an adult."

E: Yeah, that's where I'm at right now.

TH: This is another way of saying what I've often said before: the job of more constructive living, very often, is to act over, in spite of, and beyond the feeling in your guts. "I have a fear. I feel deprived. But I act productively in spite of it. I *feel* like an infant, but I'm going to *act* like an adult." The "as if" art of living. Netty?

NETTY: And part of an important inner-dialog, it seems to me, is "I sure did a damn good job." A self-stroking.

D: And my additional sentence is, "Then who needs that guy to tell me I've done a good job? It would be nice, but I can live without it and I can learn to give myself strokes."

Therapist Comments: The differing realities of intimate relationships and work relationships have to be clearly faced. The freedoms one allows oneself in intimacy are often inappropriate in a shop or office. The work situation usually has clearly defined job and power specifications and is more or less impersonal depending upon the type of organization and who heads it. In intimate relations one has the power to negotiate differences, the freedom to set limits, and the joy of emotional support and nourishment as realistic expectations when these are clearly set forth, and where there is trust and good will.

A MATTER OF ALIENATION

The following dialogue with the therapist focuses on a mother's concern about the alienation of her seventeen year-old son.

MONA: My son is going to Europe and I feel shut out of his life. I know he's deeply resentful of me. I could never get across to him my concern for him or that I feel he's really a fine person—that I love him. I don't like to see him go away so alienated.

THERAPIST: Let's rehearse what you would like to do. As I see the situation at this time, the only contact now possible is by phone, since he's in another city and is leaving tomorrow. *(Mona nods)* Okay, pick up the phone in fantasy. He has just answered the ring—now you make contact.

M: Hello, Dick. I know you're leaving for Europe tomorrow and I want to tell you to be sure to take your winter coat. Things get easily lost so I hope you have traveler's checks and not cash. Be sure to contact our friends in London—they'll take good care of you. Remember to give them my regards. Call dad to tell him goodbye. He'd like that.

TH: Mona, I heard a series of messages that *might* imply to your son:

1. My mother doesn't think much of me, not even that I know enough to dress properly.
2. My mother doesn't trust me to take care of myself.
3. My mother thinks I'm irresponsible socially and economically.
4. My mother considers me a thoughtless child.

Are these the messages you want to give your son?

M: No! I see what you mean. He *is* responsible and he does know how to relate to people.

TH: What messages do you want to give your son? What do you want to accomplish by a telephone call?

M: I want to decrease our alienation and tell him I love him.

TH: Then limit your conversation to two basic messages:

1. A statement of love;
2. An expression that you hope he will have a good time.

This time Mona actually went to the phone and made the connection.

M: I just want to tell you I love you and have a real good time.

DICK *(silence—long pause, then):* Anything else?

M: No. *(Another long pause)*

D: Gee, ma, thanks. I love you, too.

M *(putting down the receiver in very happy tears):* I think I will remember that lesson a long time, but I will need the help of my other children to change me. I don't trust myself to remember.

Chapter 10

Expectations:
Reality or Fantasy?

An important conflict area in intimacy arises from the failure to communicate the expectations partners have of each other. "Proper" ways of behavior in a relationship are *assumed* to be so well known that the possibility of *different* concepts is not considered. My "oughts" and "shoulds" are assumed to be your "oughts" and "shoulds." In it's effect, this assumption acts as a script one expects the other to know without handing over the detailed contents.

A reading of expectations one has of the other is an exercise in checking out the *reality fit* of the expectations as well as giving information about the expectations. Out of this mutual reading exchange, issues of conflict may arise. What is expected may not be possible for the partner to give. Limitations of each have to be clearly defined and other alternatives and choices considered.

The following lists of expectations are presented in order to realistically confront the mate with responsibilities and goals one partner expects of oneself and the other in an intimate relationship.

EVE'S EXPECTATIONS

OF SELF	OF MATE
Be loving and tender all the time.	To protect me from hurts.
Be lively and humorous.	To know my needs without my spelling them out.
Be a good cook and housekeeper.	To let me be free, yet secure that he will be with me.
	To allow me to be quiet or closed if I choose to be.
	To jolt me into action when I'm dragging my ass on an issue.

150

In the above list of expectations of self and mate, Eve states three beautiful goals of 100% accomplishment which might be difficult for an ordinary mortal to live up to. To be "loving and tender *all the time*" denies oneself the power to set limitations upon others in order to escape full enslavement by others. "To be lively and humorous" as a style of *being* denies the need to relax, the reality of frustration and conflict as part of intimate living. "To be a good cook and housekeeper" is fine, provided that allows imperfections from time to time.

Eve's list of expectations of her mate needs to be examined for reality fit. The expectation "to protect me from hurts" assumes the mate knows when Eve is hurt or under what circumstances she could be hurt—an assumption that might be questionable. This expectation also places responsibility for care unrealistically. It is Eve's job to deal with hurts as realistically as she has the courage to do and to enlist her mate's aid as effectively as she can.

The expectation "to know my needs without spelling them out" is a fantasy expectation. No human being can "know" another this well. It is Eve's job and responsibility to SPELL OUT HER NEEDS as elementary practice in Self-Care.

"To let me be free, yet secure that he will be with me," needs a more detailed spelling out of the specifics of "being free"—and a checking out with the mate's value system.

"To let me be quiet or closed if I choose to be" discloses a need for distance at times and needs to be negotiated.

"To jolt me into action when I'm dragging my ass on an issue" sounds like a request for an ally to change a pattern I want changed—another negotiation in which to engage.

ADAM'S EXPECTATIONS

OF SELF	OF MATE
To be more secure.	To be nurturing.
To be more assertive.	To be supportive.
Provide support for my family	To be forgiving.
Not to hurt people.	To be faithful.
To be happy.	To be loving.
	Not to use the silent treatment on me.

Adam's expectation of self "to be more secure" cannot come about automatically. The process of making and carrying out decisions is the groundwork of attaining security. This involves risking bad decisions and using such experiences as growth learnings.

"To be more assertive" necessitates detective work on oneself: to what areas of living does this apply and what specific tasks must I set myself to attain better Self-Care?

"To provide support for my family" states acceptance of the role of breadwinner.

"Not to hurt people" is a fantasy expectation. A better reality might be "not to *willfully* hurt people." Whenever one sets a limit on another's impingement on oneself, a hurt is given. In intimate living we rub our rough edges against each other. The process of dealing with them (recognizing and negotiating differences) may be very painful at times and is a normal aspect of the growth process.

A generalized "to be happy" is an Utopian expectation. To work at making differences less painful, to set realistic goals with specific ways and means of attaining such goals, to critically assess oneself and a relationship may be the means of attaining more happiness and minimizing pains.

"To be faithful" is the declaration of expectation of exclusivity and primacy in a relationship. This statement of a value system must be checked out with the mate for compatability and "fit."

The expectation "not to use the silent treatment on me" may be an issue in intimate living to negotiate and set as a ground rule in living.

ALICE'S EXPECTATIONS

OF SELF	OF MATE
To know what I want.	To operate in your "Adult" most of the time.
To be more playful.	
To share my anger.	To accept me as I am.
To tell you my expectations of you physically & sexually.	To take care of yourself.
	To get a more helpful, productive job rather than the one you have since you're a caring person.
	Be more direct about what you want and stop asking me what I want.

Alice's expectation "to know what I want" implies deep knowledge of oneself arising out of many processes of learning through experience, meeting goals and relating to others. Such "knowing" is a lifetime quest.

"To be more playful" might be a commitment to self to bring more joy into living.

"To share my anger" assumes the healthy right to be angry and the responsibility to give information of anger content to the mate.

"To tell you of my expectations of you physically and sexually" is a statement that implies I expect to have the courage to let you know what turns me on. It is not a demand for performance.

Alice's expectations of her mate may be the basis of bitter warfare or an opportunity to give basic information about each other and to determine what is negotiable and what is not negotiable, what is fantasy and what is reality fit.

The expectation of another to "operate in your 'Adult' most of the time" assumes that perceptions of the meaning and expression of "adulthood" are mutually alike. This is often not so.

The expectation "to accept me as I am" leaves too little consideration of the need to adapt to the realities of a relationship in order to make room for mutual growth in the relationship. There is no growth without some change. "To accept me as I am" stultifies the person and eliminates facing differences that might necessitate changing the way I am in some respects in order to maintain a relationship that is wanted.

The expectation that "you take care of yourself" needs more clarification—the specifics of this must be spelled out.

The expectation of job-change sets a goal that needs consensus to become reality.

The last expectation "be more direct about what you want and stop asking me what I want" incorporates two specific requests for behavior change that might be negotiated.

JOHN'S EXPECTATIONS

OF SELF

To make a contribution to mankind.
To establish goals.
To be an initiator instead of a
    follower.

OF MATE

John's expectations of himself, "to make a contribution to mankind, to establish goals, to be an initiator instead of a follower" will be tested for reality fit as he actually works at implementing them.

At this particular time, John is not able to focus on any particular expectation of his mate. It is conceivable that in the process of dealing with his mate's expectations, an awareness of his own expectations in the relationship may emerge.

COUPLE'S EXPECTATIONS

PEGGY'S EXPECTATIONS

OF SELF	OF ED
Be a good companion.	Be a good companion.
Help support the family financially.	Support family financially.
Keep house neat, be responsible for budgeting house money.	Help with housework.
Help nurture & discipline the children.	Help nurture and discipline the children.
Be willing to grow in the relationship.	Be willing to grow in the relationship.

ED'S EXPECTATIONS

OF SELF	OF PEGGY
Be a father to the kids.	Be a playmate and mother to the kids.
Support the family.	Sexual exclusivity ("Be mine exclusively")

Peggy's expectations of herself are clearly set out. She sees herself as an economic contributor to the family in addition to the more traditional responsibilities of housekeeper and mother. Her expectation that she "be willing to grow in the relationship" presumably implies the ability to change behavior that hinders a growth process.

Peggy's expectations of Ed that he "be a good companion" need to be more explicit. Her expectation that Ed support the family financially is in total agreement with his expectation of himself in this regard.

Peggy's expectation that Ed help with the housework needs to be negotiated with Ed to determine its reality fit.

The expectation that Ed help nurture and discipline the kids seems to be validated in Ed's expectation that he "be father to the kids." The specifics in actual behavior need to be spelled out.

Ed's expectation of "sexual exclusivity (Be mine exclusively)" has no similar counterpart in Peggy's list of expectations. This may or may not be a reality expectation. It clearly states that there is no expectation of an "open marriage" style of relationship. When there is no disagreement in style of living, such an expectation "fits."

JANICE'S EXPECTATIONS

OF SELF

Be an individual.
Be sensitive to his needs and meet them when possible.
Be joyful.
Be tolerant of small irritations.
Be specific and eloquent in negotiating change.
Be appreciative.
Be honest and open.
Be sexually aggressive.
Be sexually responsive.
Love him.
Tell him my love frames.
Share how I see him impacting others.
Tell him what I like & don't like.
Try to think of people, places, and activities to enhance the relationship.

OF MIKE

Make some of the plans.
Be open.
Give me feedback and not withdraw.
Trust me.
Be loving, caring, strong.
Be complete without me.
Enjoy being with me.
Choose being with me.
Give straight messages.
Help me see things clearly.
Support me when I'm frightened.
Speak softly.
Be joyful.
Resist teasing me or my children.
Be kind to me and children.
Put down the toilet seat.

MIKE'S EXPECTATIONS

OF SELF

To take care of myself.
Make sure there is time for important relationships.
Be precise about time commitments.
Make my expectations explicit as I become aware of them.
To check out impact on others; be sensitive to them.
Be appreciative.

OF JANICE

Share joy, perceptions of life and successes with me.
Use me as a sounding board and safety valve.
To be my ally in developing a warmer voice; clarifying my needs.
Be sensitive to my needs and frailties.

Be joyous & open; to continue and evolve our magical love making. \ Be specific in stating my needs.

Continue joy and enthusiasm in our sex.

Janice's list of expectations of herself clearly expresses her rights in a relationship as well as her responsibilities to the relationship. Her expectations of her mate allow him the freedom of independence ("be complete without me") and the possible joy of interdependence.

Mike's expectations of himself also clearly define his responsibilities for Self-Care and other care. Each opens doors to the other to be allies for mutual growth. They open avenues of confrontation and negotiation.

LILA'S EXPECTATIONS

OF SELF

Make myself physically attractive.
Be well-read and conversant on
current subjects.
Show concern and interest in mate.
Be honest and open.
Be sensitive to mate's needs.
Sexual exclusivity.

OF MATE

Balance of closeness and distance.
Sexual exclusivity.
To be neat and clean in appearance
and in good physical condition.
To be well-educated and intelligent.
To be interested in sports.
Similar values and goals to mine.
To be honest and open, someone I
can trust.

Lila's expectations of herself in an intimate relationship are specific guides to her own action: to make herself attractive physically, to be informed on current subjects, to care for and consider her mate, to be authentic and to limit sexual intercourse to her mate.

Lila expects of her mate the same value system returned with the addition that he be "interested in sports"—a traditionally expected male orientation.

The "balance of closeness and distance" may have to be checked out to see to what extent a mutually agreed "balance" is possible.

Tests of "honesty and openness" need to be disclosed and "sensitivity to the other's needs" is a developmental process to attain through getting to know one another over a long period of time.

CYNTHIA'S EXPECTATIONS

OF SELF	OF MATE
Be friendly.	Same as for self, except:
Be willing to negotiate.	
Actively involved in decision-making.	Be equal partners (with division of labor) in rearing children of the
Able to listen.	marriage.
Be sexually interested in mate and exclusive.	
Be tolerant of those behaviors which cannot be changed if they are not central.	

Cynthia's list of expectations of herself and mate are the kinds of goals, which, when carried out in actual behavior, become the building blocks of a fruitful interrelationship. It paves the way for productive confrontation of differences, allows the possibility and need for change, permits idiosyncratic behavior and sets guide rules for intimate living.

ANTHONY'S EXPECTATIONS

OF SELF	OF MATE
Truth to myself as a person.	Same as for myself except:
Integrity in my relations with my mate.	
Respect for my mate's individuality/similarities and differences from me.	instead of providing an adequate living, her area of functioning would be the administration of the household.
Marital fidelity (sexual)	
Sharing my growth experiences with her.	
Enough maturity to give my mate "living space" so that she can exercise herself and form relationships which she wants and needs.	
Provision of an adequate living.	
Listening to her.	
Awareness of my fantasies of who she *might* be (what she'd be like if. . .) so I don't expect that of her.	

Honesty regarding my "living
space" needs.
Be an adequate sexual partner,
growing in adequacy.

Anthony's basic role expectations are in the traditional pattern of the
husband as provider and the wife as housekeeper. To this basic pattern
Anthony widens the horizons of intimacy to allow mutual and differing
growth possibilities. The self challenge expressed, "awareness of my
fantasies. . ." in order not to confuse reality but to deal with it, is a potent input in making intimacy work for mutual fulfillment.

COUPLE'S EXPECTATIONS
SUSAN'S EXPECTATIONS

OF SELF

I expect to be honest in my feelings
relating to myself and mate regardless of the nature of those
feelings.
To listen and share.
To share my frustrations and imperfections with my mate listening rather than criticizing.
I would expect to be allowed my
angry feelings without being
told I'm acting "dumb" or
"stupid."

OF JEFF

To be self-respecting and honest.
To be open with his feelings.
To respect me as an individual and
not expect perfection. That would
include listening (at times) without criticism.
To share more in household
responsibilities.
To let me know what he's thinking,
to express it verbally without
assuming I *know* what he's
thinking and becoming frustrated
because I can't "mind read" him.

JEFF'S EXPECTATIONS
(OF THE RELATIONSHIP)

As a mate I expect myself to be approximately half (depending on each other's
needs) of a mutually loving, understanding, feeling, communicative and working (ongoing) relationship.

My expectation of my mate in this relationship is the same as I expect of myself.

Defined: Spontaneity (in sex and approach to life)
Humor
Individuality—for each other in the relationship.
To take time to relax.
Time to enjoy each other.
Fair division of household jobs.

Susan's self-dedication to honesty and integrity are admirable concepts that need method and process to put into action—the how and what of productive communication:

How to express feelings without alienating the partner;

How to share frustrations and imperfections without seeming to whine and self-deprecate;

How to give a negative message without ego destruction;

How to express anger in order to release tension and give information to the mate;

How to limit labeling "dumb" and stupid" in order to build bridges to one another instead of barriers against one another.

Susan's expectations of self are complemented by Jeff's expectations of self in their intimate relationship. Susan's expectations of Jeff are more specific than Jeff's expectations of Susan. There seems to be no basic discrepancy in importances.

The details of the communication each wants from the other need further clarification and issues of mutual concern offer possibilities of specific negotiations.

The following is an actual confrontation between current temporary roommates. Clara and Marian are contemplating sharing an apartment and started the process of communicating expectations in such a relationship.

CLARA'S EXPECTATIONS
(OF THE RELATIONSHIP)

"I expect honesty, openness, sharing communication, a weekly 'talk' session with freedom, willingness to accept (understand) the need for quiet alone time. I expect the kind of trust that enables us to listen to the kind of thing that hurts and not use it against the other. I expect us to express 'hurts,' share strengths, be willing to help each other in the ways we can. I expect us to each put ourselves first, but have consideration for the other and independence from the other. I expect us to reinforce one another in growth."

To all of the above Marian readily agreed and then read her own list of expectations to Clara:

"I expect to be considerate of your needs and my needs in the relationship; to be independent of you and do things without you; to be able to be dependent on you when I need to. I expect to share money matters—half the bills. I expect to express my feelings directly, stick to the issue, and I want you to feel free to express back. I expect to have freedom to have men over with your permission. I expect you to ask to borrow clothes. I expect us to be free to get mad and to listen to the other person. I expect us to share in housekeeping at a specific time. I expect to be able to say 'no.' I expect you to water plants alternate weeks. I expect us to keep our own property separate and consider and ask permission to use it. I expect to be concerned about you and able to express my concern about your best interest. I expect to be free to change. I expect to be free to express my need for an evening alone with you to express concerns (clearinghouse). I expect freedom to say when I do not want your grandchild over. I expect you to tell me when I do something wrong. I expect honesty and openness and to express my own feelings.''

Some of the above expectations were soon subjected to experiential tests of validity.

Clara immediately took issue with Marian's expectation that she say when she does not want Clara's grandchild in the apartment and the issue of inclusion and exclusion of family and friends brought discord.

In the actual living as roommates for a brief time the details of ''sharing in housekeeping'' surfaced different concepts of work loads and imbalances, of importances and values.

Three weeks of living together as roommates brought each to the conclusion that they would be happier apart. The honesty and openness of their communication brought to light basic incompatibilities in life styles. The grandiose words did not guarantee the grandiose behavior.

SUE'S EXPECTATIONS
(OF THE RELATIONSHIP)

"I expect that my mate and I both would be nurturing to each other during special times such as illness or work stress situations. I expect that we would both share work and financial responsibility of the home.

"I expect that we would both be open to each other. By this I mean that we would both have the freedom to develop ourselves as individuals, enjoy relationships of either sex.

"I expect that we would have a primary relationship in which our relationship is given consideration above others, and caring is given to the mate.''

Sue's expectations of intimate living presents the ideal of a mutual partnership envisioning responsibilities and freedoms and avenues for individual differences and growth opportunities. It anticipates a mutual congruence of style of living that allows for sexual freedom in a primary relationship. These have to be checked out with the mate for reality fit.

BESS'S EXPECTATIONS

OF SELF	OF MATE
Be honest and open.	Same as for myself, except:
Take equal part in money matters and plans for future.	Be fun to be with.
Be independent of my mate (have other friends and activities).	Share equally in household chores.
Be sexually attractive and a satisfied sexual partner.	
Be sexually exclusive.	
Be creative in problem-solving.	
Risk asking my mate for fulfillment of my needs.	

Bess's expectations of herself are also expectations of her mate. She accepts equal responsibility in the intimate relationship in all spheres of living—allowing for togetherness and separateness and broadening the scope of intimacy to include other people and other interests. She opens herself to rejection or acceptance of specific needs as a risk of her own authenticity.

Her stated expectation of sexual exclusivity in the relationship leaves no doubt about the limitation of enjoyment of "other friends".

The necessary homework assignment: to check out with her mate congruencies and incongruencies in the specifics of expectations.

CLARIFYING EXPECTATIONS AND DIFFERENCES

The following series of confrontations and negotiations illustrate some specifics of clarifying expectations and productively managing and clarifying differences.

Preceding the following encounter, Emma and Hugo came into a group session obviously alienated from and deeply angry with one another. Emma requested permission of the group to work first to deal with a fight that was not resolved. The group assented. She asked Hugo to join her and he assented to deal with the problem.

THERAPIST: What is the issue?

EMMA: We were discussing which furniture to move first: the living room or bedroom furniture. He said he'd help me, but then he didn't want to do the whole job.

Tн: You got the message that he was only going to do one room. Is that right? *(She nods)* Let me dialogue with Hugo just as an information-eliciting session. *(To Hugo)* What was the message you felt you gave?

HUGO: She was undetermined which to do first, so I said, "We'll move the living room."
She said, *"And* the bedroom."
I said, "We'll move the living room!"
She said, *"And* the bedroom!"
I said, "We'll move the the living room *first*."

TH *(to Emma):* Are you ready to make peace?

E: I am, but he did the whole thing with such a sour look on his face! I don't want his help with that attitude!

TH *(to Hugo):* May I talk *for* you for a moment? *(He agrees)* *(To Emma)* Look, when I'm tied up in knots, I'm not going to be pleased about complying with your requests. But you're important enough to me to do it. But hell, don't expect me to like it!"

H: That's it exactly! *(To Emma)* Would you engage me in a beef for change? *(She agrees)* Until this move is over, you shut up about my facial expression or how I answer you when you ask me to move something. Would you repeat what I said?

E: You want me not to remark on your looks or your answers when I ask you to move something until the move is over. I'll go along with that. *(The couple embrace)*

TH: Fine. Emma, what have you just learned?

E: That Hugo loves me and is willing to help. But he gripes and groans when he doesn't like it!

In effect, Hugo was fighting for his person specific *identity*—the right to BE *his way*—a way that doesn't sabotage the *behavior* or cooperation in doing unpleasurable tasks that need to be done.

In the following engagement, a stated conflict exposes *differences* in BEING.

DAN: I have a fantasy world. I want my mate to make a show of more overt affection spontaneously.

THERAPIST: If you want a changed behavior, you have to make it happen, if the other person is willing. To make it happen, you have to do it because your mind tells you: "This is the goal I want." And after you do it often enough the guts and the head become more congruent. And then you have the possibility of spontaneity when it's thoroughly learned; when the behavior becomes thoroughly familiar. When it's thoroughly familiar, it's easy. When it's easy, it could be spontaneous. You can't be spontaneous with something new. Learning to walk is a difficult procedure. The baby stands up and makes a hesitant step and sits down again. And you have to encourage him to stand up and to walk. Soon he is running. Only because he has learned to use his legs well can he run spontaneously. We're in the learning process. Am I making sense to you?

D: It makes sense logically, but the problem is "spontaneity," and I don't like the manipulation. Then you go about solving the problem by manipulation. And that creates a hang-up.

TH: You see, we manipulate or contrive not to *exploit* but to *grow.* Are you ready to work on it?

D: Okay. I want to raise another point and then you can decide how to integrate it because it's sort of related. I would like Carla to express her sexual desires more overtly so I know where she's at.

TH: Okay. That's where you'd rather start. Is that what you're saying?

D: Once you start with that, some of the first one can be implied in it then.

TH: Any way you want to do it. Ask her if she will engage you.

D: Will you engage me in this? *(Carla consents)* I would like you to give me recognizable signs of your sexual desires.

TH *(to Carla):* Repeat that.

CARLA: You would like me to tell you what my desires are.

D: No.

TH: You rephrase it. What is the message?

D: I would like you to communicate to me what your sexual desires are, and it may be other than verbal so we can get congruent messages across—maybe by touch.

C: You would like me to let you know in specific ways so that you know what I mean, what my sexual desires are.

D: Yes and no. Add to that "some way that is recognizable to me."

C: I thought I said that. To let you know.

TH: Do you want to huddle or can you answer it?

C: I want to huddle.

TH: How do you feel about this? First of all, do you have sexual desires for him?

C: Yes, I do.

TH: Do you recognize them? *(Carla nods)* Okay, how do you feel about it?

C: I feel okay about it. One of the things I have a problem with is that he wants me to feel the same way he does about it. He seems to be unwilling to accept me as a different player.

TH: Now, the issue is: *only* at a moment of time, will you overtly express in such a way that he understands what you're driving at, your sexual desire for him?

C: I think I could do that.

TH: What did she just say?

D: She said that she could.

TH: All right. Now, will you commit yourself to that?

C: Yes, I will.

TH: What are you hearing?

D: I heard that she would agree to communicate and express her sexual desires to me when she has them in a manner that's understandable to me.

TH: Okay. Seal that. *(The pair embrace) (To Carla)* What I also hear, in what has transpired, is that you feel he has expectations of you. Check out your assumption.

C: Okay. I feel that you expect me to be feeling as strongly about sex at a certain time as you do and are unwilling to settle for less.

TH: True or false?

D: False.

TH: Carla, did you hear him?

C: I heard him. May I rephrase what I said? I feel that you would prefer that we not have intercourse when I am doing it out of wanting to give to you.

D: That's true.

TH: Okay, this is what I want to work on. I just heard a beautiful demonstration of communicating a love message. "When you want me sexually and I am not turned on sexually, I make myself available to you because I love you. That's not a *sacrifice!* That's a delight!" *(To Carla)* Was I speaking for you accurately?

C: Yes!

D: But I have a mixed reaction to that. As you say it, I have an awareness that that's okay. But the back of my mind says that's prostitution.

TH: That kind of mental set, that kind of value judgment on a beautiful gift, is how we sabotage ourselves and throw back a gift of love in the other's face. And watch that carefully. It says, "I have a concept of the proper way of engaging in sexual intercourse, and my concept says that if it is to be acceptable and right, we both must be turned on at the same time.'' And that is sheer nonsense. When you sit down to dinner, do you expect of each other that you take the exact portions with the same appetite, and the same quantity, and chew the same number of times?

D: You know, I understand your point. And it feels okay.

TH: Okay. She has given you a tremendous compliment. And understand, communicate long enough and straight enough to understand each other's love frames. There are many love frames. When I cut the flowers and arrange them, take the trouble, this is my gift of love to you. Or whatever detail of living that means something significant to you for the other. When I iron your shirt, a special shirt that I don't send to the laundry, because I know this is your favorite, that's a gift of love. Whatever. Just communicate it. Do you want to take this any further?

BOTH: No.

TH: Fine. Any comments? *(Addressed to the group.)*

KAY: How do I know if I'm doing that out of guilt or as a gift of love or because I should be?

TH: Get acquainted with yourself. Does *"I should be,"* mean a mate should be always available and how dare I deprive my loved one of my role of accommodation? Okay, is it ''guilt,'' or ''should,'' or a ''gift of love?'' Come to terms with yourself and find out. Because it could be many ways. And see what you do to yourself.

K: I think I can feel the difference.

D: When you made the point of differentiating between my expectations and reality, I realized how presumptuous I've been. But we're really going to fly with it now.

C: That would happen more often, too, if you'll let me be where I am.

TH: Did you hear that? Repeat it verbatim to her.

D: That will happen more often if you'll let me be where I am.

TH: Fine. You heard it.

D: She hates to be pushed anyway. And it would be presumptuous.

Such a new understanding may be the catalyst that opens questioning doors on other unrealistic expectations.

FOGGY EXPECTATIONS AND PERSONAL GROWTH

The following is another instance where the presenting problem is just a start at dealing with a more pervading dissatisfaction about personal growth and foggy expectations.

BILL: I want to work with Joan. We started on one problem last night so maybe I'll pursue that. However, there are others I could pursue.

THERAPIST: Start where it is most important and timely to you.

B: Well, I'm going to give a series of things that relate. . . .

TH: Let's huddle.

B: I guess you could put all these under a beef for change, especially the problem of timing. You, Joan, get very tired after dinner, and very often go to bed about eight o'clock or so. Not always, but on frequent occasions. As a result, when we have sex it's normally either in the middle of the night or in the morning. It's very infrequent that we go to bed together. Also, we have twin beds with a common headboard and when Joan comes over to my bed in the middle of the night, she expects that I'll know she wants sex, just by her being there. If I fail to wake up or respond, then I get berated the next morning because I didn't respond. So my beef for change is that we be able to talk this through so that we can spend a communicative evening together and go to bed together, and try to get our timing worked out. This is rather complex and has many facets, but I've tried to outline some of the elements.

TH: Now, come out with a definite suggestion. What would you prefer? I'm fishing for information, Bill. Suppose she wants to be in bed at nine o'clock and you're nowhere near ready to go to bed at nine o'clock, but you may be ready to make love?

B: Not really.

TH: Could you be?

B: No, because at nine o'clock I usually haven't unwound from the way things were during the day.

TH: Are you saying you are unwinding at that time?

B: That's right.

TH: All right. How long do you take to unwind?

B: Well, I unwind by reading the newspaper.

TH: All right, and by what time are you unwound?

B: About ten o'clock.

TH: About ten o'clock. Okay. Let me check something out. Joan, by 10:00 are you sound asleep?

J: Not if we go to a movie or do something.

TH: Now, we're talking about your being in bed at nine o'clock and I'm asking you, the times you're in bed at 9:00, are you sound asleep by 10? Or, if you are, would you like to be awakened?

J: I'd love that. As far as I'm concerned, it's a nice time to kind of nap, rest up and then I'll feel like making love. I don't think that's so terrible.

TH: Okay, we've got some information. And where are we?

B: We're back with me. When I'm ready to go to bed at 10:00 I shouldn't feel reticent about waking my wife up.

TH: Do you want to formalize it?

B: Yes, I would be happy to formalize that. When I get ready to go to bed at night and I find that you're sleeping at maybe 10:00 or 11:00, can I feel free to awaken you so that we can have sex?

J: Absolutely. You certainly may. I don't want to interfere with this at all except I feel this is an excuse.

TH: SHHH, Joan! You have a sabotaging way of saying things. Are you saying, "For this particular freedom, I am more than agreeable." Am I reading you correctly?

J: Right, correct.

TH: Okay. No further comment. "I agree." Is that where it is?

J: I even agreed this morning to other things.

TH: Stick to the issue and only the issue.

J: I agree.

TH: Seal that agreement. *(Bill eagerly embraces Joan)*That's good now I want to work on something else.

J: I have a problem regarding my individuality and self-respect.

TH: Pick one item.

J: I would love not to be so dependent on my husband.

TH: What do you depend on him for?

J: A certain kind of stability which he doesn't recognize. I feel that I need him much more than he needs me. I would love not to feel that way. I wish I could say, "The hell with you." And I can't do that. I feel that's my weak spot and he senses it. I couldn't say to him I'm not going someplace he wants to go, because if I didn't I feel I would be letting him down. I would be losing him, I wouldn't be sharing with him. I feel I don't want to risk it. I need him. And I'd love to get rid of this feeling.

TH: Do you know what *you* want out of you, Joan?

J: I don't know anymore. I don't know. I used to think I wanted to be a good wife, a good mother. I don't know anymore. Except that I'm not going to be floored by it.

TH: The only way to independence I know of is to be aware of your own needs. And saying "I'm not getting this from you and you're not getting it from me—I want to be independent of you," is too global. What are you depending on him for that you can't do for yourself?

J: Physically, I can do anything I want for myself. I depend on him emotionally.

Th: To do what?

J: Oh, like when we're with people, it's Bill who talks. I used to trail after him completely until he told me one time that I should mix more, be on my own more. Then last night he said I should stand right next to him so he knows right where I am. I said, you used to tell me to go talk to people.

Th: So what you are saying is he "double-binds" you?

J: Yes. I don't know what he wants from me anymore.

Th: Let's check it out. Bill, what do you want from her? Do you want her glued to your side when you go into a social affair?

B: I really don't want Joan glued to my side, but there are times when I like Joan at my side. And what I would like is her awareness and I would be glad to be specific. Last night we went to a party, and I was greeting the host to begin with and then, as we walked on I turned because I wanted to say hello to our hostess. I thought Joan was right at my side and I wanted both of us to be talking to the hostess. All of a sudden I saw that she wasn't even there, that she had just gone right back to take care of her coat. Now in that specific instance, it appeared to me that this is a time when she ought to have been aware that I had stopped and so forth.

Th: Bill, she "ought to be aware" is the sheerest nonsense. She could never be aware. Even if you're married a hundred years, neither of you will ever be aware of the expectations in the other's guts unless those expectations are expressed.

B: I expressed them. *After the fact.* I was unable to express them at the moment because I myself wasn't aware that she had just walked away.

Th: All right. So at the moment, when you find that your wife is not at your side, you give yourself the message that "my expectations are unrealistic."

B: Check.

Th: Do you see?

B: I accept that.

Th: And then, if you want her, you go and find her and say, "Hey, I want to talk to our hostess with you," and she has the right to say, "Pardon me, I'm engaged here," or to comply with your request. You give each other the right of freedom of movement. And she has a legitimate complaint, when she says, on one hand you tell me to independent and make my own way, and on the other you bawl me out for not being at your side. So, from the word go, everytime you expect something and it doesn't happen, check out the reality of the expectation. Because you're being told it right then and there. And if you have an expectation about a social engagement *before* the social engagement, *you tell her* the expectation as information about you. Say, we're going to such-and-such next week, and I expect you to do so-and-so. She has the right and the privilege and the responsibility to say: "Your expectations, dear husband, are not in line with my desires," or "Now that you make yourself clear, that sounds like fun," or anywhere in between.

EXPECTATIONS OF SELF: GOD OR HUMAN?

Coming to terms with the necessity of setting limitations on self—challenging impossibly high standards of performance, suffering the pain of making choices: what do I have to give up in order to relieve *unnecessary* pressure is the problem Ted presents.

TED: I've been thinking more about my problem as an individual I just feel unrealized. I do a lot of very good things: I have many wonderful relationships, I do very good work, I'm a physician, I teach and have very good classes. I have some very fine relationships in my practice. I've written some very good things. I've done some very good research. But somehow, I haven't put it all together.

THERAPIST: What criteria are you putting up that spells out the details of "full realization" of yourself?

T: Well, my criteria would be working independently or more independently. I'm tied now with an institution; a university. I have gotten myself into a profession where I do very much what I want in the way I want, but I'm still obligated to the institution. And I don't like that. But I hang onto it for reasons of security.

TH: And how much time does this take?

T: It's hard—I avoid questions like that.

TH: And I'm going to poke you with questions like that to get at the reality of your situation. How much time does this commitment to the university take?

T: I don't know. One reason it's hard to calculate is that I work in many different places because the university is located in different places. I think I'm the first person to hold a joint appointment in two departments. But they're phasing out one department; so technically I'm now full-time in the other.

TH: All right. How much time does this full-time assignment take?

T: I do some work at two hospitals and I manage to continue my teaching on the university campuses, so I'm in about five different places—

TH: Do you have to be?

T: And then I have my private practice. Do I have to do that? Well, it's my deal with the university to maintain the full-time status.

TH: In five different places? Does it have to be five?

T: There's an aspect of the places being scattered that I like. Working in different places. I actually go downtown just about two days a week. But I guess I'd really like my work to be more centralized.

TH: How can you manage that? "I'd really like my work to be more centralized." Realistically, what can you do?

T: It gets back to the big problem I stated before—if I did more that was my own thing..

TH: What is your own thing? You just told me you enjoyed this university commitment.

T: I didn't say I enjoyed it; that's my security.

TH: Didn't you say you enjoyed some aspects of it?

T: I like moving around, meeting different people, teaching undergraduates, teaching graduates, supervising professional staff. I like the clients. . . I confuse myself as I talk because when I get into that kind of thing, it contrasts so much with the original feelings of fear and inadequacy, and so on.

TH: And you're talking about adequate functioning in many aspects.

T: That's right.

TH: That's what *you're talking* about.

T: There's a real contrast between what I do and the way I feel about it. I can think of two tremendous examples of the gap. One, I remember playing tennis last summer with a guy who was very competitive, and I am very competitive. It comes out on the tennis court.

TH: Only on the tennis court?

T: He's head of one center at the university and we play often. Sometimes I beat him, sometimes he beats me, but this time I was beating him which was very bad for him—and I felt like I was losing! I got more and more ahead, I felt more and more like I was fighting from behind, and finally, I won—but at the end I was exhausted.

TH: You won, but you were exhausted. Does that depreciate the winning, the fact that you were exhausted?

T: Yes, it did, but I didn't enjoy putting out that much effort.

TH: So what I hear you say is I don't want to play that hard to win. It should come easier.

T: That's right. Not that way, I don't want to get like that. I want to enjoy myself. I don't want to sweat that much. I don't want to play in fear. I want to win when I can, but not feel I have to win.

TH: Okay, you can change the inner dialogue. Does it now go like this: the diversification of my life is still enjoyable, self-expanding and realistic in one aspect because I not only have the university connection, in itself not boring by the variety of experiences it affords me.

T: Not by itself, it's not boring.

TH: But in addition I have my own private practice. So you have your penny and your cake.

T: But I'm not happy with it.

TH: Okay. Where does that come from? "I have my penny and my cake, but I'm never satisfied."

T: Again it's like the tennis 'cause I feel I have to have my university connection like I had to play with Bill—I had to win.

TH: You had to win to prove what?

T: To prove, in one case—tennis—that I'm okay.

TH: And you're not okay if you lose a game?

T: I feel with the university it's to gain the security I feel I wouldn't have if I were on my own.

TH: Okay, so for security you always have to pay a price. . . and if you can add to the price of security another outlet of freedom, man, you are flowing and you don't know it. Just another attitude about the same thing.

T: I feel bad about my situation, I feel worse about it than I feel you are aware.

TH: I hear your pain loudly and clearly. I'm saying it's coming from your inner dialogue. "I am worth something *only if* I meet certain standards; only if I stand alone completely, successfully, and don't need security."

T: You're saying I'm being too hard on myself.

TH: That's an understatement! "I can't be like normal people," would be closer.

T: I don't know if I can describe that these inner feelings of inadequacy and fear and so on contrast with the pose that I've worked very hard at and have maintained kind of successfully—calm and un-ruffled, very much in control and functioning very well.

TH: "That I can't show that I could sometimes be under stress."

T: That's right.

TH: That would be a sign of weakness?

T: I was terrified of coming up here.

TH: It seems to me you're terrified to show the human aspects of you. *(Ted nods)* You *can* join the human race, it's your option. It's your option to say, "Ouch! That hurts, this is too much pressure." What are you going to do for yourself now?

T: I'm going to try to stop being so hard on myself.

TH: How?

T: I'm trying to implement what we've been talking about.

TH: What are you going to give up in order to make that possible?

T: Some security.

TH: You can't survive without taking risks.

T: It seems obvious, but I just hadn't seen that.

TH: Do you have a direction to go?

T: Yes! I have to seal it with you. *(Ted and Therapist embrace)*

TH: Fine! Any comments?

GROUP MEMBER: I could see myself in this, only I feel that way at the *end* of a tennis game that I usually lose. I had to learn this lesson, too—when you keep filling the glass up, it begins to spill over when you get to the top. Then you have to know when you are at the top. And it's something I have to keep telling myself all the time.

TH: Very well put. Any other comment?

G. M.: I always wonder how somebody can look so greatly adequate and *feel* so inadequate.

G. M.: I know about that winning and losing because I've felt that way. I can't find anything that's going wrong and yet I'm sure that I'm losing everything.

T: I would have preferred having a lot more fun, devoting myself to having fun along the way. When I was in the army, I was an en-listed man first, then I was an officer and that was the worst thing that happened to me. As I became an officer, I became terribly out of it. I still think back to the wonderful fun I had as a private, sit-ting in the barracks and laughing, just not being responsible.

G. M.: Another aspect that is hard for me to accept is having fun or enjoying a project without having to justify it as useful or productive, not pretending that I'm doing it for some useful purpose.

G. M.: You said something that really rang a bell and that is the price you pay. It's a question of how much what you're getting is worth in terms of that price. And the price fluctuates, too. I have to keep asking myself all the time.

T: Part of what I have to do is realize that to soar higher than maybe is realistic is an unrealistic price to pay and that I'd better be happy with maybe the low-level flying that I can accomplish. That's a tough job for me, but I'll work at it.

DISAPPOINTED EXPECTATIONS

Disappointed *expectations* are implicit in the following list of "wants."

KATE: I want to have a monologue and I want Hal to listen. I don't mind hearing about your business, but then I want you to show some interest in my concerns. I want you to get involved with the kids. TV has turned off our life. Rather than watch it, when it's nothing that great, let's leave the TV off and talk. Now that it's the Christmas season, I have a lot of shopping for both our families. It's supposed to be a family thing. I'd like to share that with you. I also want us to go to bed at a reasonable hour when you're home in the evening—ten or eleven at the latest. And by the time we do go to bed, I want to have a chance to discuss *my* day.

HAL: I hired a plant manager—

K: You also bought a dune buggy! I don't need a dune buggy—I need a friend!

THERAPIST *(to Hal):* Did you get the message from her monologue, or did you get: "You're not living up to my idea of your role as husband and father?"

H: Both.

TH: I want to go on a fishing expedition. Are you, Hal, able to help with Christmas shopping?

H: It's hard for me to get home early right now. We have a new branch opening.

TH: Are you saying to Kate that her demands on you regarding Christmas shopping are unrealistic?

K: He's going out of town on the thirteenth.

TH *(to Kate):* All right. But I want to show you how to determine the reality of a request by fishing for information. *(To Hal)* Are there any evenings between now and the thirteenth when you'll be available?

H *(to Kate):* How many evenings would you like?

TH: Hold it! How many evenings can you offer?

H: Four.

TH: Are you saying Wednesday, Thursday, Friday, and Saturday evenings of this week?

K: Not Thursday. We have a social engagement.

TH *(to Kate):* Then any time after six—is that late enough? *(Hal nods)* Any time after six on Wednesday, Friday and Saturday, he's yours. How do you like that?

K: Fine, but I don't like his way of doing things. I want help on ideas for gifts.

TH: If you don't like his way of doing something, you have a right to do it your way. But you're in trouble when you insist *he* do it your way automatically. Your concept of his responsibility may not be *his* concept of his responsibility. Now how can you make this gift-giving easier on yourself?

K: Hal, it would help me a lot if you would tell me what you want me to give the business associates on our list. I want you to tell me something specific. I'll find it, but I want you to name the item.

TH: This is a process of milking information. And the fishing and milking for information is a process I want you to follow at home. *(To Kate)* You came up with a specific that bugs you. *(To Hal)* You didn't know it bugged her, but you know it now.

K: Yetta, I've done this before!

TH: Whenever you say that, you sabotage a new behavior track and let the old acid corrode the present. There is a different context now. What happened before is necessarily different from what is happening now. For one thing, you now have an umpire or coach who's directing communication traffic, as well as being an arbitrary rules-maker by consent only!

K: Very well. *(To Hal)* Do you want me to help you with business gifts?

H: Yes, I do.

K: Will you make a list of who gets what?

H: I will.

K: Do you mean you'll say how much you want to spend and what you want to buy?

H: I said I'd make a list of who gets what. Stop pinning me down. I don't know exact costs of things. Use your discretion.

TH: Kate, you have been offered cooperation in a specific task with the freedom to use your discretion in amounts spent.

The choice of an issue to focus on is person-and pair-specific. Any subject of negotiation is practice in establishing a process of dealing with specific conflicts, gripes, or hurts. Any thorn pulled out of a relationship eases the pain in the relationship and points the way to further ease of stress.

UNMET EXPECTATIONS

The following illustrates the process by which an unmet *expectation* can be transformed into a mutually agreed-upon negotiation.

TINA: I belong to a Hot Line group. I've assumed some of the director's job with regard to the screening and training of new people. It takes a lot of time, but I really dig it. The first meeting was Monday night. It was *great*. I came across the way I wanted to, and the feedback was terrific. But Paul's been getting increasingly upset about my involvement. And I feel I've been neglecting the family somewhat. Last night he said, "You're always on the phone." I didn't check out what he meant, but I want to now. *(To Paul)* Do you mean I'm not doing the work you expect me to do because I'm on the phone?

PAUL: *Yes!*

T *(to Yetta):* That's the problem. He's concerned about the house, and I could care less. That's really not where I'm at. I want to get into business eventually and away from the house.

THERAPIST: First let me find out where Paul's at.

P: The house needs to be picked up at least once a day.

TH: What do you mean by "picked up?" Give me a verbal picture of what you come home to.

P: I come home to full ashtrays and glasses and cups all over the place! The children's things are strewn around, and I think the place looks terrible!

T: It bothers you, but not anyone else.

P: Apparently not!

TH: Tina, do you want to do anything about this?

T: Yes, I do. But between three and five, the children are *living* in that home. I'd like it to be picked up as a gift of love for him, but the pressure's tremendous. And it has nothing to do with the Hot Line!

Between the car pools for ballet and piano—and the phone—and the dog—

TH: Can you organize a family conference where you can discuss how this can be done by five o'clock as a gift of love?

T: Sure. The other night I had the children pick up—and it was done in ten minutes. But sometimes they're not there, and sometimes they forget. I have a counter-suggestion.

P: Let's hear it.

T: Part of the problem seems to be the differences in our perceptions of "neat." For a week, I'd like you to simply point out what you've seen that hasn't been cleaned up, and I'll take care of it.

P *(to Yetta):* It doesn't seem as if I should monitor her.

TH: What I hear her saying is, she's not in your skin. Sometimes she doesn't know what bugs you.

P: Okay, I'll agree to do that for a week. Then I want a re-negotiation on the basis that you'll have some pretty clear information of how I want the house to look.

T: Fine. We can establish a checklist if you want, and I'll check it off before you arrive! *(Sarcastically)*

TH: Hold it. *(To Tina)* You can make of this a chore that you resent, or you can make it a non-stressful routine that you have agreed to initiate. Is there any way you can eliminate some of your resentment?

T: Sure. Ignore his criticism. But that doesn't help him.

TH: What I've heard in the past, though, is that Paul has lowered his standards of housekeeping in several areas and does do things around the house—and that you're grateful.

T: Maybe I'm resentful because I think I do a damn good job! I'm proud of the way I keep the house; it's just not the way he thinks it should be.

TH: And it may never be. Can you make this a one-week gift of love—a unilateral commitment?

T: All right. For one week I will see that the house is straightened up before he arrives. I won't ask him to go around with me and tell me what he wants done, unless he wants to do that.

P: For one week I'd rather that you take care of it. Then if we need to discuss it further and negotiate my involvement, I'd be more willing.

TH: What have you agreed then?

T: I'm giving Paul a unilateral commitment for one week to see that the house is tidy when he arrives home.

TH: Seal that! *(Paul kisses Tina)*

I see this negotiation as tentative steps in a process toward using each other as allies in attaining agreed upon changes in behavior, with consideration for differences in values and needs and importances.

Tina's self-expansion and self-respect demand interests and work outside her home and family.

Paul sees this, not as an addition to his world but as an encroachment upon him—her expansion at his expense—his decreasing importance and primacy in her world.

Tina's acceptance of Paul's gripe as legitimate *for him* and her willingness to honor it reinforces Paul's importance in her life. The door is now open for future consideration of each other's differences in a more productive manner.

Chapter 11

Conflict and Sex:
Freedoms, Fantasies, and Taboos

Taking the responsibility of communicating impact of the other and needs of oneself in sexual encounters enhances a relationship, deepens intimacy, and heightens sensation through the mutual confidence that each partner will take the freedom to guide the other explicitly to this end. When this becomes a commitment and a responsibility to do so, the sex act becomes both a very self-centered engagement and a knowing of the other—a complete enjoyment of physical sensations, with no goal set as criteria of adequacy.

This eliminates the too frequent "detective" game—watching for and anticipating the other's orgasm and feeling disappointed if sensations do not reach the "proper" peak at the "proper" time. The confidence that one will be told what to do and what to avoid frees one to BE and takes away all pressure to perform to set standards. To attain this degree of freedom—to act and feel—a communication system that guarantees hearing without interpretative analysis must be built into the relationship. This does not come easily. There are basic requirements which take time to create.

The first is self-awareness—a concentration on and evaluation of one's own prejudices, attitudes, and expectations of sexual fulfillment.

The second requirement is the testing out of "reality fit" by communicating what *is*. Does your partner have the same prejudices, attitudes, and expectations? Are they compatible or at war? What is fantasy and what is reality? To what extent can you meet the other's expectations?

The third requirement is a dealing with your own and your mate's taboos. What may be currently a "no-no" may in months or years—through the ease of attained freedom and knowledge—become a delightful and wanted experience.

178

Another requirement is the acceptance of Self-Care as a personal responsibility in sexual intimacy. This can only be built on self-awareness of what turns you on and what turns you off. It demands a knowledge of your body and how it "sings." It demands a knowledge of what currently violates your body and repulses—and the courage to outlaw such behavior. This, in action, means the mutually agreed-upon power to limit the other and actively engage in what pleases and actively avoid what displeases.

The practice of authentic communication also means exposing behavior misuses of sex:

> withholding as punishment for "sins"—transgressions
> against the other.
> as a bargaining item.
> as assertion of power.
> as an act of hostility.

This focuses on the pair-relationship—the pair-specific behavior patterns challenged for *meaning* in their effect.

When couples are angry, they often resort to hostility games—but the rules are not made public. In relatively indirect, seemingly innocent ways, partners can punish each other sexually. One particular hostility game is the double-bind.

A DOUBLE-BIND

A classic sexual double-bind is this complaint by one of my clients: "I resent your ignoring my requests for sex and your saying I don't want it when you do. When I want sex, you ignore me. When you want sex, you won't *tell* me. Later you accuse me of not wanting it when you want it!"

Instead of using passive-aggressive styles to hurt each other sexually, I teach my clients to negotiate for the kind of sexual behavior they want. Here is an example of one couple's attempt to arrive at sexual satisfaction.

BETTY: Both of us feel there's not enough sexual intercourse during the week. One of us will frustrate the other and then the other pouts.

THERAPIST: Describe the mutually frustrating behavior—what goes on?

B: I'll get frustrated, and I won't talk with him about it, and that way he can't know how to help me get over it. I am left frustrated at times, and I don't know how to get Jim to follow through—I've told him at other times, and I expect him to remember.

TH: This needs a *change of inner dialogue*.

FROM: "You ought to remember, and if you don't it means you don't care or are unconcerned."

TO: "It is my responsibility to communicate where I'm at and what I want—*all* the time." *Spell out* your expectations as a responsible act of Self-Care. Only then can we get rid of the trap of: Why can't you do *what I think you should do?* Our romantic fantasies can be quite destructive!

Since this was Betty's gripe, the emphasis is on Betty's responsibility to deal with her own desires. There are many alternative actions possible, but I suggested to her that she make a self-commitment to take the risk for one week to initiate sex whenever she wanted it. The risk involved was that she may be refused. The commitment, the acting against her initial feeling of giving up, involved trying again and again as often as she felt the need, and a change of attitude that incorporated "I am worth this trouble." Her advances were to be based on her desire notwithstanding any prior refusals. She agreed to try.

In group discussion the alternatives for Jim in this regard centered on the options for response available even if his penis was inert at the time but his feeling was one of interest in Betty's satisfaction. Suggestions were made that he might consider physical or oral manipulation if that was mutually agreeable. The use of a dildo or vibrator was suggested as a satisfactory substitute for Jim's unresponsive penis in certain instances where masturbation was preferable to sexual abstinence. When the pressure is taken off the penis—when alternative gratifications are available—impotency becomes less of a problem functionally and emotionally.

Obviously the work involved in this instance is self-oriented as well as other-oriented. If you want to change, you need to practice behavior consistent with whatever new goal you have set for yourself. For Betty and Jim much of their attention, as a result of this discussion, now is focused on their mutual Self-Care, using the other as an ally for certain of the desired changes.

THE POSSIBLE PROBLEM OF ALCOHOL

Another issue that sometimes causes difficulty in a couples' sexual relationship is the problem of drinking. Drinking to excess can be used to punish a partner, to threaten a partner, or to distance a partner. Even the "social" drinker occasionally experiences the abusive power drunkenness can give over a significant other. The partner of one who drinks to excess is seen either as victim or persecutor—sometimes as both—by the drinking partner. The following example of "sexploitation," that I taught Mary and Dick to confront, is only one of the several possible ways in which drinking can be used to distance people.

MARY *(to Dick):* Will you hear me monologue?

DICK: Yes.

M: After six or seven drinks—which you don't consider that much—you usually come home in the mood to be romantic. Sometimes I want to get romantic too; sometimes I don't. When I don't, you get hurt. And when I do, the time element involved for you to attain orgasm is so long that I lose interest and the act becomes painful. And then either I get so that I don't complete sex satisfactorily or I say something that you take as a personal affront.

THERAPIST *(to Dick):* What did you hear?

D: I hear her say that the love play is prolonged when I've been drinking. And I know we have problems in that area which have never existed before.

TH: You didn't hear her total message, which was overloaded. *(It was then given item by item.)*

> Missed information:
> our moods don't always match,
> you get hurt when I am not turned on,
> when you drink it takes too long for you to attain orgasm and
> I get hurt physically or I lose interest, then . . .
> I get frustrated and say something that you interpret as an insult.

Some general considerations, as I see them: in discussing sex there is often a fear that our message will be some sort of "ego crusher." Yet this area of intimate living involves the need to communicate differences, expectations, and fantasies just as much as any other—even more so because it has been such a "taboo" subject for so many of us for so long. And it is a reality that the male and female in sexual response do differ. Only the male reaches a point of no return. The female can "turn off" at any moment. When a man physiologically reaches a certain peak, there's no turning back. A woman can be distracted at any time, depending on her sensitivity to distracting influences. Besides, a man is dependent on his penis being fairly erect during intercourse. There is no intramission without some erection. No performance without some attainment. A woman can have intercourse, if she wishes, by spreading her legs and lubricating the passage! Recognize the difference! If you learn to appreciate your partner's need, you can learn to focus not on being *used* but on being needed. With good will you can develop an attitude of giving. You can be complimented if your mate desires you. You don't both have to be turned on to effect union *when there is good will between you.* You have different sexual appetites just the way you get hungry for food at different times. And attaining orgasm is not solely dependent on the penis for a woman. How you attain orgasm is open to variation, so your partner doesn't always have to be "in the mood" for you to be satisfied.

M: There's something else in that line. There's a sense that there's something wrong. Somehow I always feel that I have to bring it up.

TH: What's wrong with that?

M: It has to do with timing. I'm *tired* when we go to bed. I don't act interested. Dick becomes irritated. In the morning I get cozy, and he doesn't get enthusiastic. That's bad enough, but the few times we do get together is in bed. I don't want to feel used, but it's as if sex is the *only* thing we share. All he does otherwise is listen, and all I do is talk. You have to share something in life besides sex—and the business.

TH *(to Dick):* What did you hear?

D: That she gets turned off and doesn't want sex, and that she feels used because all I want is sex.

TH: Let me talk for her. *(To Mary)* May I? *(She nods)* I also told you I don't mind the sexual encounter. I just want it *preceded* by some interest in my person and my concerns. I need to be turned on first by some communication other than sexual—some personal communication.

M: That's exactly it!

D: I'd be willing to try if I knew what she wanted.

TH *(to Mary):* All right. He's coming home—it's late. You're tired and he's horny. Give him *specific* instructions about how to turn you on.

M: I'm not sure I know what you mean.

TH: Okay. Let me give you a few examples of how I could get turned on by a man. Then you give your list. Don't forget this sort of thing is *pair-and-person-specific*. What I like you may not, and vice versa. If I were giving this list, I'd say.

When you come home, say you are glad to see me.

Hear my pain when I share it, but don't lecture me about how I should feel or act.

Hold me and fondle me for several minutes without speaking *before* touching me erotically.

M: That's enough! I hear you! Dick, here's what you can do before we go to bed:

Give me a kiss hello as if you meant, "Darling, I love you!"

Let me know *in words* that you're glad to be home.

Then tell me something nice you've noticed about me or the house—something specific.

TH: Dick, did you hear Mary's message?

D: Sure. She wants me to kiss her romantically, tell her I'm glad I'm with her, and compliment her on the house.

TH: And what I'm trying to teach you is how to train each other in behavior that will help create a climate of interest, warmth, and mutual appreciation. How about it?

There is a further area to be negotiated, and that is the idea of allowing Mary to place limits on sexual intercourse when you've been drinking.

Can we negotiate this immediately? *(Dick nods)* Mary, how about asking this:

"Give me the power, the right and the freedom to terminate the sexual act when I need to terminate it—this negotiation is necessary to me if there is to be any sex activity when you have had more than six drinks—the excessive thrusting necessary for you to attain a very uncertain goal *(your orgasm)* causes me physical pain—and I feel abused and resentful later." Does this fit you, Mary?

M: Perfectly!

TH: The options involved here are simple: they are either Mary's right to stop the copulating process or reaching an agreement not to have sex when Dick has overindulged in drinking. Try out either or both for one week. If they work, then re-negotiate them week by week.

This was agreed upon
Comment:

The process of dealing with a behavior pattern has begun in this negotiation. The possibility of changing the pattern is introduced. Dick now has a choice. He has started assessing his behavior pattern in the light of the new information that this negotiation has surfaced. He also may now make a decision based on a self-evaluation of his own needs and not on coercion of his partner: "Do I want the drinks more than I want the sex?"

SEXUAL POSSESSIVENESS

The next form of "sexploitation" that concerns me is related to sexual possessiveness. The following example is of a wife so jealous of her husband's orgasm that she spies on him when he masturbates. Yet, although the example is unusual, there is nothing unusual in a couple or an individual misusing sex as a symbol of ownership, or misusing masturbation as an act of deprecation and exclusion of the other.

NOLA: There's something I have to tell you. *(To Therapist)* I don't know how to explain.

THERAPIST: Paint me a verbal picture. We are now dialoguing.

N: I get immobilized when I think John's been with a female client, or when I find out he's been masturbating. It's not fair. . .

TH: Wait a minute. How do you find out he's been masturbating?

N: Well, I have a habit of looking at his shorts before I put them in the wash. I hate it when he masturbates! I can't; it's no real pleasure for me. I think that's a difference between men and women psychologically.

TH: Let's stay with the immediate issue and not philosophise about male-female differences. The habit of examining his shorts— being a sperm detector—is this something you want to continue?

N: No. It makes me miserable. It reminds me of the time I was being rejected sexually in favor of masturbatory preference.

TH: Then how about giving it up?

N: How?

TH: By acting *as if* you trust him—no matter what you fantasize. And by refusing to look at his shorts when you're doing the wash!

N: I know. I tried that once—just throwing his shorts in the laundry, and it was such a relief. But then I started again.

TH: Does he want sex with you now?

N: Yes, but I'm still very, very, very angry about that past history.

TH: How long do you intend to punish him?

N: I don't think it punishes him. I think it punishes me. I think I'm jealous because I have an orgasm so seldom.

TH: It seems to me this problem is many-faceted and needs much more time than we have available at the moment.

N: I'd like to talk with you privately before group meeting.

TH: Fine. *(An appointment is made)* Now let me give you a homework assignment. When you handle *any* of his underwear, just throw it in the washer without looking. Can you accept that and try it for a week?

N: Of course. I feel like crawling in a hole right now.

TH: I just saw you courageously facing a problem. Give yourself strokes for courage. You're addicted to giving yourself bad grades, and you don't deserve them.

JOHN: Yetta, there's something else I'd like to discuss that's related to this.

TH: Do you want to dialogue with me first or—

J: I want to dialogue with you first.

TH: Nola, you realize that you're free to listen, but you're not to interrupt. All right? *(Nola nods)*

J: Well, Nola used to ask me to report my wet dreams to her.

TH: And you used to do this?

J: Yes.

TH: How did you feel doing this—did it upset you?

J: Well, yes. I think there's a point where honesty becomes sadistic. The feeling I have when I wake up is *fear* because I realize it will cause a hassle.

TH *(to group):* We can literally drive ourselves and our partner crazy with this kind of investigation! *(To Nola)* Do you want to live with this man?

N: Yes.

TH: All right. If you want to stay married, how can you make your relationship a little less painful for you both?

N: I know I shouldn't ask him about such things—

TH: It's not a question of *should*. It's a question of negotiating a livable situation for the two of you. I hear John saying that his reporting of his wet dreams makes him feel uncomfortable, even fearful. Am I right?

J: Yes.

TH: Is the commitment to report irrevocable?

J: No, except it's pretty hard to deny the evidence!

T<small>H</small>: Don't avoid my question. Do you want to discuss your wet dreams with your wife?

J: No, I don't.

T<small>H</small>: Then outlaw that topic between you!

J: Nola, I don't want to discuss my wet dreams with you from now on. And I don't want you asking me about them. Will you respect that request?

N: Yes, but I resent the way you've made me look in the wrong! You weren't unwilling at first.

J: I wasn't unwilling because I didn't know how you wanted to use the information.

N: You can lie your way out of anything! You could have an affair and I'd never know it!

T<small>H</small>: Stop this right now both of you! You are derailing from the issue being negotiated. You've agreed to outlaw the topic of wet dreams and *(To Nola)* you've got a homework assignment in *trust-building*. Let's leave it at that for the moment, and take up the accusation of extra-marital affairs at a future time when your tempers are cooler. Meanwhile Nola how would you like to de-escalate your obvious rage?

N: I'd like to have a Vesuvius with all the men. I hate men! They have a million outlets, and we're stuck with one!

T<small>H</small>: Get permission, Nola! Ask the men in the group if they will hear your Vesuvius.

N: Would you be willing to listen to my hostility?

T<small>H</small> *(when all of the men have agreed to listen):* How long are you willing to listen to Nola's Vesuvius?

H<small>ENRY</small> *(after some discussion):* We'll listen for three minutes maximum.

T<small>H</small>: All right. Nola, how would you like to arrange the group?

N: I want them all to stand together. And don't smoke. Please don't smile. I want you to take it seriously. *(Pause while Nola meditates; one of the women is to time her.)*

Nola's Vesuvius starts off with a *SCREAM OF RAGE*. Then: Men are crummy, lousy, awful creatures—I hate you! You never reach out and ask us what we want. You use sex on us—the only outlet we've got is you, and you can screw the universe! I'm done. *(Nola sobs, and one of the women comforts her.)*

T<small>H</small> *(after a pause, to Nola):* Are you a little relieved? *(Nola nods)* Good. How do you feel about your commitments now?

N: I feel better. I want to stay with them and try to change.

Comments:

It was readily apparent that much work on sex attitudes, expectations, and roles was needed by both Nola and John. The present negotiation was almost sabotaged by the long history preceding this conflict—disappointed expectations and betrayal—*(as Nola interpreted John's sexual activity).*

Private sessions were arranged dealing with the reality factors of this relationship—possible misconceptions, challenging pre-judgments, building trust, changing attitudes, giving information. This included definite reading assignments—basically, a scientific study of sex and the person-and pair-specific application of new knowledge and mutually agreed-upon values.

The area of sexual concern most commonly used to hurt a partner is the question of *exclusivity*—"Are you mine alone?" The decision to "confess" a sexual encounter with someone other than one's legal partner is often a thinly disguised form of hostility.

Before asking for such information, ask yourself:

"Can I tolerate hearing 'the worst' without vindictiveness?"

"Would I really rather *not* know?"

"What effect is this suspected behavior having on *our* sex life?"

One case of sexual possessiveness that boomeranged involved two couples; one couple were clients of mine. The issue at question was the accusation of infidelity:

KAY: Yetta, I must tell you something that happened this weekend. I know it's not something that I should be angry at Fred for, but I am!

THERAPIST: Hold it! You're not discussing anything. A monologue is simply a one-way communication intended to provide background information about your perceptions and feelings.

FRED: If it's a monologue, fine—I don't want a discussion, though—I'm sick and tired of hearing about it!

K *(to Yetta):* May I dialogue with *you?*

TH: If you'll let me coach you, of course!

K: I had to work Friday night, and I was late getting home—Fred was asleep when I came in, and I got ready for bed. I'd just turned off the light, and the phone rang. It was Ted. His voice was *shaking* with rage, and he said Fred had called Beth—not knowing he was there—and that Beth and Fred were having an affair! I told him I didn't appreciate his calling me about it and hung up on him. *Then* I woke up Fred.

He said he'd called Beth because he was lonely and pissed at me for being late, and he didn't know Ted was there until they'd talked for about ten minutes. He denied ever having had sex with her, and he got mad at *me* for suggesting it!

TH: So despite your brave words to Ted, you took the bait!

K: Yes, I did. And I think Beth set us up by not telling Fred that Ted was there. Ted's her fiancé, and he's extremely jealous, and I hope he drops dead!

TH: You sound disillusioned with your friends, but I'm not sure what's happening in your gut regarding Fred.

K: Now I'm ready to give a Haircut—may I have your permission, Fred?

F: One minute—no more.

K: It won't take that long.

TH: All right, then. Stand up, if you wish and begin—

K *(screaming):* You phony, drunken bum! I hate you!

You sit there acting so pure and wholesome—*you* didn't have any responsibility for what happened. Oh, no! You didn't do anything wrong!

The hell you didn't! *You called her.* You got pissed at me for not being home, and you'd been drinking, and you called her!

You'd love to fuck her if you got the chance! No wonder Ted's jealous—you eye her boobs like they're the the greatest pair in creation! You're a lousy lech—you make passes at all my girlfriends and then play innocent! I have *contempt* for you when you do that—

TH: Sit down—time's up. Has your rage subsided somewhat?

K: Yes. I feel better.

TH: Where do you want to go from here?

K: Now I can look at Fred without feeling resentful. As a matter of fact, I'd like to hug him!

TH: Do so.

K *(to Fred):* Is that okay with you?

F: I can't believe it! *(Said with a smile)*

TH: Just get into action. You can analyze it later. *(Kay hugs Fred and kisses him)*

Comment: In effect, in actual living, the body contact of validation of a loving relationship in spite of the intensity and content of the garbage just expressed removes the barrier between you. The process of giving information followed by a loving gesture actually validates the relationship.

The experience of surviving hurt and insult is the path to freedom in a relationship. The right to BE—even stormy—does not necessarily threaten the other when based on a commitment to a relationship. Sexual issues, even when the cause of great hostility, need not necessarily lead to "sexploitation!" The delight or frustration of a sexual encounter is dependent upon the context or emotional climate the couples generate—and the courage to *say* what is!

FROM GLOBAL TO SPECIFIC

The following transcript of an encounter demonstrates the process of going from global issues to a specific concern.

The dealing with a specific concern starts the exercise of more precise communication and feedback—a practice in giving clear messages and assuring the hearing of them; a process of checking out assumptions (mind reading).

This encounter also shows the process of the therapist's use of her own experiences to share mutual humanness and to model possible alternatives of action. The encounter developed following the assignment to bring to the group personal lists of corrosives (museums) in an intimate relationship. The group was dealing with the disposition of items on these lists

ELLA: I want to deal with Tom's attitude that I'm the one who has to work on our problems and he doesn't have to because he's okay bugs me, and I want *him* to work.

THERAPIST: Show him where he's not okay, so he can start working.

E: *(Sigh)* You're not sharing your feelings; being so dead and uncommunicative a lot of the time. Sitting there looking like you're sitting on a bombshell and not saying anything—and I feel threatened and fearful.

TH: What is she telling you, Tom?

TOM: She's saying that I don't tell her how I feel.

TH: And she's saying more than that. Give the whole message.

T: She's saying that *I* don't realize how I feel.

TH: And what else?

T: And I'm not sensitive to how she feels.

TH: You've missed the thing about fright and a bombshell exploding. What are you feeling now? Give her information about your guts right now.

T: Uneasy.

TH: Keep going.

T: I've never had this urge. I feel like you're pushing me.

TH: I *am* pushing you, Tom.

T: She wants me to be more sensitive.

TH: What do you feel? What are you feeling right now as you look at that massive list?

T: I feel she hasn't really been cooperative with me about telling me. I don't remember all those things. I must have an awfully poor memory.

TH: That's important. A poor memory and a closed ear maybe to each other's pain. So take one particular—that you are too insensitive, that you are not communicative; while true, these are global things that we can't latch on to specifically. *(To Ella)* Pick one specific thing that you would like him to change, to start a process of bonding your relationship, such as, "One of my major complaints is. . ."

E: Okay. He wants to use me for sex without seeing where I'm at, without first establishing contact at other levels.

TH: And how does that make you feel?

E: I withdraw.

TH: Okay. And what would make you not withdraw? Give him information.

E: If you would not make a sexual approach when we haven't been in contact. Establish other contact first.

TH: Tom, do you know what she's talking about?

T: Yeah, I know what she's talking about.

TH: All right, let me hear what she's talking about and we'll check it out. What information are you getting right now?

T: She's telling me that she is turned off by me in every way when I approach her sexually without having some sort of mental communication contact first.

TH: Is he reading you correctly.

E: Un-hum.

TH: How can you establish contact, Tom?

T: By communication, which is very vague.

TH: Exactly.

TH: What we're into now is a basic fact—that bedroom activity starts 'way outside the bedroom. And, Ella, how can you help him listen to you, make contact with you, long before you get into bed? What does it take to open his ears and get his attention? Let's have a dialogue.

E: I can initiate this kind of communication. I do sometimes. I resent that most often he leaves it up to me to initiate it.

Th: Let me focus on information just given—you are saying that when you do initiate it you do make contact with him?

E: Sometimes it's hard.

Th: I want to check out a mind-reading: when he approaches you sexually, you are turned off when there's been no previous communication? The impression is that you feel violated and used.

E *(affirmed):* Yes.

Th: How can we reverse that procedure? Give him an education right now. What I'm driving at, folks, is that there are many ways in which you could validate yourself and it could go as creatively as you will permit it to go depending on your feelings about yourself. For instance, in this area of sexual activity, when you are absolutely emotionally turned off from your mate, instead of hugging and kissing and closer contact, you feel like kicking and screaming. What alternatives do you have? I remember very clearly something that became not a pattern, but a fun deal with my husband and me. When I said out in front when asked to make love, "I'd rather hit you than make love to you," he laid down flat on the bed with his rear up and said go ahead. I was startled - but immediately went at it with vigor. *(Group laughter)* And I pounded his rear until it was red. *(More group laughter)* And it just cleared the air! Then all he had to do was turn over. It was a very simple matter to just fall into his arms because by that time I was laughing and I had really given him "what for." I felt relieved of my anger and free to love. Now it depends upon the level of anger, the freedom with which you go at each other and accept each other's anger, not as rejection, but as legitimate, permissible feeling; not fearing that this whole business is going to destroy us, but as a normal part of an intimate relationship. Okay, so you're angry, do something about it, get over it, it's not lethal. I am not going to be divorced. That exit door is closed *(if it is)*. And ask yourselves that question: is the exit door closed? Are you committed to the relationship and to dealing with conflict as problems to solve and not as a threat to the continued relationship? If so, all you have is the problem of solving the problem. Where is it here? Is the exit door closed or no? Do you threaten each other with divorce when you get angry?

T: No.

Tʜ: Ella, tell Tom what alternatives you would like to take when Tom approaches you when you are turned off.

E: I would like to give you a Haircut or have a Vesuvius—right then and there—and I don't guarantee that I'll fall into your arms right afterward—though I might. And I want you to accept this and not sulk for days.

T: That's okay, but I can't pretend to like it when you reject me.

Tʜ: *(to Ella):* Would you like to set a *(to you)* reasonable time limit on the sulking?

E: Could I do that?

Tʜ: Ask Tom specifically.

E: When I reject your sexual advances I want you to limit your sulking to one day—no more. Will you do that?

T: I'll try.

Tʜ: Now we're into the area of breaking a habit. To do that we need an ally and the created power to do what we don't *feel* like doing but *want* to do; a process of working over our feelings, of extending ourselves beyond the content of our guts—a process of change, of growth in a relationship. To act "as if" we are not aggrieved after the set duration of sinking into the feeling is up—that is the immediate job of work to do. It is Tom's job to explore himself and get information about himself and then tell Ella how she can help him validate this mutually agreed-upon commitment. This was accepted as a homework assignment.

Gʀᴏᴜᴘ

Mᴇᴍʙᴇʀ: Is there an alternative to sulk?

Tʜ: Always. There are always alternatives and other choices. I just pick on a possible alternative and you take it from there.

GM: So, she can give him permission to sulk for an hour or whatever else he.wants to do?

Tʜ: Exactly! Exactly! So I feel rejected. So what? So I *am* rejected at this moment. What's the big deal? But since it has been established that the exit doors are closed, then we know it's only for a limited time. And for a limited time we can take pretty much anything.

GM: Isn't it giving permission to make your own space?

Tʜ: Exactly

GM: And I need space.

Tʜ: And making space is not always mutually compatible. When I need space for me, I have to frustrate you. And vice versa.

REMOVING RIGID ATTITUDES

A possible process of removing rigid attitudes and unrealistic expectations of the sexual encounter is illustrated in the following.

BEN: When I attempt to get intimate, I feel very apprehensive.

THERAPIST: What are you apprehensive about? What arc you saying to yourself?

B: I'm not sure I know why I'm apprehensive, but I feel apprehensive.

TH: All right. When you feel apprehensive, what are the possible things it could be? For instance, will I have an erection? Will I be able to carry through? Will I ejaculate prematurely? What are *your* fears?

B: Impotency is one of them. But this is triggered off, there's something that triggers this off, and I think it's a fear of getting close. I have some apprehension about being dependent.

TH: If I let myself go, I will become too dependent on her?

B: I think so. I think that's how it feels. It's very hard to grab hold of that.

TH: All right, so what? So therefore, "I can't let myself go?"

B: That's ridiculous.

TH. Uh huh.

B: But, I have a lot of problems letting myself go.

TH: All right, do you want to experiment?

B: It depends on what the experiment is.

TH: And so you're cautious from the word go.

B: Yeah, I'll try.

TH: Okay. In spite of the fact that you are apprehensive and you fear dire consequences if you let yourself go, can you for one week experiment in just *being* sexually? I'll detail what I mean.

B: Um-hum.

TH: I heard a fear of failure in back of this apprehension. Okay, now we're deep into the bedroom in this whole business of fear of failure. *I have to perform* is the command I hear in this man's guts. Am I hearing accurately? *(This is confirmed.)* When a man gives himself the task of performing, he is already testing himself and giving himself a scale to measure up to. And I say throw that goddamn scale out the window. Because an orgasm is an orgasm is an orgasm. . . .

TH: . . . and it can be attained in many ways if you insist it must be attained everytime. You're not solely dependent upon the operation of that sometimes helpless penis.

TH: You have fingers, you have a mouth, you have a whole body that can be stimulated and is stimulating. When you confine yourself to only one avenue to giving or receiving sexual pleasure or attaining heaven, you are being self-limiting. You always have alternatives and choices. So when you gleefully go to bed and say let's have fun in bed—and if this doesn't operate, this does. . .

B: You're delightful.

TH: Am I making sense?

B: I'll have to ask Doris.

TH: Okay, here she is.

B: Doris, do you agree?

D: I don't find that very satisfying at all. No.

TH: All right, what do you find satisfying?

D: The thing that makes me most angry about Ben is that when he gets me excited and leaves me hung up I could kill him. Just kill him at that moment.

TH: Leave you hung up. Does that mean you can only attain an orgasm with his penis?

D: No, I don't think so.

TH: All right, does that mean that you will not be hung up if he gently and lovingly manipulates you to orgasm? Is this acceptable to you?

D: No, not really; what do I need him for then?

TH: Well, is he anything but a sex machine?

D: Yeah.

TH: What else is he valuable for?

D: He's pretty tender and cuddly and nice to have around.

TH: So there're a few good reasons to need him. What else? And we're on very delicate ground here. And are you also assuming that if there is manual manipulation this will be a way of life? And what I'm talking about is there are many ways of living and no one way is forever. That the manual manipulation may ease and strengthen the physical manipulation—the action with the penis itself. When you give yourself alternatives, the pressure is off the penis. And when you give yourself alternatives the penis may well act more alive. As you give each other the freedom to be where you are at—at that sexual moment.

D: It sounds good. I don't know if I can do that, because I get so angry with him.

TH: It sounds like the anger has more content to it than just the sexual reason. True or false?

D: I don't really know. That's when I become very angry with him, but I know that triggers other feelings, you know, that have accumulated.

TH: All right. Can we go for an experiment in this. For just one week?

D: If we can.

TH: All right, for just one week. Just the freedom to attain orgasm in any way that it can be attained. Just that freedom.

D: But a corollary problem we have is that we walk around one another all the time. Neither of us really initiates it. This I don't entirely understand. Maybe I'm afraid that I will give him some fears, because it's been so. I don't know—we just tend to avoid it.

B: We find other things to do or something else.

TH: All right, now would you like an experiment? Because we can go many ways with that. For instance, for the next week, and I don't know, you can take it and modify it any way it makes sense, but this is what might be possible, every day or every other day. Every other evening or every evening you go to bed early for the pure joy of sexual stimulation. And when the penis works you use it. And when the penis doesn't work you use the fingers or whatever loving caresses that will be acceptable. And there's another thing, here; sometimes orgasm is not wanted—it is not a *necessity*, but depends on how you're feeling, entirely. So this is what I mean when I say don't have a goal in mind, just let yourself BE. Wherever you are to whatever state you want to attain. Am I making sense to you?

D: Yeah, I guess so, I'm not sure what would happen.

TH: No, I'm not either!

D: What do you think would happen? *(To Ben)*

B: Can I ask you a question, and I don't want to press the answer. But are you afraid of my impotency, if that be the case?

D: I can't answer that.

TH: All right. Now I'd like to erase that question. Are you willing to risk? I don't know what will happen. It's certainly different from what you were doing.

D: Yeah, that's why I came. I'm willing to risk something. How far I want to go, I don't know. Yeah, I'm willing to risk.

TH: Will you accept then this exercise?

D: For a week, yeah.

TH: Exactly. What do you accept?

D: I'm accepting that for a week either daily or every other day, we go

to bed early and have fun in bed, whether we actually have intercourse or not. And when wanted, obtain orgasm by any acceptable
and practical means.

B: *(Confirms above)*

TH: You both understand the same thing and you're both committed to
the same thing, so seal it. *(They kiss)*

GROUP EFFECT

Following an encounter in a workshop, the group relates to the experience as it has meaning to each member—as it elicits problem areas,
similar or dissimilar. The technique of probing for further information
or analyzing another is avoided by mutual agreement.

FRED: I don't think I have any problems with impotency, ordinarily.
But one angry word can cause it. Or my *anticipating* an angry
word. That is as bad as any angry word.

THERAPIST: Then you put yourself into a real double-bind—your mate,
too—anticipating.

F: Yeah, and that can turn me off in a big hurry.

TH: You'd better check out what you're anticipating. What you are saying is, "I'm acting as if I'm on a mind-reading trip," and acting as
if the mind-reading is scientific fact, and this is what we call
mind-raping. So check out your mind-reading before it becomes a
mind-raping. As soon as you detect a climate that is a turn-off for
you, check it out immediately.

F: You have to have the courage to check it out!

TH: Yes, that's why I so frequently use the words *courage* and *intelligence* as a wedding of words to get where you want to go.

DORIS: I want to check out with Ben—do you feel that way? That I'm
going to be angry with you?

BEN: At times this appeared, but I don't think this is the case now. If
you had asked me two years ago, yeah.

D: Well, what's going to happen if I do get angry with you?

B: That's a good question. We'll have to experience it—I don't know.

D: Well, I'm going to express the anger I feel, and if it turns you off,
that's too bad. Now maybe you're going to have to do something
else and you're going to have to be angry back, if you want. But I
can't be responsible for turning you off. You're going to have to
do something about that.

TH: Excellent. Do you accept the challenge?

B: By all means.

TH: And an open confrontation may end in a happy love encounter. Do I hear Doris talking about the anger about his performance?

D: Yeah, that's when I seem to get so damn angry.

TESS *(to Doris):* It was interesting for me to hear you say that you were angry when he didn't satisfy you. I feel anger in that situation and yet I'm afraid to express it because I don't want to take his masculinity away. I feel that if I'm not satisfied and I express it, that I'm going to make my mate feel inadequate.

TH: Check it out.

T: If I told you that you didn't satisfy me, would it make you feel like you were not performing well?

ALLAN: No, because I have a lot of confidence in my own performance. I'd have to put it back on to you. I'd think it's your problem and I would do what I can to help it, but I wouldn't accept the blame for it.

T: Then the other thing I'm afraid of is that he's going to have to prove that he is a good performer elsewhere, that it's not because he's not satisfying—

TH: Bess, you're not listening. What was the answer to your question?

A: She doesn't listen.

T: He thinks that it's my problem; it doesn't affect him.

TH: He gave you more information than that. Allan, this is what I heard you say. And if I heard incorrectly, you correct me. I heard Allan say to you: ''Your orgasm is not my responsibility. I expect you to tell me that you're not satisfied and I will do whatever I can to make you satisfied, under your direction.'' Did I hear you correctly?

A: Yes, you heard me correctly.

T: Wow! We'll have to start at noon.

TH: And we're back to fundamentals again. We are not responsible for each other's orgasm. It's *our* responsibility; it's our body that is responding and we have to direct the other into the mechanics of *our* body. It's a mutual communication. *This* is not stimulating, *this is*. You're sensation traffic managers for each other. And it's not *you* who didn't satisfy me, but *I'm* not satisfied, this is yet to be done—this way, that way, any way.

T: Then I have to go a step further. I think in terms of if he can't satisfy me, somebody else can.

TH: So, it's not that *he's* going out!

T: It's getting warm in here. So what do I do about that?

TH: So what do you do about it? You have a value judgment to make according to what fits in your own guts and what is mutually-tolerable for you two, because I know of no one way of living that is suitable for everybody—any style of living is pair-specific. What can you tolerate in each other? What limitations must you put on each other in order to maintain a relationship, or what freedoms can you give to each other in order to maintain a relationship? That's between you two. But see, if it is a question of, "You can't satisfy me," that's the wrong question from the word go. Can you satisfy yourself? Can you masturbate successfully? Then you can teach him how to satisfy you, or any "him." Where do you want to play? What is meaningful to you? What kind of relationship do you want to establish and under what conditions that you can both tolerate? Where do you want to take it, Tess?

T: That is a hard question.

TH: Will you accept the assignment to discuss what style of intimate living is compatible to you two at present? *(Both agree)*

ELAINE: Our situation has some characteristics similar to yours. I've considered that, too. You know—would it be better with somebody else? And in times past—should I even stick with this marriage? We have decided to do so, each of us individually, I think. So that's no longer an issue. But one of the turning points came when I said to myself, "It's because of me that I'm not getting anything out of it." And I said to myself that I didn't think it would be that much different with anybody else. And I had it out with my husband and I thought it through and decided that it wasn't that meaningful for me that I should engage in sex with other men. Plus, I thought it was destructive to what I thought we had together. It would drain away some of my emotional energy.

TH: Long ago I gave up even the idea of considering what is best. I don't *know* what's best. *You* have to find the best—what fits where you two are at emotionally at any given time. You do have the responsibility of verbalizing your expectations of sexual living. Are they mutually compatable? Find your areas of anger, hostility, frustration. Your areas of *fear*—of deprecating self-judgments. Risk exposing them and dealing with them.

T: I don't know where I am sexually. It really makes me very happy to know that Allan is satisfied with me. That's really a good feeling, but I have a lot of sexual hang-ups in that area. I've been into it since I was seventeen, and there's been a lot. I'm just not satisfied with my whole sexual life. I'm looking for something, and I'm sure it doesn't involve Allan, because he's fine. But there's something missing and I seem to be like—*looking*. I wish I weren't. I wish I could be satisfied, but I have wild fantasies, I have childish—

TH: How do those fantasies go?

T: Oh, wow, I can't even tell him my fantasies! They're just very freaky and I'm immature, I think, in that I have a need to act out my fantasies.

TH: Are you willing to take a risk?

T: Right now?

TH: Right now! I'd like to know what you *mean* by freaky fantasies—

T: My fantasies involve other people, men, women, children *(slight laugh)*, animals, groups.

TH: All right, and they have to be acted out? —men women, children, animals, groups?

T: Not all.

TH: So there's no compulsion for total acting-out. I hear you putting limitations on some of the acting out of fantasies.

T: Yes. And then there's the other thing—the intrigue of an extramarital affair, the sweet talk, the sly glances, the games. And I just don't seem to—sometimes I think I'm getting better and then I just regress. I meet somebody. It seems the more Allan progresses, and the better he is—the kinder he is—and the more he tries to please me, the less he appeals to me sexually.

TH: That's one hell of a double-bind.

T: I'm aware of the fact of sex punishment. That's part of my torture, and I'm mind-fucking this thing all the time. I need the pain. Right now there's somebody else, and when I'm busy and I feel good about myself and I like myself and my life, then I can put this out of my mind. When I don't like myself, when I have a minute and this creeps in, I'm playing this game with myself—should I or shouldn't I? When I was with the other guy, I felt really alive; I need to have that feeling again, and after 12 years, I don't have that feeling all the time. When I get into it, when Allan and I have sex, I can be aroused, but like last night when I said, "Shall we?" And he said, "Now!" That was okay. Then this other guy called me on the phone and said, "Oh, Baby!" He is very much like the kind of guy that Allan was when I first met him, driving a hundred miles an hour—self-destructive and all.

TH: So you ask yourself, how long am I going to tie myself up in knots and where does the work of frustration tolerance begin, at what point, in order to have a better sense of whatever you want to have.

T: How long?

TH: How long do I ride my impulses to whatever destructive point I might be headed for? You could make it destructive or you could make it constructive. You could say according to what the two of you, the pair, can tolerate. Occasionally I need a sprint on the outside to satisfy my spirit of romance and daring and whatever.

T: And that's okay?

TH: If it's okay with you two. I'm not setting any moral standards for anybody.

T: Well, he's told me that that's not okay with him.

TH: Just a moment. Let's check it out. Is an occasional sprint, to relieve the tension in her guts, according to her romantic fantasies, okay with you or not okay?

A: Not okay.

TH: Not okay. But tolerable?

A: With a lot of pain and hurt, yes.

TH: But tolerable with a lot of pain and hurt. Are you saying these occasional sprints will break your relationship?

A: I don't know. They could have some very bad, adverse effects. I might lose my particular sense of dedication to our relationship. I don't know and I'm not threatening.

TH: I heard you. Now I also heard that *(We're dialoguing again, Tess)* you're jealously possessive of him. True or false?

T: True.

TH: Baby, you can't have it both ways. That's what I mean when I say what price are you willing to pay for what relationship? So if you want him, you begin the process of toleration for monogamy—if this is important to you. And the concept of sexual freedom may be a fantasy in this particular relationship.

A: She lays the rap on me, though, that I'm putting heavy limitations on her.

TH: Just a moment. I'm talking about the limitation she's putting on herself in order to preserve a relationship that she says she wants.

Comments: I can only say: try certain processes and the primary one is frustration of impulse that you consider destructive, based on what you cognitively recognize as destructive. It means self-deprivation, it means curtailment of the experience, it means what value system do you honor and what is the cost of it in order to live with yourself in self-respect. You can go on a fantasy trip and enjoy yourself to the point of a sexual orgasm at imagining animal contact, group contact, and so on. There's nothing wrong with this, providing it doesn't destroy you or the relationship. That's why we have such creative minds, we can give ourselves so much fun. But to act it out can cause a hell of a lot of trouble. But to act it out in fantasy has no effect on anybody else. So you can imagine an orgy, with men, women, children, and animals—everything, and you could create a whole television scene, and enjoy it thoroughly. The thing to remember is that sex in your relationship is not always going to live up to the fantasies. And what do you do with that? Enjoy the relationship and enjoy your fantasies!

Chapter 12

Aspects and Content of Loving: Sabotages and Implementations

The oft-repeated admonition, "love is not enough" to insure a reasonably happy life together is too often a meaningful hindsight after the termination of a stressful relationship.

Basic to a productive relationship is self-liking and self-respect. When these are lacking we tend to pass the responsibility for attainment of comfort with ourselves to the significant other. Often an endless stream of tests of one's worth are given the other to pass (usually in the form of "oughts" and "shoulds" that are not spelled out). To the testor, there's never enough proof of worth, and to the tested there is the burdensome job of performing from unclear scripts and resentment of having to meet tests. The partner is made to feel responsible for shoring up the ego of the other—a too frequently impossible task.

AS I SEE IT:

LOVE'S SABOTAGING INGREDIENTS are:

Possessiveness: A guarding of relationship "rights," a turning of the significant other into an object of ownership. An *object* has no life of its own beyond the whim of the owner. The significant other loses separate identity. In its extreme, a master-slave style of living develops—an impossible state for the possessor to maintain or the possessed to abide. The history of slavery is usually a history of rebellion.

Jealousy: A resentful suspicion of motives and influence of others, especially of the opposite sex; a demand of exclusive loyalty; a seeing as a threat to self the outside interests (job, hobbies, friends, relatives) of the significant other. Jealousy, as I see it, is a feeling that gives some distinct messages, such as:

"When you make appointments without clearing with me, I feel bypassed and without rights."

"When you admire another, it's at my expense; you are saying I don't measure up."

"When you show interest in another, my primacy in your life is threatened."

"When you defend your mother or a friend's position against mine, you are being disloyal to me."

"When you work overtime, get engrossed in your stamp collection, go on a fishing trip with friends, or insist on spending time with relatives, I feel you are more interested in others and other things than in me, and I resent it."

Jealousy is a basic mistrust of the other's commitment to the relationship. It is sabotaging when one puts the responsibility of being free from jealousy upon the other's shoulders. It becomes a demand to "take care of me in the way it is meaningful to me—in a way that makes me feel important and significant to you."

In our unequal endowments of beauty, intelligence, health, wealth, and so on, there is always someone better endowed. When this is a threat to security in a specific relationship the problem of trust in the commitment is questioned and the challenge of acting as if trust exists may be the catalyst that changes the "as if" behavior to a congruency between the feelings and the behavior.

Jealousy implies an unhappy measuring of self against others—an evaluation that deprecates the self. This becomes destructive of the relationship when the job of attaining personal security in the relationship is put upon the other as tests one has to meet and pass to prove the other's worth. The task is one of building one's own security through an investment in the pain of change: changing attitudes and changing behavior "as if" one is important enough to invest in the work of caring for. This may well become the road to attaining self-importance, self-worth and self-liking.

Intimate relationship also is sabotaged when bound by the ideology of *legal contracts* (a basic equal balance of give and take; that is, I give this amount of service for this specific return). Another saboteur to intimacy is the win/lose concept in conflicts—the ideology of adversaries.

Fear of hurting and being hurt: acting as a barrier to authenticity; a sabotage to communication; a hoarding of unresolved "minor" grievances. The oft-repeated phrase *"I can't hurt him (or her)"* often becomes the accumulated content of an atomic bomb explosion. In action, it shuts out from the partner knowledge of the emotional BE-ING and sensitivities of the other and serves as stored ammunition of hostility and stress in the guts of the "nice person" who can't hurt anyone. This kind of "protection" of the other serves as a camouflage of real feelings for fear of "rocking the boat"—a self-erasure to escape pain.

As I see it, the art of intimate living is in the process of making the hurts one gives the other an investment in mutual growth.

Use or Abuse of Sex: Using masturbation as deliberate punishment or cut-off of the other or as a retaliatory measure to pay back for an offense is a potent weapon to deprecate and alienate.

The expectation, *"If you loved me you would know how I feel and should not have to ask,"* adds another content of sabotage in a relationship. Love is not a magician's wand that suddenly gives us insight in the emotional being of another. What the other "ought" to know is one's responsibility to tell.

The inner brake on oneself that says, *"I can't do what I want to do because that would be selfish and I would feel guilty,"* can be another sabotage to the self and the significant other. When the desired action is not harmful or destructive (by mutual agreement) to a relationship, a so-called "selfish" act may be a necessary act of Self-Care. Our "oughts" and "shoulds" of behavior, when counter to our legitimate non-harmful wanted behavior, do inspire guilt; so I say: Suffer the guilt and enjoy the behavior!

FUNDAMENTALS OF REALISTIC LOVE

Trust and Goodwill: this means taking the risk of believing MUTUAL COMMITMENT to the relationship. In action, to trust means to risk disclosure of oneself:

To risk that such disclosure will not boomerang; that one's confidences will not be used against oneself,

To believe or act "as if" you believe that what is said is what is meant,

To accept that "goofs" are not deliberate attempts to hurt but issues with which to deal,

To eliminate the scale that measures one against the other, that makes of intimacy an ongoing competition for power and importance,

To accept differences as not "better or worse," "good or bad," "right or wrong," but just as differing behaviors or attitudes one has to confront realistically.

Dealing with these differences may include creating the frustration tolerance one has to build for that which can't be changed; negotiating that which can be changed; forgiving "goofs" of self and other and turning such goofs into learning processes through confrontation and critical analysis, leading to more productive behavior.

A mutual commitment to the relationship is very pair-and time-specific. It allows for change and growth. A style of intimate living that "fits" today may not "fit" tomorrow. For instance, the decision for sexual exclusivity (you are my only sexual partner) or sexual primacy (you are my most important sexual partner) may change in the life space of the committed pair. Such mutual commitment may incorporate various attitudes about sex, giving this act of intimate living different meanings, like seeing the sex act as pure recreation without meaning as content of commitment or threat to the stability of the relationship; or seeing the sex act as part of expanded relationships with the mate as primary sex partner; or seeing the sex act as a behavior exclusive of others, sexual intercourse limited to the significant other.

A decision to engage in a particular sexual life style when carried out in action often brings to conscious awareness unsuspected intolerances and unforeseen complications making necessary a re-evaluation and possible new choices.

Trust in intimacy means a developed tolerance of *imbalances*-- recognizing individual differences, disparities and resources unique to each individual. "Win or Lose" is the ideology of opponents. The ideology of intimate partners is based on goodwill and double wins.

A person who is not sure about the goodwill of his significant other may have questions such as:

Dare I confide in you? Will you use my confidences against me? Will you betray me?

Can I rely on your carrying out commitments?

Do you care?

Are you committed to our relationship?

Am I of prime significance in your life?

When a relationship is so stressed that goodwill is at a minimum and trust is lacking, "as if" behavior can promote a different climate in the relationship. Acting "as if" you care, when persistent enough, may develop into gut-level caring.

Risking self-exposure often results in a freeing of the individual, a strengthening of personhood, and a developing sense of self respect and self worth. Verbalizing one's fears and concerns may start the process of doing something about them.

Freedom to BE: This involves total responsibility for self in the pursuit of one's own identity and validation as a human being in a growth process. It involves establishing:

Authenticity–the giving of clear, unambiguous messages; the avoidance of phony games, the courage to risk possible temporary discord and hostility—and to deal with it.

Transparency–taking the risk of openness, of disclosing impact of the other on the self; making oneself vulnerable to the "other" by disclosing where it hurts—disclosing your Achilles heel.

Power–making oneself significant to the other, setting limitations, carving out areas of autonomy, declaring one's bill of rights.

Separation–establishing time and place to be alone—to recharge one's own batteries; a time of separation and freedom from intimacy (according to person and pair-specifics) in order to avoid becoming smothered in the relationship.

These are roads to self liking, self worth, and self respect.

AGGRESSIVE EMOTIONAL NOURISHMENT
(PART OF THE ART OF SELF-CARE)

Concepts to consider:

Taking responsibility for bringing joy to oneself—emotional, intellectual, and sexual.

Establishing the right to USE (not abuse or exploit) the Significant Other for mutual enhancement.

Communicating information of what meaningful actions indicate primacy (my importance in your life) and specific significance in our relationship. Equally important to disclosing hurts in order to attain a closer relationship is to disclose the joys in the relationship—the things one does that make the other feel important, significant, special and primary in the significant other's life. Positive impact needs to be nourished by recognition and thus reinforce a behavior that is bonding a relationship. It is also important to disclose to the other what behavior is desired that has the meaning and message "I am special to you, I am of primary significance in your life, I am your VIP." The following are specific examples (not related to one another).

FEMALE	MALE
I feel like a VIP when he: smiles when he sees me; leaves the garage	*I feel like a VIP when she:* takes my arm when we're walking; looks ex-

door open for me when I come home late; listens to me; has fun when he is with me; makes love sexually *only* with me; cares to know my feelings; touches me (physically & emotionally); shares his feelings with me; sees beauty in me; gets up in the morning to cook my egg, even when he could sleep in himself; remembers my birthday; when he does all these things even though I am angry, or sad, or sick, or tired, or old, or empty, or scared.

(Female with a female friend)
I feel like a VIP when she: shares her feelings about her other important concerns & relationships; actively listens to my feelings; initiates times for us to get together, both as adults only and with the kids; takes responsibility for her needs and feelings; surprises me by doing things she knows are special treats for me.

I feel like a VIP when he: trusts me enough to show me his guts—to cry in front of me; is willing to negotiate our differences and accept those that are non-negotiable; chooses me as a sex partner; brings me coffee in bed every morning.

cited when I arrive after a fairly long absence; tells me the specific things that she appreciates about me; tells me I am the most important person in her life; goes out of her way to do something special for me that she knows I'd like—like make strawberry shortcake; wants or needs to share a problem with me; risks revealing a feeling that is threatening to her; physically touches or "strokes" me—I enjoy making love, too; says to our girls that I'm a neat father; allows me my free way and time to accomplish without pushing; takes care of my home and provides good food and drink; recognizes my life space, i.e., hobbies, friendships, professional abilities.

I feel like a VIP when she: shows she loves me; initiates touch, sex, caress; does not have relationships with other men; stays over time and after a fight; accepts sexually—has orgasm with me; takes good care of me at home (food, clothes, house); gives me good children.

The following are random examples that seem to cross gender lines:
I feel like a VIP when you:

use the pronoun "we;"

show me your willingness to confront a difficult problem we have;

tell me you're ready to make a deeper commitment to our relationship;

choose to spend time with me even though you have other inviting alternatives;

ask me to marry you—you've chosen me!

One of the few things I can guarantee is that whenever people get together in a close relationship there will be differences with which to deal—differences in attitudes, differences in role concepts, differences in expectations, and differences in values and importances. Where there is difference, there is conflict—that is, conflicting pulls to do things "my way." This often creates hostility, anger, and rage when your way is not my way. I maintain the art of living lies in the way we deal with or resolve our differences. We can do so constructively or we can do so destructively.

The first challenge is to surface or make apparent what these conflicted differences are. These include the pain of not being understood, the humiliations suffered in silence, the information not disclosed for fear of hurting or being hurt, the frustration of not meeting tests of love and importance. Making apparent where you are is risk-taking—which means opening yourself to being vulnerable—opening yourself to the possibility of acceptance or rejection. This means acknowledging the acid in your guts as well as the honey or glue that keeps people together.

Consider the fact that no matter what your decision—to be open or secretive—the cost of either decision is some pain: the pain of frustration; the pain of subtle, camouflaged hostilities; dissipated energy with no productive payoff. The pain of hearing something—a criticism, a judgment on impact not meant—is a pain that can be the base of a learning process for future avoidance and productive resolution.

When the disclosure of acid in a relationship is ritualized (structured procedures of freedom and containment) we have the possibility of giving information and the release of a cathartic exercise. The content of anger, frustration, and pain in a relationship can be dealt with effectively only if we have a listening ear. So we start on a basis of good will. The assumption is, "you would like to know how you impact me, you would like to know the pain and frustration I suffer in relation to you or others." Another basic assumption is the acknowledgment that we both contribute to the acid and discord between us. One is not a devil and the other is not an angel. This also assumes the legitimacy of mutual criticism as information on which to grow.

Common concerns in intimacy are problems of trust, power, centricity (significance and importance), social boundaries, distance, expectations, and sex. Each pair must find that method of communicating the acid in the relationship which is most effective in decreasing the alienation between the mates.

We can only know what works for us by experiencing new ways of relating when the old ways are destructive. Each technique, process and procedure must be adapted to the reality-fit of any paired relationship.

Goals to strive for are embodied in the following words of Virginia Satir, which leave enough room to breathe separately and also to build bridges to one another to secure a relationship.

> "I want to love you without clutching,
> Appreciate you without judging,
> Join you without invading,
> Invite you without demanding,
> Leave you without guilt,
> Criticize you without blaming,
> And help you without insulting.
> If I can have the same from you
> Then we can truly meet and enrich each other."*

"To love you without clutching" means the power to give without strings attached—and the freedom of necessary separateness.

"To appreciate you without judging" eliminates the sabotage of having to fit in another's molds.

"To join you without invading" allows the necessary distance in closeness—an assumption of the right to privacy.

"To invite you without demanding" allows choices and alternatives.

"To leave you without guilt" presumes mutual responsibility for Self-Care in separateness.

"To criticize you without blaming" allows the possibility of mutual growth.

"To help you without insulting" acknowledges our need for one another and the joy and comfort of dependence and the freedom of independence.

* With permission to quote granted by Virginia Satir.

GLOSSARY

ACCOMMODATION:

> *Self-Expanding Accommodation:* Behavior preceded with an authentic statement of being and ending with an act of love, free of strings and martyrdom.

> *Self-Erasing Accommodation:* Doing what you don't want to do for fear of "rocking the boat" and pretending it's "okay."

ANALYSIS: A negative manipulation; when the message is interpreted as meaning something else.

"AS-IF" TRUST: Receiving a message one doesn't believe but acts "as if" the message is true and risks that the trust is validated.

AUTONOMOUS AREAS OF LIVING: A statement of power in a relationship, subject to mutual acceptance and negotiation, in which each gives to the other the power of final decision-making in defined areas of living.

BEEFS FOR CHANGE: A communication technique which zeros in on a specific, single gripe about an alienating *behavior* with a demand for change by the partner initiating the process.

BILL OF RIGHTS: Reference to a basic need of one individual in order to guarantee personal integrity, around which another is asked to live in order to maintain a bonding relationship. It is a declarative statement—*non-negotiable power*—setting boundaries and limitations of togetherness.

CLEARINGHOUSE: A time-and-place-designated meeting to present the emotional stresses of the day—*as information giving only,* not for discussion.

DERAILING: Diverting from the immediate issue of concern by reference to other matters.

DIALOGUE (HUDDLE): A method of giving background information about the issue of negotiation.

DOUBLE-BIND: A no-win situation: "I'm damned if I do and damned if I don't!"

EXPECTATIONS: "Proper" ways of behavior assumed to be mutual values; "oughts" and "shoulds;" this assumption acts as a script one expects the other to know without handing over the detailed contents.

FAIR FIGHT SCORE SHEET: An instrument used to analyze a "fight" style. (See Chapter 2)

GUNNY SACK: Hoarded grievances—ammunition for retaliation and retribution.

HAIRCUT: A hostility release of rage on one issue only, by consent and time-limited.

IDENTITY DENIAL: A negation of thought or feeling by self or another.

IDIOSYNCRATIC RAGE-RELEASE: Person-specific method of releasing rage; as a solo performance.

INVENTORY OF CORROSIVES IN INTIMACY: A list of aches, pains, and gripes in the relationship. (I. C. I. list)

MIND-READING: An unchecked assumption of another.

MUSEUM: (See: Inventory of Corrosives of Intimacy - Above).

NEGATIVE MANIPULATIONS: Methods by which intimates attempt to control one another indirectly or to avoid direct confrontation. (See: Analysis, Double-Bind, Identity Denial, Derailing, Unchecked Assumptions, Overloading).

OVERLOADING: Overdoing a negotiation for change (incorporating too many additions) losing the original issue in the process.

PICKBONE: A method of turning acid into honey—living around what will not be changed by mutual consent.

SELF-CARE: Behavior that honors one's own authenticity.

SELF-EXPANSION: An extension of interests and concerns beyond the self.

STATE OF THE UNION MESSAGE: A confrontation of perceptions of a relationship.

UNCHECKED ASSUMPTIONS: Acting on perceptions of another without checking for reality fit.

VESUVIUS: A hostility ritual allowing verbalization of rage on many issues, by consent and time-limited.

V. I. P. MESSAGES: Verbalization of the many ways you are important to me.

Index

ACKERMAN, NATHAN W., *The Psychodynamics of Family Life: Diagnosis and Treatment of Family Relationships.* New York: Basic Books, Inc., 1958.

ASSAGIOLI, ROBERTO, *The Act of Will.* New York: Viking Press, 1973.

ASSAGIOLI, ROBERTO, *Psychosynthesis: A Manual of Principles and Techniques.* New York: Viking Press, 1971.

BACH, GEORGE R., AND YETTA M. BARNHARD, *Aggression Lab: The Fair Fight Training Manual.* Dubuque, Iowa: Kendall/Hunt Publishing Co., 1971.

BACH, GEORGE R., AND RONALD M. DEUTSCH, *Pairing.* New York: Peter H. Wyden, 1970.

BACH, GEORGE R., AND HERBERT GOLDBERG, *Creative Aggression.* Garden City, N.Y.: Doubleday & Co., 1974.

BACH, GEORGE R., AND PETER WYDEN, *The Intimate Enemy: How to Fight Fair in Love and Marriage.* New York: William Morrow & Co., 1969.

BERNHARD, YETTA M., *How To Be Somebody,* Millbrae, Ca.: Celestial Arts, 1975.

BERNE, ERIC, *Games People Play: The Psychology of Human Relationships.* New York: Grove Press, 1964.

BERNE, ERIC, *The Structure and Dynamics of Organizations and Groups.* New York: Grove Press, 1966.

BERNE, ERIC, *Transactional Analysis in Psychotherapy.* New York: Grove Press, 1961.

BOSZORMENYI-NAGI, I., AND JAMES L. FRAMO, *Intensive Family Therapy.* New York: Harper & Row, 1965.

BUGENTAL, J.F.T., *The Search for Authenticity: An Existential-Analytic Approach to Psychotherapy.* New York: Holt, Rinehart & Winston, 1965.

ELLIS, ALBERT, *Humanistic Psychotherapy: the Rational-Emotive Approach.* New York: Julian Press, Inc., 1973.

ELLIS, ALBERT, AND ROBERT HARPER, *A Guide to Rational Living.* Englewood Cliffs, N.J.: Prentice-Hall, 1961.

GESELL, ARNOLD, AND FRANCES L. ILG, *The Child from Five to Ten.* New York: Harper & Row, 1946.

GLASSER, WILLIAM, *Mental Health or Mental Illness.* New York: Harper & Row, 1961.

GLASSER, WILLIAM, *Reality Therapy.* New York: Harper & Row. 1965.

GREENE, BERNARD L., ed., *The Psychotherapies of Marital Disharmony.* New York: The Free Press, 1965.

HARRIS, THOMAS A., *I'm OK — You're OK: A Practical Guide to Transactional Analysis.* New York: Harper & Row, 1969.

HARTMAN, WILLIAM E., AND MARILYN A. FITHIAN, *Treatment of Sexual Dysfunction.* Long Beach, Ca.: Center for Marital and Sexual Studies, 1972.

JOHNSON, WENDELL, *People in Quandaries; The Semantics of Personal Adjustment.* New York: Harper & Row., 1946.

JOURARD, SIDNEY M., *The Transparent Self: Self-Disclosure and Well-Being,* 2nd ed. New York: Van Nostrand Reinhold, 1971.

KUBLER-ROSS, ELISABETH, *On Death and Dying.* New York: Macmillan, 1969.

LAING, R.D., *The Divided Self.* New York: Pantheon, 1969.

LEVY, JOHN, AND RUTH MUNROE, *The Happy Family.* New York: Alfred A. Knopf, 1938.

MASLOW, ABRAHAM H., *Toward A Psychology of Being,* 2nd ed. Princeton, N.J.: D. Van Nostrand Co., 1968.

MASTERS, WILLIAM H., AND VIRGINAI E. JOHNSON, *Human Sexual Inadequacy.* Boston: Little, Brown & Co., 1970.

MAY, ROLLO, *Man's Search for Himself.* New York: W. W. Norton, 1953.

MOWRER O. HOBART, *Learning Theory and Behavior,* Huntington, N.Y.: Robert E. Krieger, 1973.

PERLS, FREDERICK, et al, *Gestalt Therapy:* New York: Dell, 1965.

PIAGET, JEAN, *The Child and Reality: Problems of Genetic Psychology.* New York: Grossman Pub., 1973.

SATIR, VIRGINIA, *Conjoint Family Therapy,* rev. ed. Palo Alto, Ca.: Science & Behavior Books, Inc., 1967.

SATIR, VIRGINIA, *Peoplemaking.* Palo Alto, Ca.: Science & Behavior Books, Inc., 1972.

SELYE, HANS, *The Stress of Life.* New York: McGraw-Hill, 1956.

SHOSTROM, EVERETT, *Man, the Manipulator.* New York: Abingdon Press, 1967.

SZASZ, THOMAS S., *The Myth of Mental Illness,* rev. ed. New York: Harper & Row, 1974.

WATZLAWICK, PAUL, et al, *Change: Principles of Problem Formation and Problem Resolution.* New York: W.W. Norton, 1974.

WOLPE, JOSEPH, *Psychotherapy by Reciprocal Inhibition.* Stanford, Ca.: Stanford University Press, 1958.

YABLONSKY, LEWIS, *The Tunnel Back: Synanon.* New York: Macmillan, 1965.

YABLONSKY, LEWIS, *The Violent Gang,* rev. ed. New York: Penguin, 1971.